In Search of Buddy Bolden

Charles "Buddy" Bolden. This is the only known portrait
of Bolden and was probably done around 1894 or 1895.

In Search of
Buddy Bolden

First Man of Jazz

Revised Edition

Donald M. Marquis

Louisiana State University Press

Baton Rouge

Designer: Albert Crochet
Typeface: VIP Times Roman

LIBRARY OF CONGRESS CATALOGING IN PUBLICATION DATA

Marquis, Donald M.   1933–
    In search of Buddy Bolden, first man of jazz.

    Bibliography: p.
    Includes index.
    1.   Bolden, Buddy, 1877–1931.   2.   Jazz musicians—
Louisiana—New Orleans—Biography.   I.   Title.
ML419.B65M4   785.4'2'0924 [B]   77-10958
ISBN 0-8071-3093-1 (paper)

Published with support from the Louisiana Sea Grant College
Program, a part of the National Sea Grant College Program
maintained by the National Oceanic and Atmospheric Administration of the U.S. Department of Commerce.

The paper in this book meets the guidelines for permanence and
durability of the Committee on Production Guidelines for Book
Longevity of the Council on Library Resources.
⊗

To the memory of Charles "Buddy" Bolden,
September 6, 1877–November 4, 1931,
who would probably wonder
what all the fuss was about

What everybody believes rarely is true!

—H.L. MENCKEN

Contents

Illustrations

Front view of main hospital at Jackson
An afternoon lawn concert at the hospital
The black patients' dormitory at Jackson hospital
Section C, Holt Cemetery

following page 140

Papa John Joseph
Ed "Montudi" Garland
Ida Cambric Baker
Eugenia Jackson
Bolden heirlooms
Charles Bolden, Jr., and Albert Nicholas

following page 163

Labor Day scene, 1906
Postcard mailed from Jackson
2338 Philip Street, last residence of Mrs. Alice Bolden and daughter Cora
Gertrude Bolden Tucker, Rita Camille Bell, and Joe Brennan
Jazz funeral at Holt Cemetery
Grave marker, Holt Cemetery
Memorial marker installed by the Ken Colyer Trust
Buddy Bolden Place
Oscar V. Zahn
Original cylinder used to record Bolden's band

following page 182

Death Certificate, Augustus Bolen
Death Certificate, Frances Bowling
Marriage Certificate, West and Alice Bolden
Death Certificate, Lotta Bolden
Birth Certificate, Charles Joseph Bolden, Jr.
Marriage Certificate, Frank Lewis
Commitment Order for Buddy Bolden
Description of Insane Person: Buddy Bolden
Receipt for Bolden, signed at Jackson
Letter from Buddy's mother to Jackson
Death Certificate, Charles Bolden, Jr.
Death Certificate, Alice Bolden

Maps

Preface to the Revised Edition
Buddy Bolden in Retrospect

IN HIS AUTOBIOGRAPHY Louis Armstrong recalls, at five years old, peeking through a window at Funky Butt Hall on Perdido Street to listen to a cornet player. "He blew so hard," Armstrong said, "that I used to wonder if I would ever have enough lung power to fill one of those cornets."

Whether Louis was actually thinking about blowing a cornet at that early age is speculative. However, growing up in that neighborhood and being an adventuresome lad, he quite likely did peer through that window and was intrigued by what he heard. The year was 1906 and the cornet player that young Louis was so in awe of was Charles "Buddy" Bolden.

Bolden was the most popular musician among black New Orleanians between 1900 and 1906. By 1907, though he was not yet thirty years old, his music career, and for all practical purposes his life, was over. Yet, in that short time, he created the most lasting legend of all New Orleans jazzmen.

Fifteen years of research went into *In Search of Buddy Bolden*. Unfortunately, Bolden left no recordings, nor was he ever interviewed. There will always be unanswered questions about his sound. But as to who Buddy Bolden really was there can be some educated guesses.

It is paradoxical but true that as man makes history, so history makes the man. In the case of Buddy Bolden, it is apparent that jazz was very close at hand. Bolden played jazz in its most basic form. He may not have been the first to play jazz, but he was the first to popularize it and give the music a base from which to grow. He did not influence many cornetists directly by his playing, but he did influence the style of their music. He contributed only what he was capable of contributing. If he had not done what he did, someone else eventually would have. He was a man a short step ahead of his time, and time for him was so limited that that step was all he needed to achieve what he did.

Bolden was a pivotal figure who lacked the musical knowledge to tend to the seed he planted. Others picked it up from him, nurtured and experimented with it, and saw it blossom into the music we know as jazz.

The fact that Buddy Bolden used his own name for his band rather than follow the trend of similar bands at that time—which was to use names like Superior, Excelsior, Onward, Peerless—says something about the man. He was deliberately trying to do something different. He wanted to be out front and to be known.

He had the personality to go along with his horn. He was the forerunner of Louis Armstrong in this sense. Louis cast a lasting spell over the world, not only with his trumpet, but with his irrepressible manner and openness. What Louis Armstrong expanded and did for the world, Buddy did for a limited element in New Orleans. He cast his spell only over his own race, not out of his own limitations so much, but from the limitations that society placed on him. His music was not accepted in certain strata, but he held sway over the black population of New Orleans where he wanted to. He was the king of the dances, the picnic grounds, the parks, the streets, the barrel houses.

Buddy Bolden was a good-time sort of guy. He did not play to impress a French Opera House musician. He did not play to impress John Robichaux, nor to take jobs away from Robichaux. He played because he loved it, and what he played he played for an audience to enjoy. To put a cornet to his mouth and play it the way he felt like playing it and watch people respond by dancing and being happy was the impression he was interested in creating.

He was a man who lived one day at a time and would no doubt wonder what all the fuss is about today. He would not understand that his music and life are termed legendary. If Buddy had been blessed with good mental and physical health, it is possible he could have lived until the 1960s and there would be nothing mysterious about him.

Buddy lives on in a fairy-tale, what-might-have-been world of all who are struck down in the prime of life. He is a romantic figure, but he is no longer real. In his day he was popular, revered by some, exciting to many, different to all. He was a black man who had ideas when black men were not supposed to have ideas, even though he funneled the energy behind those ideas only to those who were open to acceptance.

Bolden was not a genius; he attempted to follow through on the music and couldn't, which caused him great frustration and led to the public displays of rebellion against society that were his downfall and acted as a catalyst in his monumental battle with alcohol. Some of the early musicians interviewed in later years were reluctant to give Bolden credit, stating that he was not a good (meaning reading) musician and that Bunk Johnson, Manuel Perez, and Freddie Keppard were better than Bolden. Manuel Manetta, for instance, commented that Bunk was a better musician than Buddy. In this case musicianship is identified with reading and writing music that conforms to known and structured guidelines. Bolden's music did not conform to those guidelines, was something new and different to Manetta; something he could not identify with and probably did not fully understand at that time.

This same situation existed in the 1960s with new rock groups doing things that were not in the established realm of musical thinking. Consequently, it was not at first understood what they were trying to do, and much artistic bias went against them. This does not mean that what they did was not worthwhile or good, only that there was no readily discernible past point of reference. There was some jealousy involved, just as musicians who studied, read, and understood music better than Buddy Bolden felt envy at his popularity—which was attained through power (a powerful sound), novelty, and personality rather than through their idea of strict musicianship. Many people evidently grouped "different," "new," and "strange" together, and what was new was usually bad to them.

Conversely, Bolden's popularity grew because he was doing something different. He made no lasting records of his music to keep him alive. There was only word of mouth, and with so much other music in the air, people did not long remember him after they could not hear him or dance to him. When he was forgotten, it was because other musicians and bands came along that were better, but it was Bolden who had established a point of reference for them.

If a loose parallel to Buddy Bolden could be drawn today, it might well be another horn man in New Orleans who plays trumpet with one of the brass bands. When he plays on the street, you can hear him above all the others. He is stigmatized by some as "the High Note Man." He is sometimes accused of playing in the wrong key, or even off-key, but when observing the parade followers who are not reading the notes as they flow from the musicians, you will see them swinging along beside this man, enjoying themselves and the music. Jamming early one morning in a French Quarter pub, he turned the place upside down until seven in the morning when he had to go to his regular job. The only people who complained were the ones who weren't there. This man, like Buddy, may not have blown all the right notes, but he did what perhaps a lot of jazz is all about—he swung the joint and the people.

Some have shrugged Bolden off as just a honky-tonk player, but there was much more to him than that. He was a remarkable person and musician. He did not just stumble across a new sound or style. He was consciously striving for something new. Unfortunately, he could never fully attain all the goals he aimed for. The ideas and desire were there; all of the necessary knowledge was not.

Numerous factors accounted for the demise of Buddy Bolden, including a failure to cope with his successes and being thrust into a limelight that his heritage had not prepared him for. But lack of desire, sincerity, and hope cannot be accurately measured among his shortcomings.

Preface
(1978)

YOU SIT IN a patio in the French Quarter and have a few cool ones, early one morning when there is no worry or commitment. About four-thirty or five o'clock the sky begins to lighten, and you slowly distinguish the outlines of buildings and treetops against the sky as it turns from black to grey. It is the quietest time of the twenty-four hours. The city is so still, you strain to catch a familiar sound and you realize what they meant— Jelly Roll and Albert Glenny and the rest—about the way sound used to carry so far in the New Orleans night. And over where Globe Hall used to be (seven or eight squares away), if Buddy were playing you know you could hear him clearly, along with the people applauding and laughing. You want to go back there, but can't; you can only imagine how it was on a New Orleans morning in 1905.

Acknowledgments

THIS BOOK COULD not have been written without the assistance of many people and without access to documents and materials contained in numerous city and state institutions. The documentation consists mostly of primary sources, and although it was necessary to make some guesses, these guesses were based on many years of researching not only the man, but anything to be found pertaining to his family, his friends, his neighborhood, and the general atmosphere of his time. The speculations, therefore, were made with a feeling of authenticity, and many have now been verified.

This research was originally intended to be a chapter in a complete history of New Orleans jazz, being prepared in collaboration with John Bentley. I offer my sincere thanks to John for his patience, understanding, and help on the Bolden endeavor while our joint effort hung in abeyance.

Other individuals lending assistance include Congressman F. Edward Hebert who found two important letters documenting phases in the life of Buddy's son, Charles Bolden, Jr., and Lionel Gremillion, assistant administrator of Jackson State Hospital, who did a great deal of field work and interviewing for me at the hospital. Richard B. Allen of the William Ransom Hogan Jazz Archive at Tulane University went out of his way to find leads and give suggestions, as did Justin Winston of the New Orleans Jazz Museum. Dan Hagerty and Dan, Jr., helped search through records in the criminal courts files, and Dave Cressy, assistant New Orleans city attorney, granted permission to search records in the city property management, city vital statistics, and police departments.

Photographers Rae Korby, Fay Rogers, Lolly Mackie, and Hans Lychou contributed their talents and resourcefulness in obtaining pictures, including those of documents otherwise unavailable for copying. Collin Hamer, Jr., head of the Louisiana department, and his staff at the New Orleans Public Library, were extremely helpful, especially in letting me know when the library came into possession of new materials. These materials opened up another two years' research after 1973 and include some of the most important documents yet found on Bolden.

Many New Orleans musicians helped with information when and where they could, particularly Alvin Alcorn, who set up the interview with his mother that resulted in the heretofore undiscovered portrait of Buddy Bolden. Louis Cottrell, Jr., recalled facts from conversations with his father, a pioneer New Orleans drummer who was active musically during Bolden's career. Papa John Joseph, Ed Garland, Eddie Dawson, Tom Albert, Willie Parker, Henry "Booker T" Glass, Louis Keppard, Chink Martin, Slow Drag Pavageau, Bill Matthews, Peter Bocage, Paul Beaulieu, and others gave firsthand accounts of incidents pertaining to Buddy, and many younger musicians helped fill in information on some of Bolden's contemporaries.

Deep appreciation goes to the octogenarians and nonagenarians, Cecile Augustine, Susannah Pickett, Mrs. Louis (Carrie) Jones, Mrs. Nelson Joseph, Beatrice Alcorn, Elizabeth Morton, Morris Dulitz, Milton "Moony" Martin, and others who searched their amazing memories to pinpoint events that occurred around the turn of the century. There were numerous others to whom I am sure I must have sounded like an old cylinder in my incessant questions about Buddy Bolden. All were very kind and patient and when they could not be of direct help, they usually had a suggestion about some other person I might seek information from.

A most important thank you and acknowledgment must go to Harlan "Woody" Wood and his wife Jayne. They believed in this book, and there is no way I can repay their help, friendship, and hospitality. Harlan read the manuscript many times and contributed invaluable editorial suggestions. Jayne volunteered to do much of the typing and put the extensive bibliography into academic form.

There were some sad moments encountered in finding out what actually happened to Buddy Bolden. I lived with the man in my mind and often went to sleep thinking about him. When I discovered the poignant report of his physical and mental condition just prior to his commitment to the hospital at Jackson, Louisiana, it was like reading about a close friend.

There was nothing, however, that affected me more than the sudden death of Jayne Wood on May 28, 1976, at age thirty-two. Jayne was a part of this book; she suffered through it with me. I wish so much she could have lived to the day that I could hand her a published copy.

One who deserves more than a mention and a thank you for her fortitude and understanding through the years in which Buddy Bolden somehow became part of so many conversations that began otherwise, is Jo Anne Yoder. I'm sure she is happy that it's finally finished.

An important credit must go to Tad Price, a good neighbor, for his highly professional work on the maps and drawings.

I am grateful for the enthusiasm of the editorial staff at Louisiana State University Press. In particular, these people include Lloyd Lyman, who guided the manuscript through to acceptance, and Mary Jane Di Piero, who quickly sensed my feelings about the book and became my right hand in the final editing stages.

This book owes a debt of gratitude to many. It is not the work of one man.

In Search of Buddy Bolden

1

Exposing
the Legend

BUDDY BOLDEN has always been an elusive, mysterious figure in the early jazz history of New Orleans. His story has hovered at the edge of local legends like Jean Lafitte and Voodoo Queen Marie Laveau, no one knowing where reality stopped and myth began. His legendary status grew as the number of inaccuracies and inconsistencies published about him increased. No one thoroughly researched his life, and documented facts were scarce since very little was written on Bolden or his music while he was living. The accepted story, which many later jazz scholars merely copied, came primarily from Bunk Johnson's interviews with the editors of *Jazzmen* and from Jelly Roll Morton.[1] Bolden, it said, was an important early jazzman; he blew a loud cornet, drank a lot, ran a barbershop, edited a scandal sheet, and died in a mental institution. This work attempts to sort through and document the Bolden legend. It is intended as a biography and historical endeavor rather than as a treatise on Bolden's contributions to jazz or a critical comment on jazz itself.

Jazz was not seriously researched until the mid-1930s, forty years after Bolden had begun playing his horn and thirty years after he had played his last notes in New Orleans. Only then was this distinctively American music considered legitimate enough to warrant a search for its beginnings. By this time, at the heart of the Great Depression, music was upon hard times. Men who had been involved in the early days of jazz and who had later lived the glory days of Storyville were making a

1. Frederic Ramsey, Jr., and Charles E. Smith (eds.), *Jazzmen* (New York: Harcourt, Brace, 1939); Alan Lomax, *Mister Jelly Roll* (New York: Grosset & Dunlap, 1950).

living as best they could. Johnny St. Cyr was a plasterer, Alphonse
Picou a tinsmith, Manuel Perez and the Tios were cigar-makers, and
others worked as stevedores, porters, drivers, or plain laborers.[2] All
were doing their best to hold themselves and their families together.
Only a few lived by their music alone, and a few—Louis Armstrong,
Sidney Bechet, and Kid Ory among others—had left the city to attain
greater fame elsewhere. Some were gone forever. Many who remained
were forgotten, their instruments in pawn, sold, or collecting dust in a
closet and hauled out only infrequently to play for a neighborhood
gathering of old friends. There was still music in New Orleans and good
jazzmen to play it, but it was sporadic.

It was up to the early researchers to locate the old-timers, listen to
what music was available, and begin to put the story together. Many of
the musicians remembered the early days of jazz as the "good old
days." They were good times, but the new interest being shown also
gave these musicians a chance to wistfully recall their youth—a reck-
less, carefree time of life. In all these reminiscences, one name continued to pop up—Buddy Bolden. The old-timers could relive his
music, some had played with him, most had heard him, and the younger
men had heard *of* him. He was not fiction, but after thirty or more years
he had become fictionalized.

The first known critical statement concerning Bolden's work and significance appeared on April 22, 1933.[3] This first nonderogatory statement about jazz music in the New Orleans press is noteworthy as the first
recognition of a need to document New Orleans jazz history. The author
of this piece, E. Belfield Spriggins, had interviewed Willie Cornish who
had played with Bolden. From this article comes a story about the origin
of the words to "Funky Butt," a song closely associated with Bolden:

> Many years ago jazz tunes in their original form were heard in the Crescent
> City. Probably one of the earliest heard was one played by King Bolden's
> band. It seems that one night while playing at Odd Fellows Hall, Perdido

2. In *Soards' New Orleans City Directory* the Tios and Perez can be found in the 1917 edition,
St. Cyr and Picou in the 1924 edition.
3. E. Belfield Spriggins, "Excavating Local Jazz," *Louisiana Weekly,* April 22, 1933. p. 5.

near Rampart, it became very hot and stuffy and a discussion among members of Bolden's band arose about the foul air. The next day William Cornish, the trombonist with the band, composed a "tune" to be played by the band. The real words are unprintable but these will answer:

"I thought I heard Old Bolden say
Rotten gut, rotten gut
Take it away."

The rendition of this number became an overnight sensation and the reputation of Bolden's band became a household word with the patrons of Odd Fellows Hall, Lincoln and Johnson Parks and several other popular dance halls around the city.[4]

By the 1940s, jazz was a popular subject. Because this music was a continually evolving phenomenon, those who followed the new forms assumed that New Orleans was the cradle of jazz (and therefore important historically), but a cradle that had been left far behind. Just a few New Orleans musicians were thought important in their own right. By the 1950s, several researchers were attempting to write the entire history of jazz, pulling together styles and places—covering the whole picture from New Orleans, Chicago, Kansas City, and New York, to California. Too often in their effort to be comprehensive these authors failed to spend time in New Orleans developing background.

Charles Edward Smith and Frederic Ramsey, Jr., the editors of *Jazzmen,* were pioneers in extensive jazz research, and theirs was the first book to explore at any length the origins of New Orleans jazz. They could not rely on what others had written, for there was little solid research to consult; they undertook a monumental task and did so in all sincerity. They operated on a limited budget and time schedule, and were responsible for many inaccuracies in subsequent jazz histories only in that *Jazzmen* was accepted as a bible and was widely quoted. Later writers failed to document their own facts, and thus both reproduced and compounded *Jazzmen*'s inaccuracies.

Bill Russell, who was working with Ramsey and Smith, interviewed people around the country about the early New Orleans jazz days. Rus-

4. *Ibid.*

sell became quite close to Willie Geary "Bunk" Johnson, an early New Orleans trumpeter, and unfortunately based much of his Bolden material in the book on what Bunk told him.

Bunk distorted the Bolden story, most importantly by claiming to have been a member of Buddy's band. His first letter, from the frontispiece of *Jazzmen*, states: "King Bolden and myself were the first men that began playing Jazz in the city of dear old New Orleans." Bunk certainly did make an important contribution to jazz, but it came later than this implies. Anyone who has listened to his recordings from the 1940s cannot doubt his talent or the enthusiasm and excitement he' brought to a music that was being revived. His reasons for misleading Russell may have stemmed from his bitterness at having been overlooked for years, while he watched others who were often less skilled musically go on to success. Along with many other New Orleans musicians, he had experienced hard times. And very probably Bunk did not realize he was opening a Pandora's box. Who could be aware when the early jazz research was being done that it would be such a continuing thing? In that respect the misinformation did not go in vain, for it caused sufficient doubt to spur further research. Still, although jazz historians who bothered to do their own digging began to question Bunk's recollections, few did enough research to refute the errors with documentation and clear up the picture.

Bunk wasn't the only person to mention that he had played with Bolden. Willie Cornish had related his story to both Spriggins and the *Jazzmen* writers and is pictured in the one photograph of Bolden's band. More of his testimony could have been weighed against Bunk's, since the evidence is overwhelming that Cornish actually played with the band, whereas Bunk's claim is not supported by other facts.

Some of Bunk's tales about Bolden are evidently true enough, but it is now clear that he moved his birthdate back about ten years to put himself into the picture. Bunk stated in *Jazzmen*: "So I told Mr. Olivier that I think I could do better with King Bolden so he told me to suit myself and so I did and went on with King Bolden in the year of 1895. When I started playing with him Bolden was a married man and [had] two children. He must of been between 25 or 30 years old at that time."[5] Buddy's baptismal document shows that he was born on September 6, 1877; thus he would have been seventeen or eighteen in 1895. His first child, Charles, Jr., was not born until May 2, 1897.[6] Bunk continues:

> Now here are the men in the band when I went into it: Cornelius Tilman, drummer, Willy Cornish, trombone, Bolden, cornet, Bunk, cornet, Willie Warner, clarinet, Mumford, guitar, and Jimmie Johnson, bass. That was the old Bolden band when I went in to it. They were all men; I was the only young one in the Band, in short pants.
> The picture you have of Bolden's first band was taken just before I started playing with his large band. In the late years Bolden's five piece band became so great in the city of New Orleans that he had to make his band bigger by putting in drums and cornet which made it a seven piece band.[7]

According to Bunk he was born on December 27, 1879.[8] Marriage certificates show that Warner was born in 1877 and Jimmy Johnson in 1884.[9] The picture Bunk speaks of (after page 78 herein), shows six members, including Frank Lewis as a second clarinet player. Tillman is not in the picture, and it is also obvious that the Jimmy Johnson pictured here is not an eleven-year-old kid. And of all the sources I consulted in writing this book, no one except Bunk mentioned Buddy Bolden using another cornet.

Further refutation of Bunk's story comes from *The Autobiography of Pops Foster*: "Bunk claims he played with Bolden, but he was in the Superior band when Bolden was around and I played with them. The first time I saw Bunk was at the Fairgrounds at a big picnic in 1908."[10] In

---

5. Ramsey and Smith (eds.), *Jazzmen*, 24–25.
6. Charles Joseph Bolden's birth was recorded in the *St. John Fourth Baptist Church (colored) Register of Births, Marriages, Members, Deaths* on March 7, 1884. This is probably when he was baptized. Charles Joseph Bolden, Jr.'s, birth was recorded on August 16, 1897, in New Orleans Vital Statistics Records.
7. Ramsey and Smith (eds.), *Jazzmen*, 25.
8. *Ibid.*, 24.
9. The ages of Johnson and Warner were obtained from their marriage certificates which are housed in the New Orleans Vital Statistics Records. Johnson was married on February 3, 1904; Warner was married on July 22, 1911.
10. Tom Stoddard (ed.), *The Autobiography of Pops Foster: New Orleans Jazzman* (Berkeley: University of California Press, 1971), 47.

an interview with Richard Allen and Bill Russell, Peter Bocage, who was born in 1887 and played cornet and violin with the Superior band, commented on a photograph of this band showing both himself and Bunk: "I was about twenty-one when that was taken . . . around 1908 and 1909."[11] Bocage and Bunk look much the same age in this picture, which is reproduced in *New Orleans Jazz: A Family Album*.[12] Another statement by Bocage suggests further that Bunk was not as old as an 1879 birthdate would make him:

"Allen: Did you help Bunk much with his reading?

"Bocage: Yes, I helped him some—sure; but he could read when I first met him. . . . He had some schooling, you understand."[13] It would be somewhat surprising that Bunk, who was very proud of his musicianship and reading ability, would at age thirty be asking help from a twenty-one year old. Bunk expresses this pride in his musicianship in *The Bunk Johnson Talking Records*: "I come out of New Orleans University in 1894 and I was fit for orchestra . . . I liked to read, and I could read good."[14]

No records have been found to substantiate Bunk's claim of being born in 1879. My conclusion, based on dates of photos, the testimony of Pops Foster and Bocage, plus the lack of mention of Bunk being with Bolden by any other musician, is that Bunk was born closer to 1889 and did not play with Buddy Bolden.

Jazzmen contains other misleading information about Bolden, as when it states: "So when Buddy Bolden, the barber of Franklin Street, gathered his orchestra together in the back room of his shop to try over a few new tunes for a special dance at Tin Type Hall, it was no ordinary group of musicians. Nor was Buddy an ordinary cornetist."[15] Bolden had no barbershop, nor was there ever a Tin Type Hall. When I asked

11. Richard Allen and William Russell, interview with Peter Bocage, January 29, 1959, in William Ransom Hogan Jazz Archive, Tulane University, New Orleans.

12. Al Rose and Edmond Souchon, *New Orleans Jazz: A Family Album* (Baton Rouge: Louisiana State University Press, 1967), 135.

13. Allen and Russell, interview with Bocage, January 29, 1959, in Hogan Jazz Archive.

14. *Bunk Johnson Talking Record,* Goodtime Jazz Records M12048, Side 2, recorded in New Orleans, June 12, 1942.

15. Ramsey and Smith (eds.), *Jazzmen,* 10–11.

Bill Russell about the origin of this hall, he said that it had been a case of his misunderstanding Jelly Roll Morton's pronounciation of the name, and the error somehow got mixed in with the writing Russell was doing on Morton.[16]

Nearly everyone who wrote about Bolden followed *Jazzmen*'s lead in saying that he was a barber, and in addition that he edited a scandal sheet called *The Cricket*. These unsubstantiated facts became part of the legend. No copies have ever been found of *The Cricket,* and *Jazzmen* seems to be the sole source of this story. (Bill Russell attributed it to "a figment of someone's imagination.")[17] The barber reputation probably grew from the fact that Bolden hung around several barbershops, including ones run by Louis Jones, Adam Haley, and Charley Galloway. Russell, in his notes on a conversation with Buddy's widow, Nora, said that "according to her he [Buddy] did not run a scandal sheet and was not a barber, although he drank a lot and hung out at barber shops." Louis Jones, a friend of Bolden's from around 1894 on, agreed that to his knowledge the barber story was not true. And another refutation of both the barber and editor labels came from Papa John Joseph, a bass player and barber who, beginning in 1905, had lived near Bolden's neighborhood. It seems reasonably certain, then, that the publisher-barber portion of the Bolden legend can be put to rest.[18]

The New Orleans *Times-Picayune* made its contribution to the legend: "It [jazz] seems to have reached a recognizable form in the 1890s with Buddy Bolden, the Negro trumpeter, as its greatest exponent. He played with such volume that it is said he could often be heard while playing across the river in Gretna and there are still living those who can testify to his imaginative improvisations."[19]

Ten years after *Jazzmen* came Rudi Blesh's *Shining Trumpets,*

16. Conversation with Bill Russell at Preservation Hall on September 12, 1970.

17. *Ibid.*

18. William Ransom Hogan and Paul Crawford, interviews with William Russell, August 31 and September 4, 1962, and Allen and Russell, interview with Louis Jones, January 19, 1959, all in Hogan Jazz Archive; author's interview with Papa John Joseph, between sets at Preservation Hall, July 3, 1962; author's interview with Mrs. Louis Jones, April 9, 30, and May 7, 1971; author's interview with Andrew Wilson, August 5, 1971.

19. New Orleans *Times-Picayune,* January 7, 1940, p. 6.

another major work in jazz history. Blesh focused on the musical influences felt by Buddy's band, and he speculated on how the band had sounded. Much of his information on Bolden came from the old bass player, Wallace Collins, but Blesh obviously used *Jazzmen* for such background as the following: "Greatest of them was the Bolden Ragtime Band and its leader born shortly after the Civil War. . . . A barber with his own shop, as well as editor and publisher of a scandal sheet, *The Cricket* . . . Buddy Bolden found time to play the cornet as few men have ever played it and to form, in the early 1890s a band which was to initiate a period and to typify, actually or potentially, nearly all that jazz has meant, even until today."[20]

In 1950, Alan Lomax published *Mister Jelly Roll*, a compilation of his interviews with Jelly Roll Morton. Jelly Roll was an articulate, if colorful spokesman for early jazz, and although his tales at times seem far-fetched, they withstand scrutiny if toned down a bit. Jelly says about Bolden: "Speaking of swell people, I might mention Buddy Bolden, the most powerful trumpet player I've ever heard of that was known and the absolute favorite of all the hangarounders in the Garden District. . . . Buddy was a light brown-skin boy from Uptown. He drank all the whiskey he could find."[21] From Jelly Roll's more detailed account on Bolden later in that book, it is apparent that he had a good knowledge of what was going on.

In poring over approximately one hundred published works containing material on Bolden, I found that more than 90 percent of them (even some published in 1975) mention his being a barber, many reiterate the *Cricket* tale, a number elaborate on Bolden's Franklin Street barbershop, and some even add detail to the fictional Tin Type Hall. *The Complete Encyclopedia of Popular Music* contains probably the best one-paragraph summation of Bolden yet printed:

> 162. BOLDEN, BUDDY
> Born c. 1868, New Orleans, La.
> Died November 4, 1931, Jackson, La.

20. Rudi Blesh, *Shining Trumpets: A History of Jazz* (New York: Alfred A. Knopf, 1949), 180.
21. Lomax, *Mister Jelly Roll,* 57–60.

Jazz pioneer, strong and colorful personality, first "king" of cornet in New Orleans (later followed by King Oliver, Louis Armstrong). Played cornet with exceptional power. His band played New Orleans parades and dances, starting around 1895 or earlier, and Bolden became very popular. Health deteriorated in 1907, committed to East Louisiana State Hospital (mental home). Remained until death. Information sparse on Bolden's jazz activities in those ancient days, and no phonograph records. Yet as first important figure in birth of jazz, Bolden became legend.[22]

Although other Bolden myths will be examined in later chapters, we have the basics of the legend. Now what about the man?

22. Roger D. Kinkle (ed. and comp.), *The Complete Encyclopedia of Popular Music and Jazz, 1900–1950* (4 vols.; New Rochelle, N.Y.: Arlington House, 1974), II, 601.

2

Family History
and City
Neighborhoods

GUSTAVUS BOLDEN was born in Louisiana in 1806, when the population of the entire state was less than 75,000. A youngster when the first steamboat, the *Orleans*, arrived in New Orleans from Pittsburgh, he saw Louisiana admitted to the Union in 1812 and was around when General Andrew Jackson with the help of Jean Lafitte and his Barataria pirates turned back the British on January 8, 1815. He was still a young man when the first railroad west of the Alleghenies, the Pontchartrain Railroad, opened.

Gustavus was most likely born into slavery, though no definite records say. Entries in the 1880 census show that a son named Thomas was born to him in New Orleans in 1838, and that in 1850 he married Frances Smith, who had been transported as a slave from Virginia about that time. Frances was twenty years old when she and Gustavus were married and they settled in the city working as domestics. It was still legal to move slaves from one United States port to another even after the Slave Act of 1807 outlawed their importation; notations in the 1860, 1870, and 1880 census records show that the ancestors of many of the men who were later to pioneer jazz arrived in the city via a Virginia port.

The 1880 census also indicates that Gustavus and Frances had a son, Westmore "West" Bolden, in 1851, and a daughter, Cora, in 1854. Shortly before the Civil War began, around 1860, Gustavus went to work for a William Walker who had a cotton drayage and omnibus business at 354 Calliope Street. This was also the site of the Walker home where Frances was employed as a domestic servant; the Bolden family lived in quarters behind the Walker house.[1]

This was an ideal location for a drayage business, as the New Canal, which ran from Lake Pontchartrain to South Rampart Street between Julia and Delord streets, was just a block away. A wagon owner in Walker's position had ample opportunity to build a thriving business, having a cotton pickery next door, a lumber yard across the street, and within a ten-block area approximately twenty lumber yards, saw mills, planing mills, and lumber sheds. There were also a number of cotton mills and pickeries, cooper shops, foundries, and coal yards close-by. A block and a half away was the Jackson Depot where the Chicago, St. Louis, and New Orleans Railroad had a terminal, and a landing on Thalia Street brought goods from the Mississippi River wharves up Calliope Street. Walker was an enterprising man who took full advantage of his surroundings. His assessments rose from $64.88 in 1871 to $105.00 in 1879. In 1869 he paid license fees of $30.00 each for five wagons, and in 1872 he owned two large wagons and six smaller ones, licensed for a total of $280.00.

On August 6, 1866, Gustavus Bolden's death was recorded. The Bolden family, however, continued to live at 354 Calliope, all being employed by Walker. The 1870 census lists Walker as a forty-one-year-old native of Virginia, a substantial property owner, and proprietor of a drayage business. Listed below him and his wife Jennie, at the same address, are Frances Bolden, age forty, domestic servant; Thomas Bolden, thirty-two, domestic servant; Westmore Bolden, nineteen, domes-

---

1. The sources for the material on the Bolden family, William Walker, and locations pertinent to both are: U.S. Bureau of the Census Population Schedules for City of New Orleans, Wards 1 and 2, for the years 1860, 1870, and 1880; Real Estate Tax Assessments, First Municipal District, Second Assessment District for the years 1860 through 1880; *Atlas of the City of New Orleans*, comp. E. Robinson and R. H. Pidgeon, (New Orleans: E. Robinson, 1883); *Soards New Orleans City Directory* for the years 1865 through 1885; City of New Orleans Register of Licenses for Drays, Carts, Four-wheeled wagons, Floats, Public and private carriages, and Omnibuses for the years 1866 through 1880, all in the Louisiana Division, New Orleans Public Library. Death certificate of Augustus Bolen (a likely misspelling for Gustavus Bolden), August 6, 1866, in New Orleans Vital Statistics Records. (See page 153 herein for a history of the repository of these records.)

tic servant; and Cora Bolden, sixteen, in school. At this time Westmore was already working as a driver for Walker, and Cora was probably attending the nearby Fisk School for Girls at Franklin and Perdido streets.

Westmore Bolden married eighteen-year-old Alice Harris, daughter of Henry and Leah Harris, on August 14, 1873. Henry was also a drayman and the families likely became acquainted through the men's work. The couple was married at the First African Baptist Church on Howard Street, a church founded in 1824 and still existing, though now at 2216 Third Street. Almost a year later Cora married Alfred Dent.[2]

Westmore and Alice continued to live at 354 Calliope and on June 24, 1875, had a daughter christened Lotta but called Lottie.[3] A year later, according to the city directory, they moved several blocks away to 319 Howard Street. Here Charles Joseph "Buddy" Bolden was born to Westmore and Alice on September 6, 1877. There has been much controversy concerning Buddy's birthdate, but on March 7, 1884— probably the day Buddy was baptized—it was recorded in the baptismal ledgers of the First Street Baptist Church (also known as St. John the Fourth Baptist Church).[4]

In the same year Buddy was born, Francis Tillou Nicholls, a general in the Confederate army who had lost an arm at Winchester and a leg at Chancellorsville, was elected governor of Louisiana and Rutherford B. Hayes became United States president. Hayes, in accordance with his promises, withdrew the last of the federal troops from South Carolina and Louisiana, officially putting an end to the Reconstruction Era and the bitter, hectic days of carpetbag rule.

In 1880 the population of New Orleans stood at 210,000, broken down by the census bureau as 155,000 whites and 55,000 colored. A year later the population dropped when a yellow fever epidemic claimed nearly 4,000 lives. Work was beginning on a monument to Robert E.

2. Marriage certificates of Westmore Bolden, August 14, 1873, and of Cora Bolden, October 26, 1874, both in New Orleans Vital Statistics Records.

3. Birth certificate of Lotta Bolden, June 24, 1875, in New Orleans Vital Statistics Records.

4. The documents were still in the hands of church archivist, Elnora McKee, as late as 1970, though she is now deceased and no one seems to know what happened to the archives.

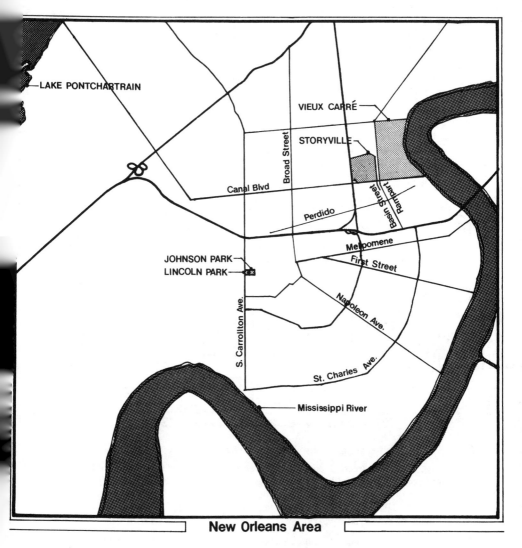

A very general map of the city of New Orleans showing major landmarks and emphasizing the areas pertaining to this book.

Birthplace of Buddy Bolden c. 1883

(This map is based on *Robinson's Atlas of the City of New Orleans,* 1883.)

A: 354 Calliope Street. Buddy's grandparents, Gustavus and Frances, lived here and worked for the William Walker family from about 1860 until 1875 and again in 1878. Buddy's father, Westmore, and his Aunt Cora were raised at this residence. His sister Lotta was born here on June 24, 1875. In 1894 the street number was changed to 2322.

B: 319 Howard Street. Westmore and Alice lived here in 1876 and 1877. This was Buddy's birthplace. The canal was called the New Canal and ran from Lake Pontchartrain down to the basin on South Rampart. The block directly above Locust between Clio and Calliope was the depot of the Chicago, St. Louis & New Orleans Railroad (Jackson Depot).

Lee, the location of which would later be known as Lee Circle. Antoine's Restaurant had been on St. Louis Street for nine years, the mysterious haunted house at 1140 Royal was a popular gambling house, and
the United States Mint on Esplanade Avenue was minting silver dollars
again, after being closed during the Civil War. The quadroon balls and
Congo Square dances were a thing of the past, though the square would
not become Beauregard Square for many years. On the literary front,
Lafcadio Hearn had taken a room at 516 Bourbon Street and was working for the New Orleans *Item*.

By 1878 Thomas Bolden had a daughter named Cora and that year
moved his family to St. Thomas Street, while West and Alice with
young Lottie and Charles moved back to the Walker residence. An an-
ticipated addition to West's family prompted a move to 225 Calliope
Street (closer to the river) in 1880, and Buddy's sister, also named Cora,
was born in that year.[5] Shortly thereafter they moved to St. Andrew
Street, between Locust and Magnolia (a location further Uptown, or
away from Canal Street), and here Buddy's sister Lottie, just short of her
sixth birthday, died of encephalitis on May 18, 1881. Westmore appeared before Dr. Joseph Jones of the New Orleans Board of Health to
have the death officially recorded, and for some reason his birthplace
was entered as Texas on this document. It appears to have been just a
clerical mistake as no other documents indicate that Westmore was born
elsewhere than in New Orleans.[6]

In these years young Charles would probably have become close to
his father, riding along on the wagon and acquainting himself with the
neighborhood and people who would later influence his life. He lived
near an area that was rife with music and possibly got his first glimpses
of the New Orleans music scene alongside his father, watching parades
and attending concerts where the brass bands played in full uniform. It is
not hard to visualize Westmore taking his son to see a parade that passed
near their home in May, 1881. The New Orleans *Louisianian*, a black

5. Cora's birthdate was obtained from her marriage certificate, dated September 11, 1902, in
New Orleans Vital Statistics Records.
6. Death certificate of Lotta Bolden, May 19, 1881, in New Orleans Vital Statistics Records.

weekly newspaper, reported preparations for this parade, which was part of a yearly celebration sponsored by the Odd Fellows:

> Joint committee of arrangements at work and has secured the two champion brass bands in the city, the Pickwick and Excelsiors for the occasion. Procession will form in Lafayette Square at 9 a.m. and move off at 10 on the following route: Down St. Charles to south side of Canal to Peters to north side of Canal to Rampart to Esplanade to Royal to Canal to Camp to Calliope to First to St. Dennis to Dryades to Calliope to St. Charles to Poydras thence to the hall where the procession will be dismissed and all proceed to the Fairgrounds in the cars. The entertainment will last all night and negotiations are being made to have the cars run all night also.[7]

Such a large parade would naturally be a big event in the area and would no doubt be a must for the Bolden family, especially since they lived on the parade route. The Excelsior band's performances that day, as described in the *Louisianian*, could not have failed to excite a youngster like Buddy:

> One important and noticeable feature of the day's celebrations was the appearance of the Excelsior Band at the head of Pelican Fire Co. No. 4, under the leadership of Mr. Sylvester Decker, in their new and beautiful uniforms, planned after the style of the Prussian military costume, with dark blue helmet hats, ribbed with burnished brass, corded in white, with long white horse hair plumes, long military coats, three rows of brass buttons, corded in white, with epaulets, pants of dark navy blue cloth with white stripes. Everywhere they appeared their approach was heralded with murmurs of admiration. It is said that a committee of Mobile firemen who were visiting our department on the Fourth, have engaged the band for their anniversary on the 9th inst., and on the 13th they will play for our Knights Templar of the Constantine Commandery. Messrs. Haggatt and Penn deserve great credit for the successful manner in which they have managed the affairs of the band.[8]

According to Isidore Barbarin, who was born in 1872 and had played with the early Eureka, Onward, and Excelsior brass bands before the turn of the century, most of the entertainments of those days were similar

7. New Orleans *Louisianian*, April 23, 1881, p. 2.
8. *Ibid.*, July 9, 1881, p. 2.

to this one, beginning with a brass band parade and ending with a concert and dance in the evening.[9] Music was also an integral part of such organizations as the Masons, the Odd Fellows, the Vidalia Social Club, Lulu Social Club, St. Joseph Young Men's Benevolent Association, Garden District Scientific and Musical Social Club, Young Men and Ladies Good Intent Social and Debating Club, and the Equal Justice Marine Association.[10]

Some of the leaders of the early (1875–1885) brass and concert bands which provided this musical entertainment were Thomas S. Kelly, Charlie Jaeger, Frank Dodson, Louis Martin, and Sylvester Decker.[11] There were smaller string bands, too, although few of the musicians' names have survived. Drummers Louis and Paul Barbarin, sons of Isidore, had an uncle named Louis Arthidore who played back then; trumpeter Peter Bocage's father had a four-piece string outfit; and the Manetta family, who will be mentioned in more detail later, were active musically in the early 1880s. The smaller bands played at picnics, dances, private entertainments, and parties.

Some of the halls where the entertainments were held survived into the 1900s, but when Buddy Bolden was a boy the popular spots, which were scattered around the city, included Loepers Park, Orange Grove Picnic Grounds, Magnolia Garden, Oakland (Riding) Park, and Turners Hall, which was close enough to Buddy's home for him to have heard the music. Another place where various clubs gathered was Cottrell's Hall, named after prominent black citizens James and Alice Cottrell.[12]

In those days the brass bands played at funerals too, and although the music may not have been "happy," it would have provided another

9. Allen and Russell, interview with Isidore Barbarin, January 7, 1959, in William Ransom Hogan Jazz Archive, Tulane University, New Orleans.
10. The New Orleans *Louisianian*, a black newspaper published every Saturday, included reports of the activities of various social clubs. These particular organizations were mentioned in each issue from May 7, 1881, to July 9, 1881, p. 3.
11. John W. Blassingame, *Black New Orleans, 1860–1880* (Chicago: University of Chicago Press, 1973), 140.
12. The halls and parks were mentioned in the New Orleans *Louisianian* between May 7, 1881, and July 9, 1881, p. 3; the locations were verified by consulting *Soards' New Orleans City Directory* for the years 1880 through 1885.

chance for Buddy to hear the bands. One can imagine him standing on the corner watching the following procession: "After the ceremony at the church, the large concourse of sympathizing friends, together with the Masonic bodies, gathered to perform the last sad offices and to the tread of muffled drum and mournful dirge he [Mr. Albert Wicker] was carried to his last home on earth."[13] Other sources of musical entertainment were the programs presented by schools, and the Boldens may well have taken Buddy and Cora to one at the Fisk School in which "the exercises were remarkably good . . . the singing and acting of numerous selections from the burlesque opera 'HMS Pinafore' showing a remarkable degree of aptness in the pupils and careful training by the teachers. . . . Professor A. P. Williams is an excellent and careful instructor, and a disciplinarian whose superiors are few."[14]

On May 29, 1883, Buddy's Grandmother Frances Bolden died at age 54. Christmas that year was bleak as well, for Westmore contacted pneumonia around December 15, and on December 22 he was admitted to Charity Hospital. After struggling through the night, he succumbed to acute pleuro-pneumonia early on the 23rd.[15] Westmore was only thirty-two years old when he died, leaving a twenty-nine-year-old widow and two children. Buddy, then six, had already lost two immediate family members.

The next few years are hard to document, but Alice, Buddy, and Cora may have lived with relatives or friends, or possibly stayed on at St. Andrew Street. They are not listed in the city directory from 1883 through 1885 and a guess would be that Alice was working during the day and the children were being looked after somewhere else. In 1886 they were listed at 468 Philip Street. Sometime during 1887 they moved to 385 First Street, which was to be the family home for nearly twenty years.

13. New Orleans *Louisianian,* April 2, 1881, p. 3.
14. *Ibid,* April 23, 1881, p. 2.
15. Death certificate of Frances Bolden, May 29, 1883, in New Orleans Vital Statistics Records; Orleans Parish, Charity Hospital Admission Book, Vol. 40, December, 1883–November, 1885; Orleans Parish, Charity Hospital, Record of Deaths, October, 1869–January, 1886.

After West died, Alice and the children seem to have become estranged from the other Boldens. Cora, the aunt, was widowed in 1884 and continued to live at 630 St. Thomas, but there is no evidence that she and Alice were close. Buddy's Uncle Thomas drops out of sight around this point, and Alice's family is no longer traceable after the mid-1880s, though she had at least two sisters. From the time they moved to First Street, Alice, Buddy, and Cora formed a close-knit group, independent of other family members.

In researching Buddy Bolden's family, the various spellings of *Bolden* cause interesting problems. The first document available— Gustavus' 1866 death certificate—spells the name *Bolen*. The city directories of 1880, 1881, 1888 and 1892 spell it *Bolding*, and the 1898 directory shows Mrs. Alice Boldan at 2309 First. Aunt Cora's wedding certificate is made out to *Cora Bolding* though her signature says *Cora Bolden*. Some of the documents were made out by ministers and others who were nearly illiterate themselves, and in digging out the Bolden history it becomes necessary to check for *Bouldings, Bowlings, Bolands, Boltons*, and *Beldens*. Information is at times incomplete as well, as when wedding certificates in giving the parentage state only "daughter of Bolden and Bolden." With enough background on dates, names, and addresses, the discrepancies in spelling can be sorted and missing information filled in.

Many researchers have assumed that marriages among blacks in the 1800s were not official and therefore were not recorded in city archives. But most of them *were*, in fact, recorded, and they are extremely helpful in pinpointing dates, ages, locations, family names, and often close friends in the musician fraternity. The only known signature of Buddy Bolden was found in this manner.[16]

16. To be fair to earlier researchers, the city archives were not open for general searching until late 1973 when the New Orleans Public Library obtained marriage and death certificates up to 1915. By some quirk of Louisiana law, the Orleans Parish vital statistics are still off-limits to anyone save immediate family members and even they must have an approximate date and proof of relationship. It is interesting to note, also, that in the census of 1870, racial categories were broken down into black, white, and mulatto; the Boldens were all listed as mulatto.

Listings of the Bolden Family in *Soards' New Orleans City Directory*

1875 - Bollen, Cora, servant, 354 Calliope
       Bollen, Francis, servant, 354 Calliope
       Bollen, West, teamster, 354 Calliope
1876 - Bolden, West, driver, 319 Howard
1877 - Bolden, West, driver, 319 Howard
1878 - Bolden, Frances, widow of Gustavus, 358 Howard
       Bolden, West, laborer, 354 Calliope
1880 - Bolding, West, drayman, 255 Calliope
1881 - Bolding, West, laborer, ns [north side] St. Andrew between Magnolia
       and Locust
1886 - Bowlan, Alice, widow of Wesley, 468 Philip
1888 - Bolding, Alice, widow of Wesley, 385 First
1890 - Bolden, Alice, widow of Louis, 385 First
1891 - Bolden, Alice, widow of Louis, laundress, 385 First
1892 - Bolding, Mrs. Alice, 385 First
1894 - Bolden, Alice, widow of Wesley, 385 First
1897 - Bolden, Alice, widow of Wesley, 2309 First
       Bolden, Charles, plasterer, 2309 First
1898 - Boldan, Mrs. Alice, 2309 First
1899 - Bolden, Mrs. Alice, 2309 First
1900 - Bolden, Mrs. Alice, 229 N. Liberty
       Bolden, Charles, plasterer, 2309 First
       Bolden, Mrs. Westmore, 2309 First
1901 - Bolden, Charles, music teacher, 2309 First
1902 - Bolden, Charles, musician, 2309 First
1903 - Bolden, Mrs. Alice, 2309 First
       Bolden, Charles, musician, 2309 First
       Bolden, Charles, musician, 2719 Philip
1904 - Bolling, Charles, musician, 2309 First
1905 - Bolden, Charles, musician, 2302 First
1906 - Bolden, Mrs. Alice, 2302 First
1907 - Bolden, Charles, musician, 2527 First
1908 - Bolden, Mrs. Alice, 2527 First
1909 - Bolden, Mrs. Alice, 2527 First
1913 - Bolden, Edward, mason, 2527 First
1923 - Bolden, Mrs. Silas, 2527 First
1924 - Bolden, Mrs. Alice, laundress, 2527 First
       Bolden, Cora, laundress, 2527 First

1925 - Bolden, Alice, 2312 First
1931 - Bolden, Alice, 2338 Philip

The 1890 and 1891 listing of Alice as "widow of Louis" is a mystery, as she never remarried after West died. In 1903, Charles Bolden is listed at two addresses; the 2719 Philip address is where he lived with his wife Nora. Edward, listed in 1913, was possibly a common-law relation. In 1923, the listing for Mrs. Silas Bolden is probably a case of mistaking the pronounciation of *Alice* for *Silas*. The 1897 street number change merely reflects a renumbering of houses on First Street.

The Boldens moved to 385 First Street when Buddy was ten years old. Mrs. Bolden made sure the children were well taken care of, even though she worked away from home and had to raise them by herself. She was evidently a conscientious parent, and her boy, Charlie—as she called him—was not a street waif. Buddy's wife, Nora, said that his mother always provided the best for him and never made him work as a kid, and Louis Jones, a good friend, agreed that Buddy did not work until he finished school.[17] Nonetheless it was not a sheltered childhood, and Buddy had a degree of independence that allowed him to follow his instincts. He was born twelve years after the Civil War, and if his mother remembered the days of slavery and the aftermath of Reconstruction, being a little uncertain of just what emancipation meant, Buddy was of a generation that didn't know or particularly care what the rules had *been* and saw life as an open challenge instead of a restricted corridor. By the time he moved to the First Street neighborhood he was already familiar with the fancy military-like uniforms and march music of the post-Civil War brass bands that had strutted through his old neighborhood, and music was one interest he must have embraced early.

The city in those days was much different from now; some of the streets and neighborhoods of Buddy's childhood no longer even exist, and other street names have changed. At that time canals ran through the heart of the city and everything was carried by barges or by horse and wagon. Entertainment was much more localized and simple; music and

17. Hogan and Crawford, interviews with Russell, August 31 and September 4, 1962, and Allen and Russell, interview with Jones, January 19, 1959, both in Hogan Jazz Archive.

dancing were a major part of most leisure-time activities. A search through *Soards' New Orleans City Directories* from 1887 to 1907 allows one to picture the area Buddy lived in during these years.

In 1887 the First Street neighborhood was primarily Irish and German, with Quinns, Mahers, McKnights, Bradys, Murrays, and Gannons living in the same block as Brinkmans, Schneiders, Durrs, Schaeffers, and Welches. It was, however, a well-integrated area—not an unusual phenomenon in New Orleans, where a "live and let live" attitude toward the person next door has always generally held. Adolph Durr had a grocery on the Howard Street corner (400 First) and Mrs. John Schneider had a bakery across the street. Steamboatmen, teamsters, carpenters, porters, teachers, plasterers, and longshoremen made up the bulk of the block's residents. When the Boldens first moved to the neighborhood a Hebrew cemetery extended between Philip and Jackson streets, just behind their home and facing White Street (now Saratoga). Another short street, Race, was a continuation of Franklin Street between Philip and Jackson. Franklin is now Loyola, the cemetery was razed in 1957, and White and Race streets no longer exist.

The ownership of the stores and homes changed hands through the years and the buildings were renumbered in 1894, but for many years the basic character of the street remained unchanged. The street maps of 1887 and 1905 illustrate the similarities over nearly twenty years. The area containing 385/2309 First Street, located above the Irish Channel between Howard (now LaSalle) and Liberty streets, was made up mostly of the double Victorian shotgun-type cottages built in New Orleans between 1870 and 1890. Many of these cottages were owned by people living in the Garden District and were rented out for revenue. They were definitely not "slave quarters" or shacks, and most of the tenants were fairly independent. A physician, Theodore R. Huston, lived at 2333; Margaret Dwyer, who taught at the William I. Rogers School on Tonti Street, lived at 2336. The famous white clarinetist Harry Shields was born in 1899 at 2319 First, just two houses from the Boldens. His half brother, Jimmy Ruth, who died in 1961 at age 72, knew young Buddy,

The Bolden family lived in this house at 2309 First Street from 1887 to early 1905. This photograph was taken in 1971.

The 2300 block of First Street shows the Bolden home as the third building from the right. When the Boldens lived here the corner building with the Barq's sign in front was Paul Mandella's Grocery.

Nelson Joseph's shaving parlor and barbershop was at the corner of First and Liberty streets, across the street from the Bolden home. Louis Jones had his shop here around 1895–1900, and Buddy spent a great deal of time here. His first cornet teacher, Manuel Hall, lived a block away.

and a half sister, Maggie Ruth (1877–1970) knew Buddy, his mother, and sister quite well.[18]

The Bolden home was half of a shotgun double and is still standing. It has a kitchen in the back, living room in front, two smaller rooms in the middle that were used as bedrooms, and a back porch, probably used mostly for storage. The street itself in those days was often a muddy quagmire, and the sidewalk consisted of diagonally laid bricks with planks used as walkways to cross the street. Frequent arrests were made in the 1880s and 1890s of people caught stealing the planks to take home and cut up for firewood. The street from 2311 toward the river on one side and from 2338 on the other has remained almost the same as when Bolden lived there. If one ignores the automobiles it is not hard to imagine things as they were at the turn of the century. Louis Jones's first barbershop still stands on the corner of First and Liberty, now shaded by a canopy with red and white supporting posts that extend over the sidewalk with the sign "N. Joseph Shaving Parlor." The original street signs are nailed to the corners of the building. Nelson Joseph and his brother John, both musicians, cut hair there from around 1907 until the 1960s. Nelson's widow, now in her nineties, owns the building and still lives beside the shop. She remembered when the Boldens lived at 2309 First Street.[19]

Police arrest records and homicide reports from 1895 to 1907 give detailed information about life in certain parts of the neighborhood. Grocery stores frequently had adjoining bars that consisted solely of a draught beer tap and a whiskey barrel—primarily a carry-out business. A patron would bring his own can or bucket and have it filled with his favorite beverage. Some of these grocery-bar combinations were relatively trouble-free, such as the one operated by the Dwyer brothers on the corner of First and Howard. Others had periodic run-ins with the police. Paul Mandella, one of several Italian immigrants who, by 1900, had taken over a neighborhood grocery, had his store and bar at 2301

18. Author's interview with Larry Ruth, nephew of Maggie Ruth, August 6, 1971.
19. Author's interview with Mrs. Nelson Joseph, April 30, 1971.

Left side			Right side
Adolph Durr GROCER	400	399	Roland Sheppard DRIVER
Henry Classen LABORER	398	397	Mrs. John Schneider BAKER
James Adams CARPENTER	396	393	Isom Ellison LABORER
James Taylor MACHINIST	394	391	Robert Anderson TEAMSTER
		387	Sara Anderson
Peter Nickerson ROOFER	386		
Conrad Welch COLLECTOR	384	385	**Mrs. Alice Bolden**
		383	Everet S. Swan LONGSHOREMAN
Ansel S. Bunton TEACHER	382	381	George L. Duvernay PLASTERER
Madison Bowles PORTER	380	379	Armstrong Payne LABORER

FIRST STREET

SOUTH LIBERTY STREET

First Street - 1887

This is a house-to-house look at Buddy Bolden's neighborhood when the family first moved to First Street in 1887. The names are taken from *Soards' New Orleans City Directory*, 1884–1887. The street numbering system changed in 1894 and this block became the 2300 block; 385 became 2309 First.

HOWARD STREET

Left side			Right side		
Richard Dwyer GROCER	2338		2339	Joseph Radosta FRUIT VENDOR	
Miss Margaret Dwyer SCHOOL TEACHER	2336		2337	Mrs. Wilhelmina Warskat HOME BREAD BAKER	
John Adams LABORER	2332		2333	Dr. Theodore R. Huston PHYSICIAN	
William Waltem LABORER	2330		2329	James McCormick	
Louis Laws WAREHOUSEMAN (for C.T. Patterson Co.)	2328		2327	Mrs. Annie Hornback	
William Taylor LABORER	2326		2325	George & William Betz MACHINIST & CLERK	
Mrs. Francis Ewing	2324		2323	John H. McLin LINEMAN	
Harry Steele SLATER	2322		2321	Daniel Leddy LINEMAN	
James Haynes CARPENTER	2320		2319	Emanuel Johnson CLERK, FIRST PRECINCT POLICE	
Edward & James Taylor PAINTER LABORER	2318		2315	Edward Toelke CARPENTER	
Mrs. Mary Ridley	2314		2313	Richard Schluter WATCHMAN	
Frank Valentine	2312		2311	John Porter LABORER	
			2309	**Charles Bolden MUSICIAN**	
Henry Schaeffer BARTENDER	2308		2307	Mrs. Susan Tillman	
William Lee CARPENTER	2306		2305	Mrs. Laura Clay	
Robert Scott DRIVER	2300		2301	Paul Mandella GROCER	

FIRST STREET

SOUTH LIBERTY STREET

First Street - 1905

A house-to-house look at the neighborhood around 1905. Most of the addresses were located in *Soards' New Orleans City Directory*, 1904 to 1906. Buddy, his mother, and his sister lived in this block from about 1887 until sometime in 1905 or 1906.

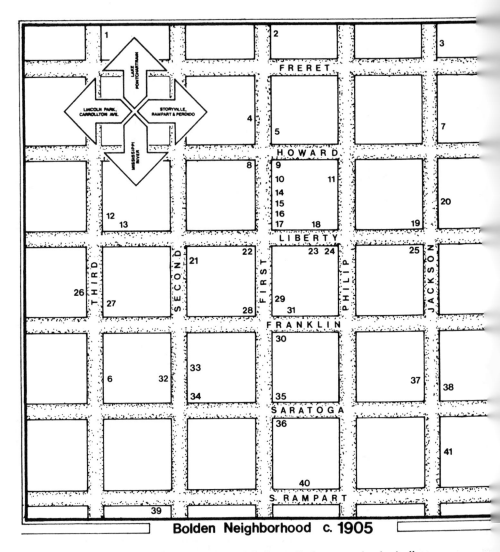

Bolden Neighborhood c. 1905

Some of the addresses include dates both before and after 1905, but basically, these were the people and businesses in the neighborhood when Buddy was in his prime music years.

Key:

1. Frederick J. Mehrtens, plasterer, 2521 Third Street.

2. Bolden family home from 1906 to 1924, 2527 First Street.

3. Mount Zion Methodist Church, 2515 Jackson.

4. St. John Fourth Baptist Church, also originally called First Street Baptist Church, 2432-36 First Street. This is where the Boldens attended church.

5. Bass family home in 1901, 2405 First Street.

6. Bass family home in 1897, 2113 Third Street.

7. McDonogh #20 School, 2407 Jackson.

8. Richard Dwyer Grocery, 2338 First.

9. Joseph Radosta Fruit Stand, 2339 First.

10. Dr. Theodore R. Huston, 2333 First.

11. Bolden home from 1925 to 1932, where Buddy's mother and sister died.

12. Mount Olive Baptist Church, 2319 Third.

13. Oscar Ellis Blacksmith Shop, 2427 Liberty.

14. Home where clarinetist Harry Shields was born in 1899, 2319 First Street.

15. The Bolden family home from the mid 1880s to 1905, 2309 First.

16. Steve Lewis, the piano player, later lived here, 2307 First.

17. Paul Mandella Grocery and Bar, 2301 First.

18. Providence Hall (Social Club and School), 2241 South Liberty. Bolden played many dances here.

19. Philip Grocery & Bar.

20. Home of Felicia Oliver Milo around 1918, 2319 Jackson. She was Charles, Jr's, aunt and was listed as next of kin on his navy enlistment papers.

21. Home of James Philips, who played trombone and drums with Bolden, 2231 Second.

22. Barbershop, 2240 First Street. Louis Jones had his first shop here before 1900. George Jackson ran it until about 1906 when it was taken over by Nelson Joseph.

23. Home of Manuel Hall, who gave Bolden his first cornet lessons, 2212 South Liberty.

24. Bertha Stark Saloon, a combination grocery, bar, and poolroom, 2200 Liberty.

25. Joseph Fallo Oyster Bar, 2100 Liberty.

26. First African Baptist Church, 2216 Third.

27. Oriental Olivet Baptist Church, 2209 Third.

28. Adam Haley Barbershop, 2200 First.

29. Albert Poree, plasterer, 2217 First.

30. Salvador Civlino Saloon and Grocery, 2139 First.

31. Fred and Samuel Deverney, plasterers, 2229 Franklin.

32. St. Frances de Sales School for Colored, 2130 Second.

33. St. Frances de Sales School for White, 2133 Second.

34. Kane Grocery, 2101 Second.

35. The Flying Horses, a tent-covered neighborhood amusement park, First and Saratoga.

36. Peter and Murphy Rondo Grocery and Saloon, 2037 First.

37. Geddes-Moss Funeral Home, 2128 Jackson.

38. Louis Jones Barbershop from before 1900 to around 1950, 2113 Jackson. His widow was still living at this location in 1973.

39. Charles A. Schneider Blacksmith Shop, 2408 South Rampart.

40. Hattie Oliver Home, where Charles, Jr., was born in 1897, 2233 South Rampart.

41. Longshoremen's Hall, originally called Hagan's Hall and also known as Jackson Hall, 2059 Jackson Avenue. Jelly Roll Morton described seeing Buddy Bolden play here.

First Street. It was a legitimate grocery and was probably the Boldens' corner store, but Mandella hassled with the police over selling merchandise on Sunday. More serious incidents resulted from illegal gambling. A murder over a card game occurred in July, 1905, in Philip Accardo's Grocery and Bar on the corner of South Rampart and First, and in September the manager of Mrs. Bertha Starck's Grocery and Barroom on the corner of Liberty and Philip was killed by police as he resisted arrest for holding dice games.[20]

The churches in the neighborhood included St. John the Fourth Baptist Church, which the Bolden family attended, the Union Bethel African Methodist Church, Mount Olive Baptist, Mount Zion Methodist, and St. Francis De Sales Roman Catholic Church. The Catholic church maintained separate schools for white boys and girls next door and also one for black children.

The Bolden family lived in the block until 1906, and Buddy did most of his growing up here. It was a busy area since several well-traveled routes intersected it. The Jackson Avenue ferry brought people from across the Mississippi River and the Jackson streetcar carried them on up to St. Charles Avenue; New Orleans and Carrollton Railroad cars also came from Downtown via St. Charles. The Cotton Exposition of 1885, held at Upper City Park—later Audubon Park—further opened up transportation and development from the heart of the city. The nearby Dryades Street market (where steak sold for ten cents a pound in 1890) was filled with livestock, produce, and seafood arriving on the New Canal barges.

Morris Square, a popular picnic ground, was close at hand, bordered by Freret, Howard, Washington, and Third streets. National Park, where many blacks played baseball and held picnics before 1900, was at Third and Willow, accessible by the Tulane Belt streetcars going up St. Charles to the dairy farms out near Dublin Street.

---

20. New Orleans Police Department Arrest Records and Police Superintendent's Office Reports of Homicide for 1905, p. 26, both in Louisiana Division, New Orleans Public Library.

3

Schooling
and Early Musical
Influences

BUDDY BOLDEN would have been old enough to begin school in the fall of 1883 or 1884. Noting the Bolden address on St. Andrew Street and the available schools for black children within a reasonable distance, the school where Bolden began his education was most likely the Fisk School for Boys. Located at 507 South Franklin near the corner of Perdido, Fisk was run by Arthur P. Williams, the strict disciplinarian whose school program was mentioned by the New Orleans *Louisianian* in 1881. His wife, Sylvanie, headed the Fisk School for Girls next door, and this is where Buddy's Aunt Cora had earned her high school diploma around 1871.

Music was part of the curriculum and the school presented operettas and special singing programs, but whether or not they had a band is unknown. John Robichaux's musicians, James and Wendell McNeil, were teachers at Fisk School for Boys in the 1890s and after, and James served as vice-principal.[1]

Because the early Fisk School records were in such bad shape they could not be transferred to microfilm or otherwise preserved, it is impossible to definitely verify Buddy's attendance there. Other schools in the area, such as the First Street School, James Lewis School, Thomy Lafon School, and St. Francis De Sales Catholic School, were not old enough for Buddy to have begun his schooling at them. The First Street School

1. *Soards' New Orleans City Directory*, 1890.

records, for example, contain the names of many of Bolden's neighbors, but they only go back to 1910.[2]

From samples of their handwriting it seems possible that Buddy and his sister Cora had the same penmanship teacher, and they must have had more than a nodding acquaintance with literacy. The following illustrations of family signatures are 1.) Buddy's, as witness to Frank Lewis' marriage on February 17, 1904, 2.) his sister Cora's, on her marriage license of September 11, 1902, and 3.) Aunt Cora's, on her marriage license dated October 26, 1874:

1.   *Chas. Bolden.*

2.   *Cora Bolden*

3.   *Cora Bolden*

How far Buddy went in school is a little uncertain, but his education continued to at least the early 1890s. Louis Jones's statement that Buddy never worked until he got out of school gives a clue, since it intimates that the two knew each other when Buddy was still in school. Jones moved to New Orleans in 1894 when Bolden was seventeen and old enough to have earned a high school diploma.[3] Also, in the city directory Buddy is not listed independently of his mother until 1897, and the frontispiece portrait of him could very well be a high school graduation portrait.

Of the early experiences that helped form Bolden's musical instincts, one of the most obvious influences would have been the Baptist church. The Boldens were Baptists as far back as can be traced and while he lived

2. Author's interview with Mrs. O. W. Nelson, October 22, 1971. The Fisk School and First Street School records are both at the Orleans Parish School Board offices, 703 Carondelet, New Orleans.
3. Allen and Russell, interview with Jones, January 19, 1959, in William Ransom Hogan Jazz Archive, Tulane University, New Orleans.

in New Orleans Buddy attended the church he was baptized in, the St. John Baptist on First Street. As a youngster, he probably suffered any typical child's impatience with too much confinement in church, but he no doubt joined in the clapping and singing and began to get a feeling for the spirituals and hymns that would remain with him. St. John's had a very musical congregation. When Buddy was older, probably around 1904 or 1905, Edward "Kid" Ory and Arthur "Bud" Scott remembered seeing him come out of church with his wife Nora and her sister Dora Bass, and said, "They were swinging."[4]

Between 1870 and 1880 the African Methodist church was predominant in black New Orleans, but the Baptist church was growing. In 1885 the city directory listed about twenty Baptist churches and by 1900 there were nearly fifty. Churches like the one the Boldens attended were emotion-oriented and somewhat primitive. The ministers, sometimes unordained and illiterate, earned their credentials by being able to stir the congregation with words and to evoke a rhythmic response that could lead individuals to a trance-like state. A combination of despair over the hard times on earth and joyful anticipation of heaven was voiced in wailing, groaning, shouting, and crying. Members sang and prayed for relief from suffering, and the responsive exchange between pastor and congregation produced a kind of jumping called the shouts. The enthusiasm of these responses at times actually shook the church buildings and led nearby residents to complain of the noise.[5]

In a December, 1899, letter to the police superintendent one man complained about Spiritual Hall on Carondelet Street: "My daughter is now sick in bed and the noise from their music and gigging [sic] is a terrible nuisance. We only ask the removal of the piano to some other part of the hall."[6] The piano, however, must have been used for a special program, as several musicians have said there were no instruments in the church services then, not even pianos. Papa John Joseph remembered

4. Author's interview with the Reverend W. E. Hausey, July 31, 1971, and Hogan and Crawford, interviews with Russell, August 31 and September 4, 1962, in Hogan Jazz Archive.
5. Blassingame, *Black New Orleans, 1860–1880,* 148–49.
6. G. Porteous to D. S. Gaster, December 14, 1899, in Louisiana Division, New Orleans Public Library.

that the Baptist churches when he was growing up had jubilee singing, which was spirituals sung with a beat accompanied by hand-clapping.[7] The musician Harrison Barnes also remembered a service in his church. "The singing was like an anthem. They would sing jubilees. They would mix them in like they do now, call them anthems. They word it out, then sing that strain, then word it out and sing some more. They'd start to clapping their hands on jubilee. Sometimes the sisters would begin to shout. That would be after the preaching and things like that would get on them. . . . They'd be shouting, it wasn't dancing, but it was so near dancing."[8]

The brass bands that so filled Buddy's musical background were part of an interesting interweaving of undertaking establishments, churches, and benevolent societies and social clubs. The societies and clubs functioned as both insurance agencies and social organizations; members paid their dues and in return received sick benefits, had their funerals taken care of, and could participate in social affairs. The entertainments included picnics and dances, and when a brother or sister died a brass band and uniformed mourners, fellow members of the society, walked the "last mile" with the body. The wakes were large affairs, too, with all the societies' members required to take part. According to Isidore Barbarin, the Odd Fellows, one of the largest societies, "had funerals every day. Our band played for the Odd Fellows, Liberty Society, Perseverance, Hobgoblins, Bulls, Friend of Orders and many others."[9]

It was important to have a proper, elaborate funeral; because death was a release from earthly burdens the inclination was to "cry at birth, rejoice at death."[10] The undertakers organized the funerals, providing a horse-drawn hearse and hiring one or more brass bands. Some of the undertaking parlors even sold insurance and sponsored their own societies. The Geddes funeral home, for example, had a large mul-

7. Allen and Russell, interview with Joseph, November 26, 1958, in Hogan Jazz Archive.

8. Paraphrased script from tape of Allen and Russell interview with Harrison Barnes, January 29, 1959, *ibid*.

9. Blassingame, *Black New Orleans, 1860–1880*, pp. 167–68, and Allen and Russell, interview with Barbarin, January 7, 1959, in Hogan Jazz Archive.

10. Blassingame, *Black New Orleans, 1860–1880*, pp. 167–68.

tivaulted tomb in Lafayette Cemetery No. 2, where members of its society were buried.[11] Other societies were sponsored by churches and many, such as the Cotton Yardmen, Teamsters & Loaders, and Cotton Screwmen, were independent.

The societies and funeral homes thus supported a number of brass bands in the city. Two of the best were the earlier mentioned Excelsior and Onward bands, but also playing in the 1880s were the Eureka, the Pickwick and Diamond bands from across the Mississippi, and the Oriental Brass Band which was formed around 1886. Country towns had their own bands, such as the one in St. Joseph's where cornetist Claiborne Williams got his start.

The parades in which the bands participated were extremely long and arduous, as illustrated by the Odd Fellows' route in Chapter 2. On occasions like Labor Day, Fireman's Day (March 4), Mardi Gras, and for some of the larger social events and funerals, the men marched all day, then played for dancing until 4 A.M. or later at a hall or park. It was, consequently, common practice to use young, aspiring musicians to beat the bass drum or snares or blow a little melody while the older musicians put down their instruments or stopped along the way for a beer. A number of boys who would later pioneer the development of jazz served their apprenticeships in the brass bands under circumstances such as these, and often they were not yet in their teens when they first appeared with the street bands.

Isidore Barbarin recalled that the brass bands then had ten to twelve pieces and would play for dances after the parades in full uniform. "Sometimes after a large parade like the Odd Fellows, they'd end up at the Fairgrounds and have maybe three bands—a brass band and a dance orchestra alternated on a stand and a small string band played in the field." Papa John Joseph said the first brass bands he saw played strictly old time marches, but they played blues and popular numbers for dancing. He thought the Oriental, Excelsior, Pickwick, and Onward bands were tops. Papa John later played with the Anthony Holmes Brass Band

11. Lafayette Cemetery No. 1 and 2 Burial Ledgers, 1910 to August 30, 1943, in Louisiana Division, New Orleans Public Library.

in Lutcher, Louisiana, and said that before he was with the band (probably around 1900) he had seen Buddy Bolden play a street job with them in Lutcher. Holmes apparently had heard Bolden in New Orleans and hired him to play a parade.[12]

Papa Jack Laine, who died in 1966 at age 93, was leading a white band as early as 1885, and suggested that his band was "ragging" the tunes. It was a large band consisting of lead cornet, two second cornets, two trombones, lead clarinet, two second clarinets, baritone horn, alto horn, tuba, and two drums. The sound was totally ensemble—no solos were taken, and although Laine played bass drum and alto horn, he was actually more the organizer and leader. At times he had several bands playing around the city and it is a good guess that Bolden heard Laine and one of his Reliance bands some time before the turn of the century. Laine did not remember hearing Bolden play, but did recall Manuel Perez (who probably began around 1895), playing a lot of parades, and a man named Perlops Lopez was leading one of the first black bands he heard. Laine mentioned that there was no musical integration in those days. He evidently did not know that one of his tromboners, Dave Perkins, was a light-skinned black who was playing both sides of the street, or that Achille Baquet, who played clarinet with him, had a father and brother playing with the black Excelsior band.[13]

The brass bands played all out when they were on the street or at an outdoor concert. Because of their size, certain restrictions were placed on the locations they could play. An 1898 letter to the police superintendent from a precinct captain explains the refusal of a permit for a complimentary entertainment that included a large brass band. The event was to be held in an unoccupied building at the corner of St. Philip and Dauphine, but according to the captain the building was too small and

12. Allen and Russell, interview with Barbarin, January 7, 1959, and with Joseph, November 26, 1958, both in Hogan Jazz Archive.
13. Allen and Russell, interview with Papa Jack Laine, April 21, 1951, *ibid*. Papa Jack Laine was interviewed twice for the Hogan Jazz Archive. On April 21, 1951, he stated that he had heard of Bolden, but had never heard him play. On April 25, 1964, when he was over ninety years old, Laine was again interviewed. At this time he stated that he knew Bolden and had heard him play. The discrepancy could be the result of his misunderstanding a leading question, but because of Laine's very advanced age in 1964, I have used the 1951 interview to document his knowledge of Bolden.

the entertainment was "not intended for good purposes." A 1907 letter from another police captain brings to light in a round-about way an additional restriction on the bands. The minister of Grace church, the Reverend Edbrooke, complained that the noise from a construction site on South Rampart between Common and Canal streets made it "impossible to hear or understand the sermon being preached." The captain, in turn, explained to the construction superintendent that although there was no law to cover this particular situation, "there was a City Ordinance which forbids the playing of music by bands in front of churches or within one block each way while services were being held."[14]

Other indirect restrictions on the bands and orchestras resulted from the strict rules that governed entertainments. Giving a ball involved complications beyond simply hiring a hall and a band, for a request had to be made to the police superintendent. After approving the request the superintendent issued a "Mayoralty of New Orleans" permit, which usually cost $5.00, and informed the appropriate precinct commander, who was then responsible for detailing police officers to the dance (at $2.50 each). An example of this formality is a letter giving Edward Garrett permission to have a July 4, 1899, entertainment at Mt. Zion Hall (also known as Providence Hall), on the corner of Liberty and Philip streets. Admission was five cents, no liquor was allowed, and— this evidently being a small affair—only one officer was detailed.[15]

As Barbarin mentioned, sometimes as many as three different types of groups played at large entertainments, and Buddy would have heard the orchestras and string bands as well as the brass bands. Some of these were and remained concert-type reading bands and "fiddle" string combos. That they were black and played in the 1880–1900 era did not by any means indicate that they were ragtime or jazz-oriented, or pickup groups making music simply because there was an occasion for it. The string quartets usually played waltzes, schottisches, mazurkas, quadrilles, and sometimes a little ragtime, and with other small string bands

14. Walsh to Gaster, May 18, 1898, and L. W. Rawlings to Gaster, March 26, 1907, both in Louisiana Division, New Orleans Public Library.
15. Original letter in author's possession.

In Search of Buddy Bolden

they continued in popularity into the twentieth century. Later on they played in some of the cabarets, but before 1900 their jobs were usually at smaller, more private parties and at picnics or complimentary entertainments.

The city was full of good musicians. John Robichaux led an orchestra of outstanding musicians, one of the top groups in the city until well into the twentieth century. The Tio brothers, Lorenzo, Sr., and Louis, were playing with the Excelsior band when it was a great hit at the 1885 Cotton Exposition. Other notable musicians of the time were Anthony and Charlie Doublet, Albert Piron, Vic and Oke Gaspard, Sylvester Cousto, Clarence Desdunes, George Filhe, Henry Peyton, and Charley Galloway. Isidore Barbarin, George Baquet, Manuel Perez, and Alphonse Picou were playing a few jobs as teenagers then but were not well known; their fame would come later.

Some older musicians who eventually either tried out or played for Bolden were Albert Glenny, bass and tuba, born 1870; Wallace Collins, tuba, born *ca.* 1858; Bob Lyons, bass, born 1870; Frank Jackson, bass and tuba, born *ca.* 1866; Lorenzo Staulz, guitar, born 1858, and Edward Clem, cornet, born *ca.* 1860. Clem and his brother Jesse came from Convent, Louisiana, and Papa John Joseph, having heard them play there, said that the brothers had strictly an ear band and that Jesse was the first man he ever saw pick the bass.[16]

Although none of these bands or musicians were classified as jazz bands at that time, even then some of their sounds probably hinted at jazz beginnings, and many of the individuals would later become well known for their jazz musicianship. During Bolden's time the "jazzy" playing was called ragtime and the word *jazz* was not used as a label for the music. In this work, however, in order to maintain a point of reference, *jazz* will denote the music of that earlier era too.

In addition to professional bands and church spirituals, Buddy would also have heard the songs and cries of the New Orleans street hawkers. The junk collectors called, "Old rags and bottles. Old rags and bottles.

16. Allen and Russell, interview with Joseph, November 26, 1958, in Hogan Jazz Archive.

I'll pay well for your rags.'' The fruit and vegetable hawkers loaded their carts with produce from the canals and markets—such markets as Treme, Poydras, Kellers, and the old French Market—and then journeyed up and down city streets, each chanting his distinctly identifiable call. Some chants were long and drawn-out, some raucous, and when the seller had a large variety of goods the calls resembled a train conductor's litany of stops—an unintelligible, run-together slur. Some of the peddlers accompanied themselves on harmonica, homemade flute or whistle, but lest they get carried away a city ordinance forbade "making a boisterous outcry." And for the horse- or mule-drawn wagons an ordinance forbidding "furious driving" took the place of a speed limit.

Another possible musical influence of the time would have been field songs and shouts. Buddy may have heard the songs, but they were not part of his background and there is little or no evidence that he used any of these sounds in his music. All of his later regular band members were city boys too and would not have been naturally influenced by the field songs. If they did use them, it was very much a second-hand use.[17] The musicians who had lived on plantations and in the country brought this aspect to the city and added it to the music after Bolden had shaped the basic foundation. The field song influence was mainly a part of the later flowering period of New Orleans jazz.

Determining the process by which Bolden incorporated these known influences into his own music necessarily involves speculation. The physical correlation of the spirited church music and the march tunes was close, and although these two can logically be separated as far as musical content is concerned, they had a cohesive element that Buddy must have recognized and was perhaps intrigued with. Apart as the two styles were, it would have been natural to wonder if and how they could be combined. Buddy may have envisioned brass bands playing the hymns instrumentally with the same enthusiasm and up-beat rhythm the

17. A process of searching the 1860, 1870, and 1880 New Orleans census records was used to trace all of the musicians most closely connected with Bolden. Their birthdates were checked out in the city directories through their parents. Marriage certificates added information and frequently mentioned individuals as being natives of New Orleans. With the exception of Cornelius Tillman, who moved to the city at age five or six, all were born locally.

worshipers voiced in church. In order to realize any ideas he might have had, however, he needed to learn an instrument.

What instruments Buddy experimented with before singling out the cornet is again guesswork. He probably did some drumming of the "sticks-on-a-chair" variety, or using homemade contraptions pretended to be playing other instruments, but his final choice seems to have been made around 1894. He chose the cornet perhaps circumstantially, but possibly, too, because he saw it as a lead instrument and pictured himself a leader. Louis Jones said that Buddy took his first formal lessons from a neighbor, Manuel Hall, who lived at 467 South Liberty between Jackson and Philip streets. Thus we can speculate that because Jones did not move to New Orleans until September, 1894, Buddy began lessons around that time and was unlikely to have played any professional jobs before 1895.[18]

Manuel Hall was a cook at Nelson Quirk's Cafe on Royal Street in the French Quarter and around 1894 was keeping company with Buddy's widowed mother. He was born in 1856 (about the same time as Mrs. Bolden), had been married in 1880, but was a widower and perhaps acted as a sort of substitute father to Buddy.[19] He was not primarily a musician, nor was he one of note, but he taught young Buddy the rudiments of reading music and playing the cornet. It is likely that Buddy had soon absorbed everything Hall could teach him and was left to practicing on his own, formulating his own ideas, and learning from listening to other musicians. He may have been somewhat precocious musically, but starting out on the cornet at age seventeen was a late start compared with many other New Orleans musicians. Many of them were playing by the time they were ten and in their early teens were playing professionally. Buddy's precociousness stemmed more from his ability to take the music he had heard around the city and adapt it to his own style.

From this profusion of music in New Orleans between the late 1880s

---

18. Allen and Russell, interview with Jones, January 19, 1959, in Hogan Jazz Archive.

19. *Soards' New Orleans City Directory*, 1895, and marriage certificate of Manuel Hall, July 8, 1880, in New Orleans Vital Statistics Records.

and 1894 or 1895, Buddy was sorting out what appealed to him, what he could handle, and what he wanted to experiment with. There was in this youth, as in Louis Armstrong after him, a natural affinity for the horn and for the music. He apparently rejected the role of copier or imitator. He wanted to innovate. The ideas in his head had to come out, had to be expressed, and Buddy's way of expressing them was, it seems, different from what had been heard before.

4

Forming the
Early Bolden Band,
1895-1900

BOLDEN'S EARLIEST DOCUMENTED musical liaisons were with Manuel Hall around 1894 and a little later with Charley Galloway. However, since the three families—Boldens, Halls, and Galloways—lived around the same general area for many years, Buddy was almost certainly acquainted with these two men long before Hall began giving him cornet lessons. In 1880 and 1881, for example, Manuel Hall lived at St. Thomas Street near Seventh, very close to Buddy's Aunt Cora and Uncle Thomas. Hall moved to South Liberty in 1882, several years before Alice Bolden and her two children moved just around the corner to their First Street location, and he remained there for more than twenty years. In 1881 the Westmore Boldens lived in the same block as William Galloway and his son Charley, on St. Andrew between Locust and Magnolia; William Galloway, like Westmore, was a coachman and driver. In 1894 or 1895 Charley opened his barbershop at 435 South Rampart, in 1897 he moved up to 761 South Rampart, a neighborhood Buddy was quite familiar with, and in 1899 he moved the shop to 1324-26 Lafayette, where it remained until 1907.[1]

Charley, born in 1869, had a small string band. He played nearby halls like Turners and Violet, at Odd Fellows' Hall, and for parties, but though he was a good guitarist his musical career was not particularly distinguished; he is remembered mainly as owner of the barbershop-

---

1. *Soards' New Orleans City Directory*, 1870-1890; New Orleans Vital Statistics Records, 1870-1890; U.S. Bureau of the Census Population Schedules, 1870-1890.

musicians' headquarters and as an organizer for some of Bolden's first music jobs.[2]

Barbershops in those days were meeting places for musicians, since without telephones it was necessary to have rendezvous points where personal contacts could be made for lining up jobs. Bolden's original musical hangout was probably Galloway's. The older man had experience, knew some musicians, and most importantly, knew where to get jobs. Already active with his string band, he answered questions and discussed music with the younger men, and there would certainly have been a guitar, fiddle, or possibly a harmonica in the shop for impromptu lessons coached by Galloway.

Buddy also frequented Louis Jones's barbershop at the corner of First and Liberty, just a few doors from the Bolden home. Jones opened this shop shortly after his 1894 move from Greenville, Mississippi, and he and Buddy became close friends. Jones, also a Baptist, was a couple of years older and apparently had a big brother-type influence over Buddy. He was admittedly not very music-minded and their relationship was mostly as drinking companions and carousers. Together the two visited the neighborhood bars, and they often got down to the rougher South Rampart-Perdido area to "hoist" a few. (Mrs. Jones called her husband one of those old time "hot poppas.") It was most likely through his friendship with Jones that Buddy got the reputation for being a barber, since that's the closest he came to entering the profession. He was not a licensed barber and certainly never owned a shop himself. Jones moved his shop several times through the years, including a move to 2226 South Franklin Street in 1903 or 1904, but he finally settled at 2113 Jackson, making his home in the back. He died in the early 1960s, but his widow was still living there in 1974. Louis' recollections of Bolden were very vivid.[3]

2. Robert Goffin, *La Nouvelle Orleans, Capitale du Jazz* (New York: Editions de la Maison Française, 1946), 52–53.

3. Allen and Russell, interview with Jones, January 19, 1959, in William Ransom Hogan Jazz Archive, Tulane University, New Orleans; author's interview with Mrs. Jones, April 9, 30, and May 7, 1971. Louis Jones and his wife both contributed a great deal toward clearing up a number of questions about Bolden and his family.

The musicians who frequented Charley Galloway's barbershop included Bob Lyons, Wallace Collins, and Albert Glenny, all bassists who
played periodically with Galloway's band, and Frank Lewis, who
played some jobs on clarinet. As Buddy became a more proficient cornetist Galloway began using him in the band, sometimes employing
strings, cornet, and clarinet, and sometimes using just four pieces, omit-
ting either clarinet or cornet. Buddy was learning his instrument quickly;
before too long was taking the lead from Galloway, booking jobs under
his own name while still using Galloway on guitar. He also continued
using Frank Lewis—who was to be one of his longest associates in
music—and the same bass and violin players that Galloway had employed.[4]

Most information indicates that Buddy developed his style in the
small string band playing for dances and parties, rather than apprentic-
ing in parades. He did play in a few parades as a sideman with other
bands, and he sometimes used a pickup group for the larger parades
when fifteen or twenty bands were out at the same time, but he did not
have a regular brass band. His brass band personnel, such as it was,
changed often. The fact that very few people remember much about
Bolden's street music career makes it seem a rather insignificant part of
his musical development. A few did mention seeing Buddy in parades
and others mentioned marching with him, but their recollections were
somewhat hazy. Papa John Joseph had seen Buddy play with the Holmes
band in Lutcher that one time, but Louis Jones didn't remember ever
seeing him play a parade. Jones's observations were generally accurate,
but because he was not much of a second-liner (parade follower) he
would not have been on the parade routes when Buddy did indeed
march.[5]

Bolden's string band personnel was not too stable those first few
years. Much experimenting was done and if someone did not like the

    4. Goffin, *La Nouvelle Orleans, Capitale du Jazz,* 52–53, and Samuel B. Charters, *Jazz: New
Orleans, 1885–1963* (New York: Oak Publications, 1963), 13.
    5. Author's interview with Joseph, July 3, 1962; and Allen and Russell, interview with Jones,
January 19, 1959, in Hogan Jazz Archive.

way Buddy played, or vice-versa, he left. Given Bolden's personality we can be sure he was looking for a novel approach—something to gain the crowd and sway the applause his way when he competed with other bands. His efforts took the form of playing "wide-open" on the cornet and of playing in up-tempo or ragging the hymns, street songs, and dance tunes to create a musical sound that people were unfamiliar with. This style did not catch on immediately and the Creoles scornfully called it honky-tonk music. But Buddy kept working, and he began to gain followers.

By 1897 the style and membership of the band was taking a definite shape. They began to get jobs that were no longer in the "kid" category. Although their sound was alien to some, it had an appeal, especially to a liberated, post-Civil War generation of young blacks. According to Louis Jones, Bolden played both by note and by ear and he liked to please the audience. Having a great ear he could hear another band play and after practicing their piece between dances was able to duplicate it by the end of the evening. As he matured musically, he would listen to a number, memorize it instrument by instrument, then teach the parts to the others.[6] Some of the musicians who played with him during this time were William "Red" Warner, who periodically substituted on clarinet, and Bill Willigan, John McMurray, Cornelius Tillman, and Frank Jackson, all of whom played drums at one time or another. Wallace Collins added his tuba when the band went on the street.[7] Later in 1897 Bolden realized the possibilities of putting more brass band sound on the bandstand and got Willie Cornish with him on valve trombone. Cornish, however, left shortly to serve in the Spanish-American War.

A few people remembered Bolden's band in its earlier days. Zue Robertson, who later played with the Original Creole Band, said he saw Bolden play before the 1898 Spanish-American War. One number he remembered was "Ride On, King," a spiritual in which "Bolden would blow so hard, he actually blew the tuning slide out of his cornet and it

6. Allen and Russell, interview with Jones, January 19, 1959, in Hogan Jazz Archive.
7. Paul Eduard Miller (ed.), *Esquire's 1945 Jazz Book* (New York: Esquire, 1945), 9.

would land twenty feet away.'' If it were not a physical impossibility this would have been a good gimmick, and it is an indication of the legendary power with which Buddy blew the horn. It would by no means be the last seemingly impossible description of Bolden's assault on his instrument. Another story came from Ray Lopez, later a renowned band leader, who recalled hearing Bolden's band play for the embarkation of a Negro regiment bound for Cuba during the Spanish-American War. As the ship moved away the band played "Home, Sweet Home," and some of the men on board were so overcome by nostalgia they jumped off and swam to shore.[8]

An intriguing mystery grew up around the possibility that this early Bolden band had made a cylinder recording. In 1939 Willie Cornish told *Jazzmen* editor Charles E. Smith that the cylinder had been made before 1898, and Smith, along with Orin Blackstone and Bill Russell, began an extensive search for it. Their leads met frustrating dead ends; in a 1957 *Saturday Review* article Smith concluded that the cylinder would never be found.[9] The search had been revived temporarily in 1951 through an article by Tom Sancton in *The Second Line*, with the magazine offering a hundred-dollar reward for information, but this effort, too, was fruitless.[10]

That the cylinder was made is quite believable; that it is gone forever is even more believable and perhaps preferable since its presence would cause insoluble problems. Because cylinders in those days were of a material that did not age well, the acoustical quality would be poor and it would be nearly impossible to insure that the band was indeed Bolden's. Also, because Cornish was positive the recording had been made before he entered his military service, the personnel would not have been the same as in the band that made Bolden famous. It would have been a less-organized unit, perhaps "ratty" sounding, the tunes more novelty than jazz. And to listeners who have as their point of reference New

8. Hogan and Crawford, interviews with Russell, August 31 and September 4, 1962, in Hogan Jazz Archive.

9. Charles Edward Smith, "The Bolden Cylinder," *Saturday Review of Literature*, March 16, 1957, pp. 34–35.

10. Thomas Sancton, "Trouble in Mind," *Second Line*, September, 1951, pp. 9, 14, 18.

Orleans jazz as it is now known, or the jazz of the 1920s when New Orleans music was first regularly recorded, the cylinder might be a disappointment. Music of the post-Bolden period lacks many of the characteristics that made Buddy's music so new and unusual, and his music can only be judged properly in its own context, against what was being played then.

Buddy, at this point in his life, was becoming a ladies' man, enjoying a taste of the music idol worship that would blossom more fully with Frank Sinatra in the 1940s and later with Elvis Presley, the Beatles, and other rock stars. He had girls holding his hat, coat, and sometimes his handkerchief—but never his horn. (According to a number of witnesses, including Kid Ory and Big Eye Louis Nelson, Buddy was never without his horn.) The girls Louis Jones remembered as being part of Bolden's "harem" were Ann Bartholomew, Leda Chapman, Emma Thorton, Hattie Oliver, and a girl named Ella.[11] Hattie Oliver was the only one with whom he had a very lasting relationship; only a little is known about the others.

Leda Chapman was a prostitute who plied her trade at North Liberty and Conti streets in the District. She was eighteen years old in 1900 and was picked up several times between 1900 and 1906 for disturbing the peace and using obscene language. Emma Thorton, also eighteen in 1900, probably knew Buddy for a short time when she lived at 2618 Josephine, only a few blocks from his address on First. She had a running feud with a neighbor that resulted in her arrest for fighting and insult and abuse, and in 1905 she was performing in Lincoln Park with Remer's Vaudeville Company.[12] Ann Bartholomew and Ella were probably casual acquaintances at best or girls who hung around the bandstand and with whom Buddy had short-lived affairs.

---

11. Allen and Russell, interview with Jones, January 19, 1959, in Hogan Jazz Archive.

12. Leda Chapman was booked in the First Precinct Police Station on December 26, 1899, August 10, 1905, February 1, 1906, and June 15, 1906, and Emma Thorton was booked at the Twelfth Precinct on July 17, 1900, September 21, 1900, and January 9, 1901, all in New Orleans Police Department Arrest Records, Louisiana Division, New Orleans Public Library. Emma Thorton is also listed as a performer in Remer's Vaudeville Company, whose Sunday, October 15, 1905, Lincoln Park performance was advertised in the New Orleans *Item*, October 11, 1905, p. 10.

Sometime around 1895 or 1896, Buddy began going with Harriet "Hattie" Oliver, a pretty, slim girl several years older than he. She lived with her father and sister about four blocks from the Boldens at 2233 South Rampart. Hattie gave birth to Charles Joseph Bolden, Jr., on May 2, 1897, and although there was no formal liaison, she helped authenticate the Bolden story by having the birth officially recorded. Between the *Hattie* and *Bolden* written on the certificate by the deputy recorder, Hattie, being illiterate, scrawled her *X*. Even though Buddy was not yet twenty, she gave his age as twenty-two and hers as twenty-three, evidently wanting to diminish the age difference. She listed his occupation as plasterer. Buddy's fascination with Hattie did not last, though he did briefly provide for her and his son.[13]

Several people close to Bolden have declared that he never did anything for a living but play music—"never earned a nickel other than by his horn."[14] This was true after 1900, but before he became a big name in New Orleans music he was not making enough by playing to sustain himself and his family very handsomely. Consequently, he worked as a laborer at several temporary jobs. One old neighborhood resident, Robert Burthlong, mentioned working with Bolden in a barrel factory, located, he thought, at the corner of First and Baronne. Buddy's menial service there did not last long.[15] Around 1896 or 1897 he began working for a plasterer, probably Albert Poree, who lived at 2217 First and contracted numerous jobs in the area. Bolden first appears in the city directory in 1897 as a plasterer and the 1900 entry is the same, which corroborates the information given on Charles, Jr.'s, birth certificate. Buddy worked days, getting off occasionally to play important afternoon jobs.

13. The information on Hattie Oliver was found in *Soards' New Orleans City Directory,* 1900 to 1905; birth certificate of Charles Joseph Bolden, Jr., dated August 16, 1897, in New Orleans Vital Statistics Records; Allen and Russell, interview with Jones, January 19, 1959, in Hogan Jazz Archive.

14. Nora Bass as related in Hogan and Crawford, interviews with Russell, August 31 and September 4, 1962, in Hogan Jazz Archive; Alice Bolden as related in author's interview with Eugenia Jackson and Laura Lawes, June 25 and July 2, 1971; Allen and Russell, interview with Jones, January 19, 1959.

15. Thomas Sancton, "Trouble in Mind, Part Two," *Second Line,* January-February, 1954, pp. 1-8.

At night he was a musician. From 1900 on his life was centered around music and he was successful enough that he no longer needed a secondary income. The city directory in 1901 listed him as a music teacher; from 1902 to 1907, it called him a musician.

Word was getting around that there was something new in the air, and Buddy's audience continued to grow. Rags and blues had been played occasionally by the brass bands; now Bolden was playing them at smaller gatherings with his smaller band. His particular brand of ragtime or blues did not occur by accident. What other bands had been doing in the street parades ("ragging" the tunes as indicated by Papa Jack Laine), Bolden began doing for a different audience—the dancers. The old string bands were being overshadowed by Bolden's brassmen, and in this new arrangement the strings became part of the rhythm section. There was no one great influence on Bolden's cornet playing, no "king" to copy or dethrone. Buddy took musical bits from his background and environment and put them together in a way that utilized what he thought was best about the music, blending the parts with his own talent and personality.

Bolden began to attain city-wide fame around the turn of the century and most people who heard him mention seeing him between 1900 and 1905, though his career was so fast and so short the dates were inevitably confused by people trying to remember what and when things actually happened. These comments, however, indicate that it had taken five years of trial and error for Bolden to make a big impression. That he was fronting a well-known band at age twenty-two is not at all unusual in New Orleans, for later musicians like Sidney Bechet and Kid Ory— whose careers are better documented—were leading bands at even earlier ages.

Also by 1900 the makeup of the band was becoming solidified. In Cornish's absence Bolden had tried using various trombone players including Ed Jones, James Philips, and Frankie Dusen, who at that time was young and inexperienced. When Cornish returned in 1899, Buddy had worked out his musical style. Cornish was a large man and like Bolden had the power to bring the brass into a more dominant role in the string band. Things began to click. Just before 1900 Jefferson Mumford joined the band as guitar player. Born in 1873 across the river, Mumford had had a rough childhood, losing his father by 1875 and contracting a case of smallpox that left his face so badly scarred he was nicknamed "Brock."[16] Jimmy Johnson, a Catholic born in 1884, turned out to be the bass player Bolden was looking for. Johnson was a close friend of some of Robichaux's musicians and would ride his bicycle to the jobs he played, his bass strapped on the back.[17] Henry Zeno, born in 1870, and Cornelius Tillman were both drivers as well as musicians, and they alternated playing drums; Tillman eventually became the regular. To round out the band's personnel, Frank Lewis and Willie Warner played clarinet. Most of the band members were from the same general Uptown area and were about the same age, though Tillman was the old man at age twenty-eight and Johnson the kid at sixteen.

16. Author's interview with Mrs. Jefferson Mumford, Jr., November 2, 1971.
17. Author's interview with Alvin Alcorn, June 23, 1971, and author's interview with Louis Cottrell, Jr., July 30, 1973.

5

Places Bolden Played: The Rampart-Perdido Area, Parks and Dance Halls 1900-1906

MUCH OF THE Bolden story took place in an area that had as its hub the intersection of South Rampart and Perdido streets. Canal Street, the city's main thoroughfare, was just three blocks away. Shortly before 1900 the neighborhood atmosphere around Rampart and Perdido began to change. The regular grocery stores became combination grocery-bars; saloons opened at every other corner. In 1897 or 1898, when Bolden began playing the area, just about every corner of Rampart, Franklin, Tulane, Howard, Liberty, Poydras, Lafayette, Gravier, and Perdido streets had either a grocery store, a saloon, or a combination of the two. The 200 to 700 blocks of South Rampart were still highly commercial, containing about twenty clothing stores, twenty shoe and boot stores, and approximately forty other business establishments, divided almost equally among dry goods stores, fancy and variety stores, furniture stores, hardwares, and crockery and china shops. In addition there were nearly twenty secondhand stores, run primarily by Jewish merchants. The Chinese community was located along Tulane Avenue, and most of the Chinese groceries, restaurants, and laundries were in the 1000 to 1400 blocks. In 1897 the area had twenty-five barbershops that also served as general meeting places. Arthur Thomas' barbershop at 1212 Perdido was one of these that was often used by musicians as a place to find sidemen and arrange jobs. Musicians looking for a gig stopped in to see what was happening and were sometimes hired on the spot.

By 1906, when this same area had been the center of Bolden's musical activities for about ten years, many of the more legitimate businesses had moved out. The number of secondhand stores had increased to thirty-five and there were about forty saloons. South Rampart's 100 to 700 blocks contained a number of pawn shops that were sometimes handy for musicians, for when a man was not actually playing, his instrument might be resting on a shelf at "Little Jake" Itzkovitch's, "Big Jake" Fink's, or at Nathan Cohen's large shop. The "sporting" crowd was moving in, inhabiting wooden cottages and places above and behind the shops.

The area was included in the boundaries of the Red Light District known as Storyville, as proposed in the following 1897 city ordinance:

> From and after the first of October, 1897, it shall be unlawful for any prostitute or woman notoriously abandoned to lewdness, to occupy, inhabit, live or sleep in any house, room or closet, situated without the following limits, viz: From the South side of Customhouse Street to the North side of St. Louis Street, and from the lower or wood side of Basin Street to the lower or wood side of Robertson Street; 2nd:—And from the upper side of Perdido Street to the lower side of Gravier Street, and from the river side of Franklin Street to the lower or wood side of Locust Street, provided that nothing herein shall be so construed as to authorize any lewd woman to occupy a house, room or closet in any portion of the city.[1]

This second part was an area one block wide and four blocks long that included the 400 blocks of South Franklin, Liberty, Howard, Freret, and Locust, and the 1200 to 1500 blocks of Perdido and Gravier streets. Although it was never officially enfranchised as "black Storyville," law officials did not generally interfere with the activities of the prostitutes living there.

It is difficult to pinpoint definite locations of brothels in black Storyville, since they were not advertised in the infamous Blue Book which extolled the talents of Storyville ladies. There were, however, enough arrests and letters of complaint like the following examples to establish its existence. A 1906 ship captain's complaint stated that

1. City Ordinance No. 13,485, July 6, 1897, in Louisiana Division, New Orleans Public Library.

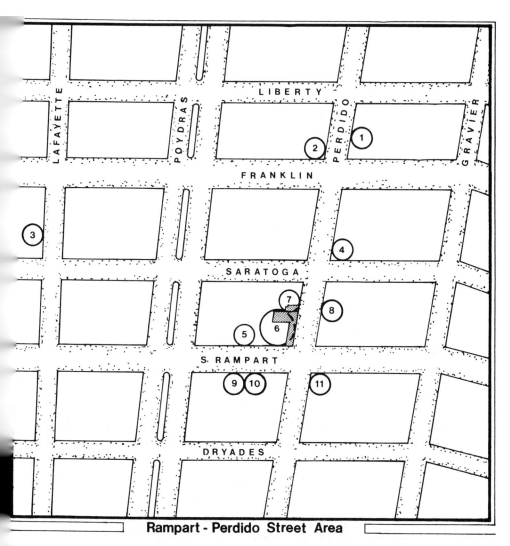

Rampart - Perdido Street Area

Key:

1. Union Sons Hall, also known as Kinney's Hall and Funky Butt Hall, 1319 Perdido Street. It is now the site of the Louisiana State Office Building complex.

2. Fisk School, 507 South Franklin.

3. Charley Galloway's Barbershop, 1326 Lafayette.

4. Arthur Thomas' Barbershop.

5. Charley Galloway's Barbershop in 1896, 435 South Rampart. In 1897 he was at 761 South Rampart.

6. Odd Fellows and Masonic Hall, 1116 Perdido St. Downstairs at 401–403 South Rampart was "Little Jake" Itzkovitch's Eagle Loan Office.

7. Bob Lyons had a shoeshine stand here in later years, 1118 Perdido Street.

8. The Zulu Social and Pleasure Club had their headquarters here during the 1920s.

9. England Tea and Coffee Company and Store, 414 South Rampart.

10. Fred Staehle Bakery, 408 South Rampart. In 1905 you could get a fresh loaf of bread for a nickel every hour on the hour.

11. Harris Dulitz Shoe Store, 360 South Rampart. Dulitz also had a hardware store at 445 South Rampart, and the family is still doing business in this block.

"$105.00 in U.S. currency" had been stolen from him after he was accosted by a prostitute living at 129 South Franklin who enticed him into spending the night. Earlier that year an investigation of Lucile Caryle's residence at 940 Tulane revealed that "Mrs. Caryle, the land lady, can be seen running from room to room in a nude condition and the other inmates following her screaming and laughing. This is a nightly occurrance, and the house is a most disorderly one, men and women frequent the house every night, the women begging the men to go to bed with them." Arrests were made for insult and abuse, lewdness and abandonedment, reviling the police, "roping in," fighting, and disturbing the peace.[2]

There were regular citizens who lived in the Rampart-Perdido neighborhood, but black Storyville, especially, hosted some rough characters who were professional criminals rather than just members of the sporting crowd or the worldly wise and hip. Most offenders, however, were reasonably tame and included pickpockets, sneak thieves, pimps, and gamblers. Police records show the following oddly named customers coming from the area: Drop a Sack, Jack the Rabbit, Jack the Ripper, Grand Jury, Cinderella, Baby Gray, Pudding Man, Willie the Pleaser, Ratty Kate, Whiskey Head, Hit 'Em Quick, Two Rooms and a Kitchen, Diamond Dick, Lead Pencil, Peckerwood, and Baggage Car Shorty.[3]

The local bars were natural spots for police attention, some being less reputable than others. One of the worst was G. W. Carrington's saloon at 818 South Rampart, described in a police report as "a Negro dive of the lowest type" where such occurrences as a man being "assaulted and knocked down with a chair" were not unusual.[4] Musicians and dance hall patrons—especially those recalling the Bolden days—mentioned many bars in the Rampart-Perdido area as "stopping off" spots or hang-

2. L. W. Rawlings to Edward S. Whitaker, September 1, 1906, and August 27, 1906, both in Louisiana Division, New Orleans Public Library. The police department arrest records identified black prostitutes with a "B."
3. New Orleans Police Department Arrest Records, First Precinct, from 1899 to 1907, *ibid*.
4. Investigative report by L. W. Rawlings, November 9, 1906, *ibid*.

outs. These bars are listed on the following pages. The number of them that became popular *after* 1900 suggests that new attractions were causing the clientele to grow. Bolden's music was no doubt one of these attractions, for although it's not clear how much time he actually spent here, Bolden is the most talked about and best-remembered personality of the area from that time. It was a much different, certainly much rowdier neighborhood than around First Street where Buddy grew up, and in a sense he was thrust into it because many of the dances for which his band played were held at the Odd Fellows and Masonic Hall at 1116 Perdido. But this is where Bolden reigned. He played many other spots and was well known at Lincoln and Johnson parks (especially around 1904 and later), but it was along Rampart and Perdido streets that his reputation was originally made. And the Rampart-Perdido crowd helped spread his reputation by following him to the parks.

Description of bars in the Rampart-Perdido area
between 1895 and 1910:[5]

Allen Saloon: Opened by Charles B. Allen in 1900 at 1024 Poydras Street. In 1904 he moved it to 500 South Rampart.

Astoria Hotel and Ballroom: 200 block of South Rampart. Did not come into existence until after Bolden was gone.

Bagnetto's: Emile Bagnetto had a saloon at 700 South Rampart from 1900 until about 1905. Philip Bagnetto opened a saloon at 534 Saratoga in 1905.

Barbara's: Frank Barbara had a saloon at 1301 Gravier from 1904 until at least 1906.

Carrington's: George Carrington opened his notorious bar at 818 South Rampart in 1906 and lasted about a year.

Deichmann's: William Deichmann opened a grocery at 1332 Perdido in 1900 and was still in business in 1907, but he combined it with a barrelhouse saloon shortly after 1902.

Durand's: Louis Durand had a grocery store-bar at 1201 Perdido from 1895 until after 1906.

Duroux's: Frank Duroux started a saloon at 449 South Rampart in 1903.

5. The information in this chapter on bars and other businesses was obtained by going through *Soards' New Orleans City Directory* for the years 1895 to 1908, and from the City of New Orleans Bar Room Investigations and Permits, 3 vols., 1896-1901, 1901-1905, and 1905-1910, all in Louisiana Division, New Orleans Public Library.

By 1910 he was leasing 403 South Rampart from Jake Itzkovitch and running a bar there, plus maintaining a bar at 446 South Rampart.

Eagle Saloon: The Eagle Saloon was mentioned by many persons in their remembrances about the area, but though the consensus located it at the corner of Rampart and Perdido, no one could pinpoint which corner. The Dulitz family's shoe store occupied one corner from 1897 until around 1910; a secondhand store was there in 1914. A second corner held Themo Scotti's saloon until his trouble with the police in 1898, and thereafter that location was not granted a permit. Morris Dulitz recalled that a man named Mulligan was associated with the Eagle Saloon.[6] Ben Mulligan had been a bartender at Frank Duroux's at 449 South Rampart in 1905 or 1906. Duroux took over part of the 401–403 South Rampart corner around 1910, perhaps earlier, and one possibility is that Jacob Itzkovitch of the Eagle Loan and Pledge Company kept one side of the corner site and leased 403 to Duroux, at which time Mulligan began tending bar for Duroux again. In keeping with the habit many musicians had of nicknaming a bar or dance hall by whatever sign hung outside or nearby, the saloon likely became identified with the Eagle loan office.

Basile Famiglio's: Famiglio, who had been a fruit vendor on Poydras Street, opened a saloon at 1233 Perdido in 1902 and maintained a grocery store-bar there until after 1906.

Ferrantelli's: In 1900, Joseph Ferrantelli opened his saloon at 301 South Rampart. His brothers Paul, Charles, Anthony, and Peter helped him run it, and shortly after 1900 he opened another at 300 South Rampart. About 1905 he sold out his 301 Rampart establishment to Dominick Lamotta, who continued its operation until 1911 when he moved to 1333 Poydras.

Locicero's: Gasper Locicero, who had learned his trade as a bartender at Sunseri's on 1200 Poydras, opened a grocery store-bar at 501 South Liberty in 1905.

August Miller's: One of the early grocers who moved out with the influx of new activity was August Miller. He was at 347–357 South Liberty until 1897, moved to 1401 Gravier in that year, and retired a year later.

Mix's: Frank Mix started the Mix Saloon at 1000 Perdido in 1902.

Mussachia's: Leon Mussachia took over from August Miller at 1401 Gravier in 1898, moved to 1333 Poydras in 1899, and left the area around 1903.

6. Author's interview with Morris Dulitz, July 11, 1971.

Pelican Club: A short-lived colored social club that began on 407 Dryades Street in 1897 and ended up at 1126 Perdido a year or so later.

Prat's: The Prat brothers, Bonaventura, Thomas, Vincent, and John began business at 358 Dryades in 1894 and moved to 943 Dryades in 1898. They were still in business after Bolden left, but were more of a legitimate restaurant enterprise.

Rexach's: John Rexach inaugurated a grocery store-bar across the street from Odd Fellows Hall in 1900 and remained in business for many years. William Cornish was one of his good customers.

Savocca's: Joseph Savocca's Tonk was opened in 1901 at 1201 Poydras. His brother, who had worked at Charlie Commander's Bar at 761 South Rampart, joined him along with brothers Charles, Peter, and Frank. They remained at 1201 Poydras for many years.

Scaffidi's: Anthony Scaffidi lived at 1227 Perdido and operated the bar at 1233 Perdido just before Famiglio took over. He then contented himself with tending bar for Frank Barbara in 1904 before joining Piarano's Bar at 1300 Tulane.

Scotti's: Themo Scotti ran the bar at 361 South Rampart from 1896 until 1898 when he ran into trouble with gambling offenses. From that point on the location could not obtain a permit for beer or liquor. It was right across the street from Odd Fellows Hall and although Jake Itzkovitch and others tried to obtain permits for the location, they were denied, and 361 became a drug store. Otto Lyncker, a well-traveled druggist, took over the location in 1905, but was too lenient in his dispersal of cocaine to the neighborhood residents. He was quickly put out of business and the address subsequently lost its notoriety.[7]

Segretto's: John Segretto ran a grocery store-bar at 401 South Basin beginning about 1895. This location became 403 Saratoga in 1898. His brother opened a grocery store at 453 South Liberty in 1902 and John took this over later. In 1915 he owned bars at 457 South Liberty and 833 Decatur and resided at 1122 Perdido.

Spano's: Paul, Anthony, and John Spano were in the saloon business at 519 South Franklin from 1895 until about 1905.

Sunseri's: Philip Sunseri and his brother Mike had a grocery store-bar at 1200 Poydras for a short time in 1901 and 1902.

Winston's: John Winston, who was a neighbor of Buddy Bolden, resided

7. New Orleans *Item*, May 5, 1906, p. 1.

at 331 Second Street. Winston had a plastering business from 1895 until 1905 with his brothers Clarence and Thadias. He had a try at the bar business in 1907, but returned to plastering within a year.

Buddy Bolden played all over town for different stratas of black society and for every conceivable function. The people who remembered his playing often associated him with Lincoln and Johnson parks and Odd Fellows and Funky Butt halls, but their recollections also place him on advertising wagons, at picnics, excursions, and parties. Mrs. Bella Cornish, in talking about her husband Willie, mentioned some of these spots: "He used to play out here on Perdido in a place him and Buddy Bolden and all of them, you know; cause he told me about it. He used to play all out on the basins and everywhere. Yeah, that was about, I guess from the way they talk, it must have been about the first little band started off. He used to play all around in them halls." Mrs. Cecile Augustine, who "loved to go dancing" in her youth, said Bolden played anywhere and for anyone who would hire him. As a teenager she was a member of the Blue Ribbon Social Club, and they frequently hired Bolden for their dances at Longshoremen's Hall on Jackson Avenue.[8]

Buddy played the lakefront area on the shores of Lake Pontchartrain, providing the music for numerous picnics and outings. Johnny St. Cyr recalled that Bolden sometimes played all afternoon for a private party or picnic at the lakefront, then went back Uptown to play a dance at Johnson or Lincoln park. St. Cyr also heard him at Mrs. Betsy Cole's lawn parties on Willow Street around 1904 and at the fairgrounds race track for picnics and postparade concerts. The infield at the fairgrounds was a popular gathering place for many years.[9] New Orleans clarinetist Albert Burbank has described a picnic typical of the ones at which Buddy must have played:

Picnics were held usually on Sunday at Milneburg. The pavilions or camps were just big rooms with tops. The band would pick a corner inside

8. Allen and Russell, interview with Bella Cornish, January 13, 1959, in William Ransom Hogan Jazz Archive, Tulane University, New Orleans, and author's interview with Mrs. Cecile Augustine, July 16, 1971.
9. Manuel Manetta and Russell, interview with Johnny St. Cyr, August 27, 1958, in Hogan Jazz Archive.

the room to set up. The people attending would not sit down. There were no chairs provided for them, but would dance. People would bring their own food. There were usually long benches around the inside walls. Keg beer was served. Bands would arrive about 11 A.M., play until 5 or 6. Perez played at picnics, so did Big Eye Louis. Usually had six pieces, banjos instead of guitar—no piano. Bands at picnics had trumpet, trombone, clarinet, bass, drums and banjo. Tempos were slower. Not a lot of solos taken, although sometimes players would take their horns down to rest. Rhythm sections never took solos. People would applaud at the end of a number, then there would be a five minute break.[10]

Manuel "Fess" Manetta, who played both brass and reeds, said he first saw Bolden play across the river at the Odd Fellows and Masonic Hall on Sequin Street near Evelina. Alphonse Picou was with the band, temporarily replacing Frank Lewis. Manetta remembered Bolden having other jobs over the river, with Henry Allen, Sr.'s, brass band, at the Algiers Masonic Hall on Olivier Street, and at Pecan Grove, a picnic grounds in Algiers. Trumpeter Alvin Alcorn's mother, Beatrice Alcorn, and her aunt Elizabeth Morton, recalled that Buddy played on advertising wagons that passed about six blocks from their house. The wagons were used to publicize dances at the halls, and Mrs. Alcorn said you didn't have to see Buddy to know who was playing.[11]

The band played on excursions, too, and were well known outside the city. They sometimes took an early train to play an all-day picnic and dance in Baton Rouge and would also play at stops along the way, performing from the baggage car. Kid Ory first heard Bolden at the train station in La Place, Louisiana.[12] The trumpet player, Charlie Love, born in 1885 in Plaquemine, Louisiana, recalled a personal encounter with Bolden during one of these excursions:

> Buddy Bolden came to Plaquemine. I was a little fella then. But, anyway, Bolden played at the Odd Fellows Hall and he had a new Conn cornet and

10. Ralph Collins and Russell, interview with Albert Burbank, March 18, 1959, *ibid*.

11. Allen, Robert Campbell, Nesuhi Ertugin, and Russell, interview with Manuel Manetta, March 21, 1957, in Hogan Jazz Archive, and author's interview with Beatrice Alcorn and Elizabeth Morton, June 23, 1971.

12. Nat Hentoff and Nat Shapiro (eds.), *Hear Me Talking to Ya* (New York: Rinehart and Co., 1955), 28.

something got the matter with it . . . the middle valve. He couldn't get it loose. So I'm standing by and I had a pot metal cornet made of nickel plate. I told him I have an instrument at home . . . you wanta borry mine, I'll go get it. He say, Yes, I can use it. I got a bicycle I jumped on and went to Fortville down by the levee. Buddy held it up and laughed at it and he say look what this boy done brought here. How in the world I'm gonna play this? And he takes it out and made out with it and finished the job with it.[13]

Despite the implication that Bolden played most everywhere, he did not play in the brothels. None of the musicians who were interviewed remembered playing with a band in a whorehouse, nor did they know of anyone who had. Piano players sometimes did, but not the bands. Nonetheless, this erroneous bit of mythology has become part of the birth of jazz story, perpetuated by authors such as Stephen Longstreet in *The Real Jazz Old and New*, when he says, "The music that came out of the cathouses on Iberville and Liberty and Franklin and Bienville is still remembered." The authenticity of this statement is called into question when Longstreet continues by endorsing inaccuracies in the Bolden legend. He talks about the new music being organized in Buddy's bar-bershop, and states, "You bowed to Buddy because his newspaper *The Cricket* was full of stuff you usually whispered before dawn." This is followed with a mention of Buddy being busy playing at Tin Type Hall.[14]

Not many of the early bands played in the Storyville honky-tonks either, primarily because owners believed that when people danced they didn't drink. This assumption was not strictly held to, however, and sometimes a piano player or other solo musician, or an occasional string trio or quartet, was hired as entertainment. New Orleans bands did not begin playing the tonks regularly until after Bolden was gone, or after 1907, except for big days like Mardi Gras. Nonetheless, according to *Jazzmen* there was one place in Storyville where Bolden did play in 1906 and after, and that was Nancy Hank's Saloon, owned by Ada Hayes and

13. Folkways Records, "The Birth of Jazz," Album No. FA2464, 1959, Vol. 4, side 1, in the four-album series, *The Music of New Orleans*.

14. Stephen Longstreet, *The Real Jazz Old and New* (Baton Rouge: Louisiana State University Press, 1956), 8–9.

John Exnicious, on the corner of Marais and Customhouse (now Iberville) streets. Ada managed the place—which was frequented by prostitutes and "sports"—and was also a madam. A 1907 police report verifies that the proprietors had been issued a permit "to sing, with cornet, and band, also for electrical piano," but unfortunately it does not say whether the cornet and band referred to were Buddy Bolden's.[15]

Catty-corner from Hank's was Pete Lala's, which also employed musicians on occasion and where Bunk Johnson played before World War I. Clarinetist Big Eye Louis Nelson said that Bolden played a few gigs at Lala's 25 on Franklin between Canal and Customhouse, a few bars away from Hank's.[16]

Two other very important spots on Bolden's performing agenda were Lincoln and Johnson parks, where many of the societies held their dances and other social functions. These gathering places opened within a month of each other in 1902 in the same part of town, but Johnson Park was in use for only around seven years, whereas Lincoln remained open until about 1930. Also, the activities in Lincoln Park were more varied.[17]

At the end of St. Charles Avenue Carrollton Avenue begins, and Lincoln Park grew from a square block of property bounded by Carrollton, Short, Fourteenth (later Oleander), and Forshey streets. The Yazoo and Mississippi Valley Railroad sold the property to the Standard Brewing Company on July 15, 1902, after the brewery had received permission from the New Orleans City Council to establish a park there.[18] The new

15. City of New Orleans Bar Room Investigations and Permits, 1905–1910, in Louisiana Division, New Orleans Public Library; Ramsey and Smith (eds.), *Jazzmen,* 14; Jim Driscoll to John P. Boyle, July 10, 1907, in Louisiana Division, New Orleans Public Library.
16. Lomax, *Mister Jelly Roll,* 91.
17. The information on Lincoln and Johnson parks came from several sources. Property owners were found in the conveyance order books in the Civil District Courts Building, New Orleans (individual transactions are listed in the bibliography under Conveyance Order Books). The New Orleans *Item* ran ads for Lincoln Park every Friday and Saturday from April 15, 1905, through December 16, 1905, and also carried articles on the park on July 11, 1905, p. 3, November 14, 1905, p. 6, and December 19, 1905, p. 7. On July 16, 1971, the author interviewed John Jules, Leonard Johnson, and Paul Caesar, all members of the Old-Timers Club at the Midget Bar, 2600 La Salle, New Orleans.
18. City Ordinance No. 1260, New Council Series, establishing Lincoln Park, May 30, 1902, in Louisiana Division, New Orleans Public Library.

owners built a wooden fence around the block and erected a large pavilion or dance hall directly behind the Carrollton Avenue entrance. The
park was accessible by the Tulane Belt streetcar that ran up St. Charles
Avenue onto Carrollton; admission to the grounds was fifteen cents.

At first the park featured mostly concerts, picnics, and dances, with
John Robichaux's orchestra, Adam Olivier's orchestra, and the Excelsior band making the music. By 1905 the place was so popular that other
attractions were added. Vaudeville acts became a regular part of the
program with a balloon ascension and parachute leap as the headliner. A
series of advertisements in the New Orleans *Item* in 1905 and 1906, give
some idea of the entertainment: "A Festival of Fire" with five hundred
dollars' worth of fireworks, billed as "Mount Vesuvius in Action"; a
burlesque drama; motion pictures of the San Francisco earthquake and
fire; Baby Glennon, "The Sweetest Little Girl and Sweetest Singer in
Vaudeville Today"; and a dirigible labeled "Astonishing, Perplexing,
Fascinating."

The balloon ascension was held in an open space to the right of the
entrance. It was somewhat dangerous, as the takeoffs sometimes hit
snags, the balloon could be blown off course, or it could be forced to
make an unscheduled landing in a weed patch or tree. Ideally the climax
was when a shot fired in the air directed the aeronaut to cut loose a
certain rope, which caused the balloon to overturn and sent the rider
parachuting down.

The balloon ascension artists were Professor L. B. Haddock of Boston and the "colored aeronaut" Buddy Bartley. Bartley also acted as
emcee and unofficial manager of Lincoln Park, and in addition he
worked as a waiter at a restaurant downstairs from his apartment on
Dryades Street. If his balloon ascension act seems a bit risky, it was in
keeping with his reputation and personality; he was a gambler most of
his life and was often arrested—for gambling, fighting, loitering, dis-
charging firearms in the city limits, disturbing the peace, and even for
"catching on behind streetcars."[19]

19. Buddy Bartley appears on the arrest books of the First Precinct on the following dates:
January 6 and October 14, 1895, April 6 and June 27, 1896, July 22, 1899, February 15, 1900, July

The corner of Liberty and Perdido streets in the 1930s. In Bolden's day both Masonic and Odd Fellows Hall and Funky Butt Hall were nearby and drummer Henry Zeno lived in a house behind the lunchroom on the left. The saloon on the right, facing Liberty Street, was Joe Segretto's Grocery and Bar in 1905.

—Photograph from William Ransom Hogan Jazz Archive

This photograph of Funky Butt Hall was taken in the 1930s when the building had become the Greater St. Matthews Baptist Church. In the early 1900s the hall was officially titled Union Sons and was also called Kenny's Hall. The site is now part of the Louisiana State Office Building complex and is directly across the street from New Orleans City Hall.

—Photograph from William Ransom Hogan Jazz Archive

Bolden played many dances at Longshoremen's or Jackson Hall, 2059 Jackson Avenue.

The Globe Exchange is on the left, facing the New Basin Canal and St. Claude Street at the St. Peter Street corner. Globe Hall, where the Bolden band often played, was on the second floor.

—Photograph from New Orleans Jazz Museum

Perseverance Hall at 907 S. Claude Avenue.

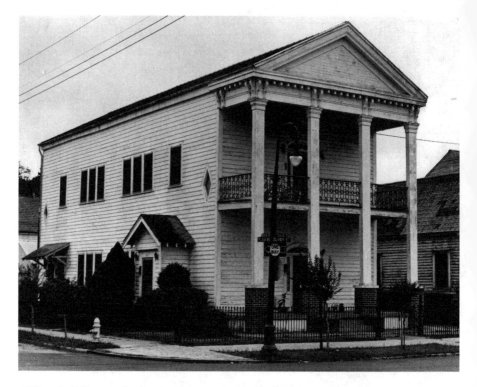

A Masonic Hall across the river in Algiers, at the corner of Olivier and Pelican streets, was the location for some of Bolden's dance jobs.

—Photograph from William Ransom Hogan Jazz Archive

Some confusion has resulted from misspellings of Bartley's name and its similarity to Buddy Bolden's. Bartley has been referred to as *Buddy Bottley* and *Buddy Bottle*. Consequently, some writers have stated that Buddy Bolden "used to go up in a balloon and play a horn,"[20] and some even remembered him playing his cornet while parachuting out of the balloon. Numerous persons who observed the events firsthand have refuted these stories, but the confusion indicates how easy it was to make erroneous connections.

Paul Caesar, a member of the Old-Timers Club at Midget's Bar near Bolden's old neighborhood, used to "live for those Sunday afternoons at Lincoln Park," and he remembered that once when Bartley sent his wife up in the balloon it sprang a leak. After her ultimate rescue, she set after her husband in a fury, cursing and yelling at the top of her lungs. Mrs. Beatrice Alcorn said that when Bartley would go up "they'd shoot the balloon and he would come down in a parachute." Bartley, she said, was not as famous as Bolden, though he admired Bolden's reputation and his way with women.[21]

After the balloon act the crowd's attention was focused on the pavilion, a somewhat decrepit building resembling a barn. It had both a stage and an orchestra pit, and near the entrance was a long counter on which kegs of beer were placed. Next to the counter were tables laden with fruits, sweets, gumbo, sandwiches, and chickens or roasted pigs; for fifty cents you could get a big plate of food. The band usually took the stage about 8:00 P.M. and played until one or two in the morning.

Other entertainments at the park included prize fights, a roller skating rink that opened in 1906, and at some point a merry-go-round for kids. Across the street at the corner of Carrollton and Oleander, the Blue Goose Saloon offered refreshment to those who desired something stronger than beer. Standard Brewing Company sold the Lincoln Park

16, 1901, December 12, 1905, January 7, 22, and July 7, 1906, New Orleans Police Department Arrest Records, in Louisiana Division, New Orleans Public Library.

20. Campbell and Ertugin, interview with Edward "Kid" Ory, April 20, 1957, in Hogan Jazz Archive.

21. Author's interview with Beatrice Alcorn, June 23, 1971.

property to Jarreau Motors in 1925 and the park itself went out of existence around 1930.

Johnson Park had opened April 14, 1902, after George W. Johnson (a
former waiter at the Arlington Saloon on North Rampart Street),
petitioned the mayor and city council to establish a baseball park on
property he had leased from Pierre Larroux. The park was located behind Lincoln Park between Forshey and Oleander, Short and Fern
streets. Johnson and James Flowers, another waiter from Arlington's,
then opened the Johnson Saloon at 7935 Oleander.[22] Johnson Park only
lasted until 1908 or 1909 and was used mostly for baseball games, but it
also became an important part of the Bolden legend because Buddy
played at the music pavilion there even before he played at Lincoln Park.
Albert Glenny remembered that both Manuel Perez and Bolden had
bands at Johnson, and it was here that Buddy first created the phenomenon of "calling his children home." Louis Jones recalled what it was
like: "Johnson Park was right next to Lincoln Park. That's where Buddy
used to say to Cornish and them, say, 'Cornish, come on, put your hands
through the window. Put your trombone out there. I'm going to call my
children home.' He would be at Johnson Park; Robichaux would be at
Lincoln Park. Buddy Bolden would start to play and all the people out of
Lincoln Park would come on over where Buddy was."[23]

Jones did not remember any particular tune that Bolden used, but
many others have verified the story of Buddy pointing his horn toward
Lincoln Park and powerfully "calling" the Lincoln crowd. And dancers
frequently abandoned the smoother Robichaux band to hear Bolden produce a newer, more raggedy, more exciting sound that stirred their dancing fancy. Buddy's dance band became as closely identified with Lincoln Park as with any other location, but the group could have been
heard by many people there while playing at Johnson, and the numerous

22. Petition for permission to create Johnson Park, submitted by George W. Johnson and approved April 14, 1902, and permission to open the saloon, granted by City Ordinance No. 1579,
New Council Series, January 2, 1903, Calendar No. 2089, in Louisiana Division, New Orleans
Public Library.
23. Thomas Sancton, "Libretto," *Second Line,* April 1951, pp. 1, 8, 13, and Allen and Russell, interview with Jones, January 19, 1959, in Hogan Jazz Archive.

stories of Bolden stealing Robichaux's crowd indicate that a majority of his jobs may, in fact, have been at Johnson. Bolden is not mentioned in any of the Lincoln Park ads for 1905 and 1906, although he was clearly playing at one of the parks during that time. Possibly the ads were intended to combat his effect on certain portions of the Lincoln crowd.

Robichaux's band continued its jobs at Lincoln Park and the two bands—the most popular in the city and thus great rivals—sometimes performed there at the same time, with Bolden playing dances at the skating rink while Robichaux played in the pavilion. The two spots were about seventy-five yards apart, and Bolden "called his children home" at such times too. Musicians were usually hired by different societies who had rented sections of the grounds for picnics or other functions.

Personal accounts of the Lincoln and Johnson park days include that of Willie Foster, brother of the late Pops Foster and an outstanding guitar player, who said that when he was about seventeen he heard Bolden's band at Johnson when Robichaux was at Lincoln. Foster thought Bolden had a rough band compared to Robichaux's nice orchestra, but when Bolden would stick his cornet out and blow, the people would go where he was. Foster recalled going there in mud up to his knees.[24] Johnny St. Cyr said that Bolden's special call was "not hot, just ordinary, a little lick he used to use. To me he was not as hot as the Golden Rule Band." (The Golden Rule Orchestra was led by Alcide Frank.) St. Cyr added, "I didn't hear many Uptown bands at this time. A few times, Mother went to a ball and I'd hear an Uptown band. Willie Cornish and Bolden. Didn't make much of an impression as I was just a young boy. Bolden had a certain theme he would insert into everything he played."[25]

The balls St. Cyr mentioned were held in dance halls, and one of the most popular of these was the Odd Fellows and Masonic Hall on Perdido. Beginning about 1898, Bolden's band played many jobs there, as did John Robichaux's and various string bands. The hall, built around 1850, fronted Rampart Street at the corner of Perdido and extended to

24. Collins and Russell, interview with Willie Foster, January 2, 1959, in Hogan Jazz Archive.
25. Letter from Johnny St. Cyr to author, August 10, 1962; and Manetta and Russell, interview with St. Cyr, August 27, 1958, in Hogan Jazz Archive.

1118 on the Perdido side. It occupied the second floor of the building, above Jacob Itzkovitch's Eagle Loan and Pledge Company, and had its entrance at the side.[26]

In May, 1897, some of the officers of the George D. Geddes undertaking parlor obtained a charter to form the Masonic and Odd Fellows Hall Association, Limited, and a close relationship between the funeral home and the Odd Fellows was thus well established. In September, 1897, the group subleased "the whole of the premises bearing the Municipal Nos. 1114 and 1116 of Perdido Street; the rear portion of the premises No. 1118 of Perdido Street and the third floor of the premises No. 403 of South Rampart Street . . . for the full term of Ten Years . . . at the rate of one hundred and twenty five dollars per month."[27]

The hall had a pool room and eating area adjoining the dance hall proper, and Salvatore Francisco had his living quarters in another room upstairs. Francisco was the manager and general handyman for the hall, so arrangements for dances had to be made through him. The dances were given by various organizations or even by individuals. On March 19, 1903, for example, the Ladies Broadway Swells gave a ball, and a barber named Wellington Smith sponsored one on October 13, 1906, that broke up at the unusually early hour of 11:00 P.M. when Smith stopped a party crasher with a bullet.[28]

The best evidence of who attended the dances comes from police arrest records. On March 10, 1903, two men got into a fight and the First Precinct mules and wagons took everyone at the dance to jail, releasing those not involved only after their names, addresses, ages, and occupations had been recorded. Out of sixty-two males and forty-four females

26. The ownership history of the building that housed Odd Fellows and Masonic Hall can be found in the conveyance order books in the Civil District Courts Building, New Orleans. Individual transactions and successions are included in the bibliography.

27. Benjamin Ory, notary public, March 7, 1897, incorporation articles for the Odd Fellows and Masonic Association, and Robert Upton, notary public, September 11, 1897, lease agreement between Jacob Itzkovitch and the heirs of Joseph B. Hubbard for the building at the corner of South Rampart and Perdido streets, both in Notarial Archives, Civil District Courts Building, New Orleans.

28. Names of social clubs and individuals sponsoring balls were obtained from New Orleans Police Superintendent's Office Reports of Homicides for the dates given in the text, in Louisiana Division, New Orleans Public Library.

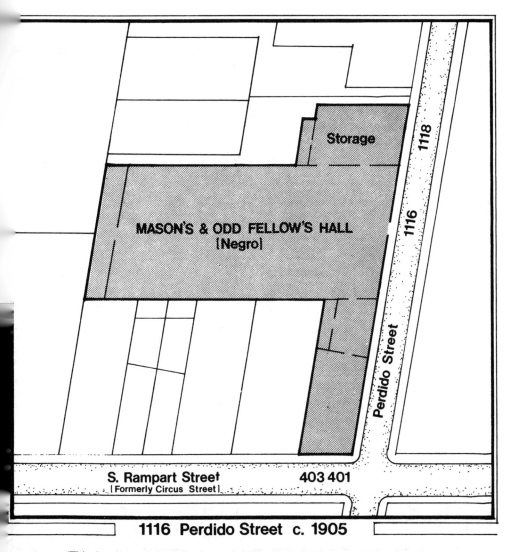

Storage

MASON'S & ODD FELLOW'S HALL
[Negro]

1118

1116

Perdido Street

S. Rampart Street
[Formerly Circus Street]

403 401

1116 Perdido Street c. 1905

(This drawing and the following one of Lincoln and Johnson parks are based on "Insurance Maps of New Orleans, Louisiana" by the Sanborn Map Company, New York, 1909).

This building housed Joseph B. Hubbard & Co. Furniture Store from 1851 until about 1897. It was leased to Jacob Itzkovitch who eventually bought the building in 1904 and ran the Eagle Loan Office at 401–403 South Rampart until his death in 1927. In 1898, Itzkovitch rented the large upstairs area (entered at 1116 Perdido Street) to the Odd Fellows as a concert hall and meeting room. It was here that Buddy Bolden played for many dances. The building was restored after a serious fire in 1908, and although it is still standing, it is different from the original structure.

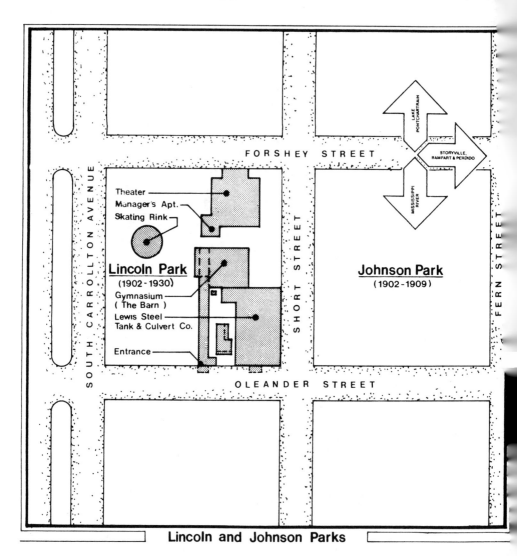

Lincoln and Johnson Parks

Based on the Sanborn Insurance Maps of New Orleans for the year 1909, this is the only detail that was found of the park's physical makeup. Vaudeville shows were performed in the theater; the prize fights and big dances were held in the barn. Bands also played in the cupola located in the center of the skating rink. Johnson Park was primarily a baseball park, but was also used for picnics. Both parks were enclosed by wooden fences. Bolden often aimed his cornet across Short Street to lure the Lincoln Park crowd to Johnson Park.

present, ninety-nine were single; only fourteen were unable to read and write. They ranged in age from thirteen to forty-four and came from all parts of the city, though nearly forty were from Bolden's First Street neighborhood. They worked mostly as laborers; there were sailors, stevedores, bricklayers, teamsters, housekeepers, coopers, valets, plasterers, bartenders, barbers, cooks, and one prostitute.[29]

For all its importance to jazz history, the Odd Fellows and Masonic Hall's connection with the bands was short-lived, since the building was shut down for a period around 1908 for renovation and even the Odd Fellows and Masonic lodges no longer met there after 1921. The building is still standing, but it now houses an antique shop and has changed considerably.[30]

Further up the street, at 1319 Perdido, was Union Sons Hall. In 1866, several men, all "free persons of color," had formed the Union Sons Relief Association of Louisiana and purchased two lots of property to make their headquarters in the hall located there. The officers of the organization all lived in the immediate area, were laborers, and evidently were not financially blessed enough to avoid leasing or renting the hall frequently to other groups for meetings and social gatherings. These gatherings usually included music and the Union Sons held many of their own dances as well. Therefore at some point toward the end of the century Bolden began playing at the hall. The dances on Saturday nights often lasted until four or five in the morning and on Sunday morning the hall served as the First Lincoln Baptist Church. Later, in the 1920s, it became a full-time church, the Greater St. Matthews Baptist.[31]

Willie Cornish, Buddy Bartley, and Bob Lyons all lived near the hall, and it was probably the roughest place that Bolden played, considering

29. New Orleans Police Department Arrest Records, First Precinct, March 10, 1903, *ibid.*

30. Author's interview with Dulitz, July 11, 1971.

31. Henry C. Dibble, notary public, March 1, 1866, incorporation papers for Union Sons Benevolent Association of Louisiana, in Notarial Archives, Civil District Courts Building, New Orleans. The history of 1319 Perdido Street was obtained from conveyance order books in the Civil District Courts Building; individual transactions are included in the bibliography. The agreement between Elder Edward A. Higgins, pastor of First Lincoln Baptist Church, and Reuben Elmore, representing the Union Sons, was witnessed by J. G. Eustis, notary public, on March 24, 1902, and is also in the Notarial Archives.

both the neighborhood and the people who attended the dances. There were frequent fights at these dances, and nearly 75 percent of the arrests made there involved women. Andrew Wilson, born in 1885, said he attended a dance at the hall when he was about twenty years old and saw some women get into a fight over Bolden. They were hauled away in the wagon. Police records for January 7, 1906, show that Margaret Hodge, thirty, Wilmena Love, seventeen, and Ida Carter, thirty, were arrested for fighting and disturbing the peace, and this may well have been the incident Wilson was talking about.[32]

Musicians and patrons had other names for Union Sons Hall. After Bolden became its most famous occupant it was popularly known as Funky Butt Hall. Before that its nicknames were "Kenna's Hall," "Kenny's Hall," and "Kinney's Hall," these nicknames quite possibly coming from one of the organization's presidents, William S. Kinney. A 1904 amendment to the Union Sons charter included the minutes of a meeting in which officers were elected, and Kinney, a laborer residing at 627 Liberty, was listed as the new president. Interestingly, Alex Reed, who for a year had been married to Buddy's sister Cora, was elected third deputy marshall.[33]

In 1950 the city of New Orleans bought the lots on which the hall was located to make way for the civic center, and the Louisiana State Office Building now occupies the site. Ironically, the office building holds Buddy Bolden's death certificate.

Other area halls where Bolden played dances included Longshoremen's and Providence. The Longshoremen's Benevolent Association had its headquarters at 2059 Jackson Avenue, about two blocks from Bolden's home on First Street. This hall had been known as Hagan's Hall in 1888 and was also called Jackson Hall, but around 1890 the longshoremen took it over and began sponsoring dances as well as rent-

---

32. Author's interview with Wilson, August 5, 1971; and New Orleans Police Department Arrest Records, First Precinct, January 7, 1906, in Louisiana Division, New Orleans Public Library.

33. Edouard Henriques, notary public, February 6, 1907, minutes of a meeting of the Union Sons Benevolent Association that includes a list of officers elected on November 9, 1904, in Notarial Archives, Civil District Courts Building, New Orleans.

ing the hall out to other groups. Although the building was badly gutted by fire several years ago, the shell was still standing in 1975. Providence Hall was located between Longshoremen's Hall and Bolden's home, on the corner of Philip and South Liberty. Mrs. Alice Bolden was a member of the Ladies Providence Society there, and old, old timers in the neighborhood still remember Buddy playing at Providence. Around 1937 the hall was torn down and a church was built in its place.

Louis Jones said that Buddy also played at the Mississippi Valley Hall on Poydras Street and at St. Elizabeth Hall near Camp Street and Napoleon Avenue, both rather ordinary halls. Frank Adams, a dancer born in 1883, as a young man used to listen to music every chance he got and the first music he remembered was "King" Bolden's playing at Love and Charity Hall at 1330 Eagle Street.[34] Musicians Tom Albert and Willie Parker recalled that Bolden also played at Electric Light Hall, a hall not mentioned in any other stories on the early days of New Orleans jazz. Old letters in the police commissioner's file, however, verify not only that the hall existed but show that "brass music" was being played there. One letter states, "The Electric Light Hall was blown down last January and was re-built recently and an entertainment was given in it Sunday July 19, 1906 with the usual Brass Music complaint of the neighbors."[35]

Bolden was more at home Uptown in New Orleans than Downtown. He did not play at the Creole society halls such as Jeunes Amis or Frans Amis, but he did play in the fringe area halls Downtown including Friends of Hope Society Hall at 922 North Liberty and Economy Hall on 1422 Ursulines, which some musicians called "Cheapskate Hall," since, as Isidore Barbarin said simply, "Rich people didn't go there." This Downtown-Uptown terminology and the rivalry between Creoles and blacks will be more fully explained in Chapter 6.

When in Downtown territory Buddy was most comfortable in the area back of North Rampart Street, near old Congo Square, in Perseverance

34. Allen and Russell, interview with Jones, January 19, 1959, and interview with Frank Adams, January 21, 1959, both in Hogan Jazz Archive.

35. Author's interview with Tom Albert, July 10, 1962, and author's interview with Willie Parker, April 19, 1962; D. S. Gaster to John B. Cooper, October 16, 1899, and Louis Madere to

and Globe halls. Globe Hall, on the Old Basin Canal at the northeast corner of St. Claude and St. Peter streets, had a long and illustrious life; it was home to New Orleans bands for over fifty years. As early as 1864 acting mayor James F. Miller granted permission for a ball at Globe ballroom,[36] and it stood until the 1920s when it was torn down to provide space for the municipal auditorium. Like many of the Downtown halls, the upper story of Globe Hall had an elevated stage for the band. There were many large windows that gave a good view of the Old Basin Canal with its barges, oyster luggers, and produce boats and the hall also looked out on Congo Square and the First Parish Prison at Treme and Orleans streets. When he had a job at Globe, Buddy would take his band outside and play to attract anyone who might be standing around the square or the basin. Perseverance Hall was not far away on Villere Street, and though Bolden did not play many jobs there it is interesting that the late Paul Barbarin, who grew up on nearby Urquhart Street, remembered his mother saying one night when she heard a loud, loud horn, "That's Buddy Bolden. He's gonna blow his brains out someday because he plays too loud." Barbarin was a small boy then, but he remembered bands playing at Globe Hall for the Monday night banquets that were a tradition in the black community. He did not recall ever seeing Bolden and did not know what he had sounded like, other than that you could sure hear him.[37]

Other people remembered seeing Bolden play at places that cannot be documented, such as Big Easy, New Hall, and Independent Hall. The nicknames of some of the halls have caused discrepancies and have made it difficult to establish their locations or even their existence. In addition, people's memories—as they try to reach back through the years for precise facts—are often understandably faulty. Jelly Roll Morton, in his tapes recorded for the Library of Congress, talks about

Edward S. Whitaker, September 4, 1906, in Louisiana Division, New Orleans Public Library.

36. James F. Miller to Hypolite Perceval, January 11, 1864, in Louisiana Division, New Orleans Public Library.

37. Allen and Russell, interview with Barbarin, January 7, 1959, in Hogan Jazz Archive.

being with Bolden several times, and one of these incidents nicely illustrates how time can play tricks with one's memory:

> I had an opportunity to be in Jackson [Longshoremen's] Hall one afternoon when Mr. Bolden was playing a matinee. A little incident happened that will show you the type environment that produced hot music. There was a man standing at the bar, a little bit of a short fellow. Seemingly he was sick with rheumatism. A great big husky guy steps on the little guy's foot, I was just between them, and they got into an argument and the little guy didn't want to stand for it and pulled out a great big gun almost as long as he was old, and shot, and if I hadn't pulled my stomach back, I wouldn't be here to tell you the history of jazz. This big guy laid there on the floor, dead, and, my goodness, Buddy Bolden—he was up on the balcony with the band—started blazing away with his trumpet, trying to keep the crowd together. Many of us realized it was a killing and we started breaking out windows and through doors and just run over the policemen they had there.[38]

Longshoremen's Hall, for one thing, was not a two-story building and thus probably had no balcony. Jelly Roll's story seems to be a composite of two separate events that over the years became mixed-up in his mind. A June 15, 1902, homicide report tells of a murder that occurred at Economy Hall on Ursulines Street near Villere in which "a difficulty took place at a Negro ball given in the Independent Pleasure Club . . . between Charles Montrell . . . and Edward Ory . . . which resulted in Ory drawing a revolver, 38 caliber, Hopkins & Allen make and firing one shot at Montrell the ball taking effect in his forehead above the right eye enflicting a mortal wound. . . . Cause of difficulty—Ory claims that Montrell stepped on his foot." The New Orleans *Daily Picayune*'s version explained: "Montrell always cuts quite a figure at the dances, but outside of the slow drag shuffle he was awkward and some of the fancy darkies did not like his style. Ory does not consider himself in the rough head class of negroes and he waxed warm when Montrell, in dancing in the hall about 3:30 yesterday morning danced on his foot." Three years

---

38. Jelly Roll Morton, "In New Orleans, The Bolden Legend," *The Saga of Mr. Jelly Lord*, Vol. XI, Pt. 1 and conclusion, Circle Records, Circle Sound Inc.

later, on March 7, 1905, another murder was reported, this one occurring at Longshoremen's Hall. "W. drew his revolver and fire[d] three shots at P., of which two took effect. . . . P. expired immediately. . . . During the shooting the Negroes in the hall made a general stampede out through the windows and doors."[39] Morton was quite likely present when both the shootings took place and from a time distance of nearly thirty-five years simply combined the high points of each.

Despite the frequency of Bolden's jobs and the many places he played, no advertising leaflets or printed references such as window posters or newspaper clippings giving written documentation of his performances were found until the summer of 1973. Mrs. Al Rose, while going through some old letters in the flea market in the old French Market, came across an invitation to a Mardi Gras ball sponsored by the Ladies of Providence and the Knights of Pleasure at Providence Hall on February 18, 1903, the music to be provided by "Prof. Bolden's Orchestra." This is the only known document advertising or mentioning a job that Bolden actually played, though he must have used printed advertisements since Kid Ory pointed out that he would learn when Bolden was to pass through his home town, La Place, "by seeing his advertisement" or by word of mouth. Bolden also advertised on wagons when he had a particularly important dance that night, and he was probably his own best advertisement. When he played you *knew* where and who he was.

Bolden got around so much and was kept so busy playing his cornet, it is easy to see how and why his fame spread throughout the city. It did not, however, extend far into white New Orleans, and the question arises as to whether he played for white audiences at all. It seems strange that Jack Laine, the white "father of jazz" who had been ragging music since 1885, said he had never heard Bolden, though he had heard Manuel Perez and Perlops Lopez.[40] Black musicians who played with Bol-

---

39. New Orleans Police Superintendent's Office Reports of Homicide, June 15, 1902, and March 7, 1905, in Louisiana Division, New Orleans Public Library, and New Orleans *Daily Picayune*, June 16, 1902, p. 3.

40. Allen and Russell, interview with Laine, April 21, 1951, in Hogan Jazz Archive.

den or knew him likewise never mentioned seeing any white musicians playing anywhere. It was quite coincidental that whites and blacks started playing ragtime around the same time and then came up with similar sounds related to ragtime. But given Bolden's inquisitive musical mind, he more than likely picked up a few ideas from the white musicians and they in turn may have used ideas of his. The debate will go on as to who influenced whom, though we can assume that Bolden played where he felt most at home and where his music was most appreciated, doing what he did best in the best way he knew how rather than playing as a reformer trying to convert the world or the city to his music.

Robichaux's band was known to have played jobs for whites, and the wealthy St. Charles Avenue and Garden District plantation owners, brokers, bankers, merchants, and professionals often hired blacks for private parties. Papa John Joseph mentioned that Bolden didn't play many private parties because he was too barrelhouse, but there are several indications that he did appeal to some whites and that some of his audiences were integrated. First of all, he would have been seen and heard in the street parades that wandered over great areas of the city, though as an individual he would not have stood out musically. Papa John Joseph said Bolden played "mostly for colored," implying that he may have played a few jobs for whites; Willie Foster said when he was a kid he heard Bolden and took some white friends to Lincoln Park to hear him play; Frank Adams stated simply, "Bolden was tops, famous, and played for white and colored."[41]

41. Allen and Russell, interview with Joseph, November 26, 1958; Collins and Russell, interview with Willie Foster, January 2, 1959; Allen and Russell, interview with Adams, January 21, 1959, all in Hogan Jazz Archive.

6

Bolden's Sidemen and Contemporaries

THE PARISH OF Orleans is made up of many small areas, most of which were originally settled by ethnic groups. Nearly all of these sections are contained within the city proper, the oldest of them being the French Quarter or Vieux Carre. As the city grew there evolved an American sector, and eventually, the Irish Channel, Garden District, Riverfront, Lakefront, East New Orleans, and University sections. The city also came to be separated into two major parts, with Canal Street as the dividing line between Uptown to the west and south and Downtown to the east and north. Uptown included the Irish Channel, Rampart-Perdido, Bolden's First Street neighborhood, the Garden District, Tulane and Loyola universities, Lincoln and Johnson parks; Downtown contained the French Quarter, Storyville, the Globe, Economy, and Perseverance halls, and the Creole society halls. Generally speaking the Creoles lived Downtown, often in beautiful homes along Esplanade Avenue and Bayou St. John; the darker-skinned Negroes, whom the Creoles referred to as blacks, lived Uptown. The Downtown-Uptown or Creole-black rivalry was not, however, exclusively a territorial one, since members of both groups lived within the other's "boundaries." The division was really more one of heritage and tradition.

The Creoles of color were descendants of the early New Orleans settlers and were a mixture of nationalities—French, Spanish, Haitian, and African. Peter Bocage's grandfather, for example, was French, his

74

grandmother Haitian.[1] The Creoles were educated, and at least at one time most of them were fairly well off. They had their own sections reserved at the opera and other social events. As members of this distinctive caste they felt a great deal of prejudice toward darker-skinned Negroes.

These differences naturally extended into the New Orleans music world, where musicians like Bocage, Perez, and the Tios specified that they had been taught to play music and, unlike Bolden, did not play jazz. Creole music had come from the professors who abounded in the city, from the French Opera, the "Red Book of Rags," and the "Manhattan Book" of dance music that Bocage utilized. Paul Barbarin's father Isidore and his uncle Louis Arthidore both were taught music by a member of the French Opera orchestra. Louis Cottrell, Sr., learned to read music around 1891 from John Cornfelt, who was about Cottrell's age.[2] The Creoles were competent musically and often took a violin, piano, or trumpet part, transposed it, and from it created parts for the other instruments. Along with their classical training, they had feeling and could interpret music in their own way much as Bolden did in his.

It was a great blow to Creole pride when an 1894 amendment to the Black Code thrust them into the same category as full-blooded blacks. Creole musicians had had the society jobs almost entirely to themselves for years, and as white bands began to take over these jobs the Creoles were forced to compete with black bands, to integrate with them or to abandon music altogether. Some remained bitter all their lives and never compromised musically or socially; most did not mix with the black bands until later. It became increasingly difficult for nonintegrated bands to survive, however, and need sometimes forced together strange bedfellows. Peter Bocage, the Creole violinist and trumpeter, found himself on occasion playing with the high-flying Eagle band. Later,

---

1. Allen and Russell, interview with Bocage, January 29, 1959, in William Ransom Hogan Jazz Archive, Tulane University, New Orleans.
2. Author's interview with Louis Cottrell, Jr., July 30, 1973.

along with Louis Tio, Manuel Manetta, and Louis Cottrell, Sr., he played at the Tuxedo Dance Hall in the District.[3]

When the Creoles did eventually combine with the Uptowners they added their various ethnic influences to the sounds that had already been assimilated by Uptown musicians, and the first melting and refining of the basic music was ready to take place. The Tio family, educated at the Mexican conservatory, added a Spanish touch; Alcibiades Jeanjacque, Oscar Duconge, Punkie and Bouboul Valentin lent their French style and background; and Robichaux and Bocage contributed the French-Haitian mixture. The men played what they felt, what their talents allowed, and each made his individual contribution to the whole. It was nobody's music and it was everybody's music.

Bolden's popularity hit its peak in 1905 and that was the only year most of his sidemen were listed as musicians in the city directory. The regular band at that time included Bolden, cornet; Willie Cornish, valve trombone; Brock Mumford, guitar; Cornelius Tillman, drums; Frank Lewis, b-flat clarinet; Willie Warner, c-clarinet, and Jimmy Johnson, bass. Bolden and Lewis, the best reading musicians in the band, taught Bolden's repertoire to the others.

The one actual photograph that has been found of the band pictures these regulars, with the exception of Cornelius Tillman, whose absence is unexplained. This photograph has been printed in nearly every major book on jazz and continues to perplex meticulous jazz scholars. The original came from Willie Cornish, who loaned it to Charles E. Smith to use in *Jazzmen*. Bella Cornish later loaned it to Leonard Bechet, Sidney's brother, and when he died the original was never recovered.[4] When it was first printed the caption stated "before 1895."[5] Bunk Johnson, however, provided this information and because he claimed to have joined the band in 1895 it was necessary for him to say that the picture had been taken before he was a member. For years the "before 1895" date was thrown in automatically whenever the picture was

3. Allen and Russell, interview with Bocage, January 29, 1959, in Hogan Jazz Archive.
4. Allen and Russell, interview with Bella Cornish, January 13, 1959, in Hogan Jazz Archive.
5. Ramsey and Smith, *Jazzmen*, pictures following page 32.

copied. There are several reasons to believe that the date was actually closer to 1905, one reason being that Bunk Johnson's other information concerning Bolden is off by almost exactly ten years. Jimmy Johnson is the key man in dating the photograph. According to his marriage certificate Jimmy was born in 1884; this date was verified by Louis Cottrell, Jr., who roomed with Johnson for seven years while both were touring with Don Albert's band in the 1930s.[6] The quality of the picture is so poor it is difficult to judge Johnson's precise age, but it is nonetheless evident that he is older than eleven.

Another puzzling aspect of the photograph is the way the musicians are holding their instruments. As originally printed in *Jazzmen* the fingering positions of the clarinetists indicate that the picture may have been printed backward. When the picture is reversed to correct these poses, however, both Johnson on bass and Mumford on guitar would seem to be playing left-handed. Johnson was not a left-handed bass player, and Mumford's family and others who knew him say he was not left-handed either. Bolden is also holding his cornet an unusual way, flat in his open palm. Whatever the explanation for these curious poses there is no doubt that this is Bolden's band. Among the many who have identified the group and its individual members are Beatrice Alcorn, Ed Garland, Tom Albert, Papa John Joseph, and Willie Parker.

The list of men who claimed to have played with Bolden is quite long; the list of those who actually played with him is considerably shorter. The Bolden alumni grew during the 1940s and 1950s when jazz research was reaching its peak. The following names of Bolden's sidemen were cross-checked and documented as carefully as was possible and consequently there are probably some who were omitted here because no documentation was available. Several persons long thought to have played with Bolden have been weeded out for various reasons, one being that not even New Orleans musicians would likely have been playing in the band at age five or younger. Bunk Johnson was one who seems to

---

6. Marriage certificate of Jimmy Johnson, February 3, 1904, New Orleans Vital Statistics Records; author's interview with Louis Cottrell, Jr., July 30, 1973.

have conveniently changed his birthdate to fit himself into Bolden's band.

There were numerous changeovers and substitutions in all the New Orleans bands. Many men had full-time jobs that conflicted with their musical activities and for this and other reasons band leaders frequently found it necessary to alter their lineups. Often parade bands were formed on the spur-of-the-moment, and a musician who played in just one brass band parade with Buddy could still claim the distinction of having played with him.

In addition to his regular band members, Bolden at one time or another used Octave Phillips on trumpet in his brass band. Phillips (1858–1907) had played in various brass and dance bands around the turn of the century. An old neighbor of his on Orleans Street, Alberta Lamkin, remembered going to dances at Odd Fellows Hall in 1906. She said that at times, when Bolden did not show up, Edward Clem or John Pendleton played in his place. She also remembered seeing trombone players Ed Jones, Bill Harrison, and Frank Dusen play with the band.[7]

A number of different drummers were used, probably for the parades. These included Bill Willigan, John or Joseph McMurray, Louis Ray, Henry Ray, Dee Dee Chandler (who was later credited with developing the first foot pedal), and Jimmy Phillips, who was noted for chewing matchsticks and falling asleep on the bandstand. Phillips also played trombone with Bolden. Some of Buddy's earlier bands used violinists Tom Adams and Dee Dee Brooks, and later, on occasion, Jimmy "Spriggs" Palao. Frank Jackson, Wallace Collins, and Bobo Lewis (from Raceland, Louisiana), all sometimes played tuba in the parades, and Jackson also doubled on the drums. Albert Glenny, Bob Lyons, Bebe Mitchell, and Ed "Montudi" Garland were bass players associated with the band. T-Boy Remy subbed for Mumford on guitar. Lorenzo Staulz, a heavy-drinking, hard-talking guitarist, played some jobs with Bolden later in his career, probably in 1906 when Frank Dusen had replaced Cornish on trombone. Staulz was known for his impromptu,

7. Author's interview with Alberta Lamkin, August 5, 1971.

The Bolden band photograph from 1905 contains the only actual photograph of Buddy. It was originally in the possession of Willie Cornish. The band regulars pictured are, back row, left to right: Jimmy Johnson, Buddy Bolden, Willie Cornish, and William Warner; front row, left to right: Jefferson Mumford and Frank Lewis.

—Photograph restored by Kenneth Pape

Because of the controversy as to whether the first publication of the photograph, in *Jazzmen*, was printed backwards, the reverse possibility is shown here, with the band members' signatures underneath.

—Photograph restored by Kenneth Bass

The John Robichaux Orchestra, 1896. Seated, left to right, are Edward "Dee Dee" Chandler, Charles McCurdy, John Robichaux, Wendell Mc Nïl. Standing, left to right, are Baptiste DeLisle, James Williams, James McNeil, Octave Gaspard.

Willie Cornish, who died in 1942 at age 67, was the last survivor of the regular Bolden band. A big man, he was "six feet and three and 297 pounds," his wife said. He is shown here with two of his music students.

—Photograph from Mrs. Bella Cornish

Louis Jones, born in 1874, was a barber and close friend to Bolden. He moved to New Orleans in 1894, lived until 1958, and his remembrances of Bolden are the closest and most accurate personal observations available. This picture was taken about 1905.

—Photograph from Mrs. Carrie Jones

Louis Jones had his barbershop in his home at 2113 Jackson Avenue from about 1909 or 1910. His widow was still living there in the 1970s.

—Photograph by Don Marquis

often obscene vocals. He often improvised words for "Buddy Bolden's Blues."

Sam Dutrey, Sr., and Alphonse Picou were employed by Buddy as clarinetists, and George Baquet, who was a regular member of the Robichaux Orchestra and whose father Theogene led the old Excelsior band, was fascinated by Bolden's music and sat in with him.[8]

Ed Garland, born before 1890 on South Basin Street and still playing great bass on the West Coast in 1977, recalled, when in New Orleans for the 1972 Jazzfest, the circumstances of his playing with Bolden:

> I substituted for Jimmy Johnson with Bolden. Johnson worked in a furniture factory and sometimes couldn't get off work. I played with Bolden at Liberty and Perdido Street at Kitty's Hall [actually Union Sons Hall at 1319 Perdido, but was also known as Kinney's and Funky Butt Hall]. Played on Saturday night and Sunday morning they had church there. The band had Jimmy Johnson, regular bass; Cornish, Lewis, Mumford, Warner and Jamesy Phillips on drums. I started out young, nine years old, had to put that bass on my shoulder. I was pretty good when I played with Bolden, though, about fifteen or sixteen years old.[9]

In 1905 when black New Orleans was in tune with the new music and Bolden was at his height, his primary rival was John Robichaux, a Creole who nevertheless lived Uptown on Tchoupitoulas Street and competed with Bolden in some of the rougher spots. Robichaux was in many ways the epitome of the New Orleans Creole of color. Born January 16, 1866, in the bayou country town of Thibodaux, he was older than Bolden and had the advantage of an excellent musical education. When he moved to New Orleans around 1891 he promptly became the bass drummer for Theogene Baquet's highly regarded Excelsior Cornet Band; shortly thereafter he organized his own band. By 1893 those playing for him were James Williams and James McNeil on cornet; Charles McCurdy, clarinet; Baptiste Delisle, trombone; Edward "Dee Dee"

---

8. Charters, *Jazz: New Orleans, 1885–1963,* 14–16; Miller (ed.), *Esquire's 1945 Jazz Yearbook,* 9–10; Rose and Souchon, *New Orleans Jazz: A Family Album,* 138, 144, 156, 158, 172, 182, 185, 197, 198.
9. Allen and Floyd Levin, interview with Ed "Montudi" Garland, April 20, 1971, in Hogan Jazz Archive.

Chandler, drums; Henry Kimball, bass; and Wendell McNeil, violin. Robichaux himself played violin and led the band, though he came to be more concerned with arranging music and managing the group. Clarence Vincent called him "more of a businessman."[10]

Of these musicians only Chandler and Kimball became significantly identified with jazz happenings. All of them, however, were mature musicians and the band was picking up many of the plush jobs in the city when Bolden was just learning the cornet. Robichaux's regular jobs included Antoine's Restaurant and the Grunewald (later Roosevelt and now Fairmont) Hotel, and he led the only Creole band to play a carnival ball in the old French Opera House. The 1894 Black Code amendment hit Robichaux's orchestra harder than any others, coming just when they seemed to be at the top of the New Orleans music scene. It was a comedown to some of these fine musicians to be thrown into competition with the Uptown blacks and to play for audiences who did not always appreciate their musical background. But Robichaux had enough determination to persevere during the difficult years that followed the transition, and even though a number of his musicians had to moonlight with the Onward Brass Band, he managed to hold on to a number of good jobs.

A second blow hit Robichaux's orchestra when, in 1898, Chandler, Delisle, and the McNeil brothers were recruited into the army while playing a job with the Onward band. Robichaux had to quickly pick up others to fill the gaps, and some of these fill-ins were Arthur "Bud" Scott on guitar, Lorenzo Tio and Paul Beaulieu on clarinet, and on some occasions Manuel Perez. Then, as the century turned and the Bolden band gained popularity, Robichaux had something else to contend with—a new sound. That he was able to hold his own without succumbing to any adulteration in his musical standards is a tribute to his talent. Usually Robichaux played for a different type of crowd than Bolden attracted, but not always. They both played at Lincoln Park, Longshoremen's Hall, Providence Hall, and Masonic and Odd Fellows Hall. Robichaux, in addition, played in the Downtown halls where Bol-

10. Allen and Crawford, interview with Clarence "Little Dad" Vincent, November 17, 1959, in Hogan Jazz Archive.

den was not hired. But Bolden could and did play a few polite society dances, and Robichaux by then had Williams and McNeil playing hot enough cornets to move an Uptown crowd.

In spite of their differences both Robichaux and Bolden had large followings, since then, as now, music was a matter of personal taste. Peter Martin Robertson, born in 1888 and porter in the building that now occupies the old Odd Fellows Hall site, was one of those who felt Bolden's music was too rough. He remembered going to dances in the hall for a dollar, and though he had heard of Bolden, he "was not a rowdy and preferred the music of John Robichaux and later A. J. Piron."[11] Whether Bolden or Robichaux won the cutting contests that took place between Johnson and Lincoln parks often depended on the type of crowd; if it was a "ratty" crowd, Robichaux's men, Williams and McNeil, did not have a chance. Bolden reportedly won the majority of these contests by popular acclaim, but both Alcide "Slow Drag" Pavageau and clarinetist George Baquet remembered times when he lost. Baquet recalled that three blocks from Mustache's, a favorite saloon of Bolden's men, was the Mix Saloon frequented by Robichaux's men. At some point the two bands decided to have a contest, the honors to be determined by the crowd's response. At first the Frenchmen seemed down; then Baquet rose and went through a stunt routine of throwing away parts of his clarinet, continuing to play as if it were all there. When he ended up with only the mouthpiece the audience gave him a tremendous hand and the contest went to Robichaux. Bolden, who didn't like losing, furiously asked, "George, why did you do it?"[12]

The rivalry between the two bands was not one of complete animosity by any means, though there may have been some sneering back and forth originally. The two pioneers cared enough about music to recognize the skills the other possessed and the contributions each was making. Bolden was known to have used ideas from the Robichaux band; some of Buddy's fans remembered seeing Robichaux seated by himself in the back of a hall where Bolden was playing, later leaving as quietly as he

---

11. Author's interview with Peter Martin Robertson, May 13, 1971.
12. George Baquet, "Baquet on Bolden," *Downbeat,* December 15, 1940.

had come in. Then too, we already have the words of some Robichaux-style musicians giving Buddy due recognition, albeit sometimes grudgingly. For the Bolden band members were good musicians too. They were not as technically proficient as the Creoles, but apparently most were readers, and Bolden and Lewis, at least, could write music. Bolden's accomplishment would not have been the same had he had a strict classical training or had he relied solely on the ideas in his head or the lessons he took. But he was able to combine these influences in a way that has made him the important pivotal figure in early jazz history. And the two bands, Bolden's and Robichaux's, provide the earliest and most clear-cut examples of the two types of music, Uptown and Downtown, that simultaneously borrowed from each other and hastened the development of jazz.

New Orleans has always prided itself on its musicians and musicianship. The old-timers made a point of differentiating between the "players" and the "musicianers," and some of them felt that Bolden did not measure up. It hurt them to see relatively untrained musicians like Bolden get all the fanfare and many of the jobs. The Creole musicians were a proud group and it took them awhile to accept the fact that their superior training and musical abilities were not putting them ahead of the Uptown bands. The distinctions, in fact, to some extent still exist; there is still talk of drum players as opposed to drum beaters and readers versus counters and fakers. This is not to say that the beaters, counters, and fakers do not merit a certain amount of respect, but the old musicians keep themselves aware of the difference. And of the two main present-day jazz emporiums, Preservation Hall features musicians like Preston Jackson, Kid Thomas, and Chester Zardis who would have been considered Uptowners, whereas Tradition Hall headlines Louis Cottrell, Jr., and Alvin Alcorn, who in earlier days would have played with the Creole orchestras.

The years 1900–1910 are considered the early major developmental years of traditional jazz; the first half of this period was almost exclusively Bolden's. He was more involved with ragtime than were most of his rivals, and his musical style was unique. Until 1905 or 1906 his was the only jazz band in town. But although they were not playing ragtime or jazz during these early years, some of Bolden's contemporaries did later become jazz musicians and others were, in retrospect, labeled as such. Peter Bocage, for example, played with the Imperial band in 1900 and the Onward in 1903 and 1904 but said that he did not begin playing jazz until he joined the Superior band around 1907 or 1908.[13] Charley Galloway and Edward Clem, though not closely identified with the new music in 1900, later were called jazz players. Galloway, in fact, had virtually dropped out of the professional music scene when Bolden was at his peak. People comparing Bolden to his contemporaries long after he was gone thought of him as being older than many of the others, when in age he was younger than such musicians as Wallace Collins, Edward Clem, Bob Lyons, Albert Glenny, Henry Zeno, Cornelius Tillman, Willie Cornish, Frank Lewis, Lorenzo Staulz, and Brock Mumford. He was older only in that he was identified with the new music before the others, and he perhaps seemed older because his career was so short.

In addition to his rivalry with Robichaux, Bolden competed with the brass bands for jobs, both on the street and with the slimmed-down versions that played for large gatherings. Other rivals were the Silver Leaf and Golden Rule orchestras and the many pickup bands that changed from night to night and were known by the name of the man who got the job. Some pickup groups probably played only once or twice as a unit.[14]

The Excelsior band, mostly Creole musicians, included Theogene Baquet, who led the group until 1904; Lorenzo, Sr., and Louis Tio; Adolphe Alexander, Sr., Edward Clem, and George Williams, cornets; Alphonse Picou, Charles McCurdy, and Sam Dutrey, Sr., clarinets; Buddy Johnson and Vic Gaspard, trombones; George Hooker, baritone horn; Clay Jiles, bass drum; and George Moret, cornet and leader in 1905. Louis Cottrell, Sr., who played snare drums, was described by

13. Allen and Russell, interview with Bocage, January 29, 1959, in Hogan Jazz Archive.

14. The best sources for personnel of New Orleans jazz bands are: Charters, *Jazz: New Orleans, 1885–1963;* Miller (ed.), *Esquire's 1945 Jazz Yearbook;* Rose and Souchon, *New Orleans Jazz: A Family Album.* Marriage certificates provided more accurate documentation of ages, dates, relationships, and friendships, and these are listed in the bibliography on pages 154–56.

Papa John Joseph as "the best drummer we had yet. That man could roll a drum."[15]

The Olympia, started by Freddie Keppard, was actually an orchestra. Its members were Alphonse Picou, Jean Vigne on drums, Joe Petit on trombone, and Keppard's brother Louis on guitar. The Superior band around 1907 or 1908 had Bunk Johnson on cornet, Billy Marrero as leader and bass, Buddy Johnson, Walter Brundy on drums, Richard Payne on guitar, Big Eye Louis Nelson on clarinet, and Peter Bocage on violin. Big Eye Louis Nelson also played for the Golden Rule Orchestra, led by Babb Frank's brother Alcide. Other players in this group were Adolphe Alexander, Sr., James Brown on bass, and Joe Brooks on guitar. Another orchestra, the Silver Leaf, was used mainly for dances, employing Hypolite Charles, cornet; Sam Dutrey, Sr., clarinet; Albert Baptiste, violin; George Sayles, guitar; and Ernest Rogers, drums.

The Peerless and Onward rosters read like an honor roll of early jazzmen. The Peerless was led by piccolo player Gilbert "Babb" Frank, who "always carried his piccolo in his pocket . . . wrapped in a piece of paper."[16] And with Frank were Vic Gaspard, Octave Gaspard, Andrew Kimball, Hamp Benson, and Walter Brundy. Manuel Perez led the Onward band, which had Peter Bocage, Lorenzo Tio, Jr., Adolphe Alexander, Andrew Kimball, Vic Gaspard, Louis Cottrell, Sr., George Filhe, and Isidore Barbarin.

Bands from across the river included the Pacific Brass Band, headquartered in Algiers, with George Hooker, Buddy Johnson, Manuel Manetta, and Frankie Dusen; and the Pickwick, which existed only a few years before and after 1900, had Norman and Jules Manetta and James Love as members, and used a number of musicians from other bands. Henry Allen, Sr., also led a brass band in Algiers and with him were Buddy Johnson, Clay Jiles, Joe Howard, Jack Carey, and George Hooker. The Eclipse Brass Band was made up of musicians from Magnolia plantation taught by Professor Jim Humphrey. Sam Morgan, Chris

15. Allen and Russell, interview with Joseph, November 26, 1958, in Hogan Jazz Archive.
16. *Ibid*.

Kelly, and Harrison Barnes were some of the later jazzmen who played in this band as young men.

Of all the musicians playing at the time, Manuel Perez was one who was nearly as busy musically as Bolden and Robichaux. Perez, a Creole, was born in 1879 and married in 1900; the timetable of his early musical career runs almost parallel to Bolden's. He was an excellent reading musician whose talents were highly respected by both Creoles and blacks in the inner circles of music. Although he did not lead a band under his own name he did lead the Onward Brass Band and the Imperial Orchestra. Perez never sought publicity, was reserved, almost shy, and lived quietly in a Downtown neighborhood, making cigars as a daytime occupation. His parade cornet was one of the best sounds in the city, and Albert Burbank observed that "although his upward range was not particularly high, he was so powerful he'd make you think he was playing high."[17] Sidney Bechet remembered that Perez used to "three time the music until it was really beautiful."[18] Perez was responsible for refining many of Bolden's ideas on the cornet, and he helped combine the best of Bolden with the Creole music so that by 1910 elemental jazz was on its way to becoming classical jazz. He was one of the true giants of the New Orleans jazz tradition and it is unfortunate that so many jazz historians have given him so little attention.

Another name that appears in researching the Bolden era is that of Louis Ned, a cornetist who at one time played with Willie Humphrey, Sr. Ned's history as a prejazz figure is even more elusive than Bolden's. Many people remembered having heard of him, but they knew little about him, and no evidence exists to support the assertion that he played with Bolden in New Orleans. Ernest "Punch" Miller described Ned as "mule-faced, strong-lipped and a first class musician."[19] As far as can be determined, he grew up in New Orleans and played with some of the

17. Collins and Russell, interview with Albert Burbank, March 18, 1959, in Hogan Jazz Archive.

18. Bechet, *Treat It Gentle*, 64.

19. Author's interview with Ernest "Punch" Miller, April 17, 1962.

kid "Spasm" bands before Bolden's time, but he later moved to Baton Rouge. This would explain his being relatively unknown in New Orleans, and it is reasonable to think that he may have played a parade with Bolden when the band went on excursion to Baton Rouge.

With the degree of overlapping from one band to another and the fact that all the bands were competing for jobs, the musicians' paths often crossed and many friendships were formed. Bolden evidently got along well with his fellow musicians, as most who knew him before 1905 spoke well of him. The occasional indications that these friendships were limited seem, at least on the surface, to stem from the much belabored Uptown-Downtown separation. Bertha McCullum, whose husband George, Sr., played cornet with Robichaux, said that she knew the Bolden family but did not see them socially. Her husband did not play with Bolden, she added, since they were not in the same class musically.[20]

One indication of friendships among musicians comes from noting the best men and witnesses listed on marriage certificates. Bolden, for example, was a witness at Frank Lewis' wedding, Walter Brundy was a witness for Henry Kimball, George Hooker for Jimmy Palao, James McNeil for Oscar Duconge, and Willie Foster, Alex Scott, and Roy Palmer for Amos Riley. There were occasional crossovers between Uptown and Downtown bands, as in Jimmy Johnson's wedding when James Williams of Robichaux's band and George Sayles of the Silver Leaf stood up with him.

Buddy's closest friends were Louis Jones and Willie Cornish. The three were about the same age, lived fairly close together, and drank most anything that could be poured. When the women helped Buddy carry his coat and other accouterments after a dance, it could be expected that Willie and Louis helped him carry some of the women. They were energetic men, and if their energies often turned to pleasure, they also managed to responsibly handle other aspects of their lives. Cornish was

20. Harold Dejan and Russell, interview with Bertha McCullum, October 16, 1960, in Hogan Jazz Archive.

never known to miss a music job and Jones cut hair every week for thirty-seven years, retiring only when his eyesight went bad.

Louis had never paid much attention to music, but as Buddy's career developed he began to attend many of the dances, going, as he put it, "to watch the people." He eventually married a girl named Caria or "Carrie," and though she was a strict Baptist and didn't attend dances, she talked affectionately of Louis' "shenanigans with Bolden and them" and remembered that before she and Louis were married he and Buddy often would not get home until the following day. Mrs. Jones, in reminiscing, said Louis had a way with the neighborhood kids; he always gave them a sucker or stick of gum when he cut their hair and found time to talk with them about school or their problems. There are middle-aged men in his old neighborhood who still speak with respect of "Papa Louis."[21]

Willie Cornish embraced life with a thoroughness that was reflected in everything he did. "He was six feet and three and weighed two hundred ninety-seven pounds," said his widow Bella, "and he could blow the horn, too, don't you think he couldn't." Cornish, raised in a large family on or near Perdido Street, worked at many jobs besides music, including as a driver, longshoreman, and laborer. He had little formal musical education, but his wife said that when he practiced at home he took his music out and played by note rather than by ear. "He could arrange music, too," she said. "He'd take them chords and he could fix the notes, all on them chords." The fact that he worked as a piano tuner for awhile indicates that he had a good ear as well. Cornish was a dedicated musician and his wife once chided him, "Lord, you love that horn don't you?" He replied, "Yeah, I love the horn better than I love you or anybody; my horn comes first; I makes my living with this horn." Cornish, in his Bolden days, would take on a rival band with his trombone and sometimes with impromptu verses, yet he had the gentleness to teach youngsters who were barely able to hold his trombone how

21. Allen and Russell, interview with Jones, January 19, 1959, in Hogan Jazz Archive; author's interview with Mrs. Jones, April 9, 30, and May 7, 1971.

to blow the notes properly.[22] Nora Bolden said that Cornish often visited Buddy at home on band business and they would go off together to some bar; Louis Jones also mentioned that Bolden and Cornish were good friends.[23]

Jazz: New Orleans, 1885–1963 mentions another contemporary of Bolden's, Tom Pickett, citing him as a gambler who took over Bolden's women around 1907.[24] There was a _Bob_ Pickett connected with the Bolden story. His widow, Susannah, who was eighty-four years old in 1971, lives across the street from the old Bolden home on First Street. She used to attend dances at Odd Fellows Hall, and it was there that she met Bob. He was a gambler and hustler who hung around the dances, keeping a sharp eye out for a card game or crap shooting event, always looking for the big break. In those days Pickett, who was twenty years older than Bolden, was only managing to maintain a hand-to-mouth existence.[25] Bolden's popularity, fame, and money-spending habits may well have irked Pickett, and if the stories are true, he sometimes jealously needled Buddy. There is no evidence, however, of any dispute between the two, and it is probably more realistic to believe that they tolerated each other's presence when necessary.

The following list of musicians comes from _Soards' New Orleans City Directory_, 1880 to 1915.

Adams, Thomas, laborer, 2229 North Prieur
Albert, Thomas, laborer, 512 Dauphine
Alexander, Adolph, shoemaker, 1801 St. Philip
Allen, Henry, longshoreman, 921 Verret
Baquet, George, laborer, 2126 Annette
Baquet, Theogene V., cigarmaker, 1820 Conti
Barbarin, Isidore, musician, 1750 St. Claude
Barnes, Harrison, helper, 503 Newton
Beaulieu, Paul W., carrier, Post Office, 1026 Burgundy

22. Allen and Russell, interview with Bella Cornish, January 13, 1959, in Hogan Jazz Archive.
23. Hogan and Crawford, interviews with Russell, August 31 and September 4, 1962, and Allen and Russell, interview with Jones, January 19, 1959, both in Hogan Jazz Archive.
24. Charters, _Jazz: New Orleans, 1885–1963_, 12.
25. Author's interview with Susannah Pickett, August 5, 1971.

Bechet, Leonard, dentist, 1716 Marais
Bocage, Peter, musician, 513 Socrates
Boisseau, Joseph, musician, 413 North Roman
Brown, James, musician, 724 North Derbigny
Cato, Augustin, laborer, 3922 Laurel
Chaligny, Paul, tailor, 919 St. Claude
Chandler, Edward, musician, 2016 Melpomene
Clem, Edward, musician, 2307 Erato
Collins, Walter, laborer, 322 North Galvez
Cornish, William, piano tuner, 1326 Erato
Cottrell, Louis, musician, 1121 North Robertson
Cousteau, Sylvester, cigarmaker, 1446 North Derbigny
Dawson, Edward, packer, Bolivar Street
Decker, Sylvester, laborer, 238 South Basin
DeLille, Louis, musician, 1631 North Robertson
DeVerges, Charles, musician, 507 Homer
Dodds, John M., boilermaker, 2437 Perdido
Dominguez, Paul, laborer, 1700 Elysian Fields
Dominique, Aniate [Natty], cigarmaker, 1723 Urquhart
Dusen, Frank, musician, 1425 Leontine
Dutrey, Samuel, barber, 3912 Laurel
Duconge, Oscar, musician, 1315 St. Peter
Elgar, Charles, workman, U.S. Mint, 1625 Burgundy
Filhe, George, musician, 1704 Laharpe
Frank, Alcide O., barber, 4838 Tchoupitoulas
Frank, Gilbert [Babb], musician, 1917 Fourth
Galloway, Charles, barber, 1326 Lafayette
Gaspard, Octave (Oke), cooper, 2022 Bourbon
Gaspard, Victor, cooper, 2028 Bourbon
Glass, Henry, laborer, 1120 Frenchmen
Glenny, Albert, laborer, 1817 Marais
Hooker, George W., porter, 221 Homer
Jackson, Frank, laborer, 1529 Gasquet
Jaeger, Charles, laborer, 528 Jackson
Jeanjacques, Alcibiades, cigarmaker, 1413 North Villere
Johnson, Arthur [Buddy], laborer, 260 Hillary
Johnson, James, musician, 613 St. James
Joseph, John, barber, 2400 South Liberty
Keeling, Frank, laborer, 1423 Perdido

Kelly, Christopher, driver, 1659 St. Thomas
Keppard, Frederick, musician, 1813 St. Ann
Keppard, Louis, musician, 1813 St. Ann
Kimball, Andrew J., carpenter, 5306 Constance
Kimball, Henry, Jr., musician, 916 Seventh
Laine, Alfred, musician, 632 Port
Lewis, Frank, musician, 1220 Joseph
Lopez, Raymond, musician, 475 Josephine
Love, Charles J., laborer, 1819 Dauphine
Lyons, Robert, musician, 421 South Liberty
Manetta, Emanuel G., laborer, 239 Pelican
Martin, Louis, cigarmaker, 808 St. Claude
McCullum, George, sexton, 3514 South Liberty
McCurdy, Charles, musician, 2133 Rousseau
McMurray, Joseph A., musician, 2431 St. Ann
McNeal [McNeil], James W., vice principal, Fisk School for Colored Boys
    and Girls, residence 1438 Euterpe
McNeal [McNeil], Wendell, teacher, Fisk School, 1438 Euterpe
Mitchell, Arthur J., 1729 Poydras
Moret, George, cigarmaker, 1818 St. Anthony
Mumford, Jefferson, musician, 7622 Macarty
Nicholas, Joseph, laborer, 2266 North Villere
Oliver, Joseph, musician, 2712 Dryades
Olivier, Adam, barber, 514 General Taylor
Ory, Edward, musician, 2135 Jackson
Parker, William, laborer, 1905 Marais
Pendleton, John, laborer, 1610 Prytania
Perez, Emanuel, musician, 1714 Urquhart
Perkins, David, musician, 1814 Sixth
Peyton, Henry, musician, ws [west side] Chestnut between Jena Cadiz
Phillips, James, porter, 2231 Second
Phillips, Octave, laborer, 2237 Orleans
Picou, Alphonse, tinner, 1720 St. Philip
Piron, Armand, musician, 1818 Columbus
Piron, Albert L., artist, 1525 Columbus
Piron, Milford, shoemaker, 1525 Columbus
Ray, Louis, laborer, 212 Port
Remy, Dominick [T-Boy], laborer, 1923 Bienville
Rena, Henry [Kid Rena], musician, 2032 Conti

Robertson, Alvin C. [Zue], musician, 3109 South Liberty
Robichaux, John P., musician, no address given
St. Cyr, John, plasterer, 2116 Burdette
Scott, Arthur, Jr., [Bud], musician, 3009 Dryades
Spillis, Willis, musician, 1923 Seventh
Staulz, Lorenzo, musician, 1427 Leontine
Tillman, Cornelius, screwman, 2912 Philip
Tio, Lorenzo, painter, 1621 St. Bernard
Tio, Louis, cigarmaker, 1704 Laharpe
Vincent, Clarence [Little Dad], yardman, 1917 Fourth
Vinet, Joseph, cigarmaker, 108 Annette
Warner, William, musician, 2707 South Liberty
Williams, Clarence, laborer, 3221 Baronne
Williams, James A., barber, 1114 Perdido, residence 2214 Valence
Williams, Norward [Gigi], porter, 1830 Philip
Wolff, Oscar, musician, 224 Toulouse
Zeno, Henry, musician, 7019 Wall

7

Personality and Family Life

BOLDEN WAS NOT a legend in his own time. Consequently it is nearly impossible to arrive at a clear idea of his character and personality, since there is no recognized authority to consult and because it is extremely difficult to prove what was happening with a black musician in those days. The information must be patched together from accounts by people who saw Bolden from 1894 to 1906, in the years when things were moving very fast in his life and when he must have appeared in different lights according to the situation he was in. Many of the "authentic" interviewees had little opportunity to observe Bolden when he was actually the "king" and some did not even consider him consequential until years later, when his reputation was established. They then made an attempt to remember and become a part of a phenomenon they hadn't paid particular attention to before. In asking questions about Bolden, if the barbershop, the *Cricket,* girls, loudness, and "Funky Butt" are all that is mentioned, one can surmise that rather than actually having known Bolden the person has merely read *Jazzmen*.

Most sources agree that Bolden was fairly light-skinned, closer to the Creoles in coloring than, for example, to the very black-skinned Cornish. He was about five feet eleven inches tall and was well-built as opposed to being slender or heavy. The available official documents add little to the description, the most detailed one stating only, "brown hair, brown eyes, no beard."[1] Kid Ory described Buddy as "kind of on the

1. State of Louisiana, Parish of Orleans, City of New Orleans, Coroner's Office, Description and Record of Insane Person, p. 408, in Louisiana Division, New Orleans Public Library.

Maroni style, hair wasn't black, was not exactly red, never combed it, always the way it was cut. He was about the size of Jim Robinson [about six feet, well-built], but not quite as tall, strong, not dark-skinned, but brown-skinned."

Bolden's band was Ory's favorite. He told how one Saturday in 1900 when he was practicing his trombone at his sister's house there was a knock, and "it was the most famous musician in New Orleans, Buddy Bolden, whose band I had heard many times." Buddy was looking for a trombone player and asked Ory if he'd like to join the band, but Ory's sister thought he was too young (he was about fourteen at the time).[2] By around 1903 or 1904 Bolden was famous enough to be given the title *King*. He had been called *Kid* previously, this being a soubriquet given to young New Orleans musicians who started and led bands. Bolden must have enjoyed being called *King* and within certain limits he tried to live like one. He frequently "held court" at one of the bars on Jackson Avenue or in the Rampart-Perdido area; he made money and then spent it. His name does not appear in property ownership records, either as owning personal property or real estate.

Albert Glenny said that Bolden was a good dresser, that women gave him money for clothes, and that although he drank heavily, his drinking did not interfere with his playing.[3] Sidney Bechet elaborated: "Bolden used to drink heavy. He lived it fast. One reason you hear his name, why he is remembered. He got a lot of attention with the things he did. You always heard how he had three or four women living with him in the same house. He'd walk down the street and one woman would have his cornet, his watch, his handkerchief, etc. He could drink and he was a real story teller. He couldn't go anywhere without making a big splash. He could play, too. He took up ragtime some, but he couldn't follow through on it, he wasn't able."[4] Bechet was not born until 1897 so much of his knowledge about Bolden was secondhand and also was filtered

2. Campbell and Ertugin, interview with Ory, April 20, 1957, in William Ransom Hogan Jazz Archive, Tulane University, New Orleans.
3. Sancton, "Libretto," 1, 8, 13.
4. Bechet, *Treat It Gentle*, 84.

through a Creole sensibility. In addition, because Bechet was one of the most outstanding all-around musicians to come out of New Orleans, his standards were extremely high.

Excerpts about Bolden from several books reinforce the comments on his drinking and women and indicate, as well, how deeply involved he was in his music. *Shining Trumpets* calls him "boldly creative, versatile, dominant. He shaped the prevailing tendencies into forms of a new period. . . . Bolden was a shrewd organizer, dynamic, a magnetic leader. He was a public figure of immense popularity."[5] Historian Harnett Kane, in *Queen New Orleans* said: "Bolden had two loves, music and women. Women fought to hold his coat. He made up songs, his rich voice stirred the girls. His playing had one indispensable feature, 'the trance.' He had an ability to immerse himself into the music until nothing mattered but himself and his cornet in fast communication. Girls threw money at him and bought him whiskey."[6]

Bolden, however, was able to adapt himself and his music to different situations. To Beatrice Alcorn and other members of the teenage girls' Blue Ribbon Social Club around 1904, he had seemed special. Mrs. Alcorn said that the girls, when meeting one another during the day, would ask, "Are you going to the dance tonight?" And when it was established that Bolden was playing, the response would be an excited, "Yes, indeed I'm going!" Bolden was a favorite at their Friday night dances. The club paid five dollars for the hall and ten dollars for the band; ice cream and punch were served as refreshments. Bolden's musicians neither wore their hats on the bandstand nor did any drinking. They played waltzes, quadrilles, the two-step and slow drag—all dance music and no fast or "jazzed-up stuff"—and no one sang lyrics as they might have at other dances. The kids liked Buddy and crowded around the bandstand; the band members in turn were all polite, well-behaved, and friendly.[7]

5. Blesh, *Shining Trumpets*, 180.
6. Harnett T. Kane, *Queen New Orleans: City by the River* (New York: William Morrow, 1949), 285–86.
7. Author's interview with Beatrice Alcorn, June 23, 1971.

Buddy was a friendly, gregarious person. When he was not playing music or spending time with his cohorts at a barbershop or bar, he frequently would sit on the steps in front of the house on First Street and talk with passersby. Kid Ory recalled that Bolden practiced outside too, "always on the box step out in the street on the sidewalk. He blew so loud, he'd blow everyone out of the house. The kids gathered around on the sidewalks, yelling 'King Bolden! King Bolden!' "[8] But though Buddy was something of an idol to the children in the area and represented what to them was greatness, he apparently was not star-struck and always had time to talk.

The stories of women giving him money, whiskey, and clothes occur frequently enough to be given some credence. Bechet hinted that Buddy may have had women working for him.[9] He would certainly have had the opportunity to take up procuring as a sideline around Rampart and Perdido streets, but once again there are not enough hard facts to say for certain. My feeling is that he did not pimp, but that the women who surrounded him he enjoyed himself. These women were probably no secret to his family, but they certainly did not live at the house and the stories of Buddy having three or four women living with him are accurate only in that the women were family members.

Alice Bolden was the family's sole support until Buddy was able to contribute his earnings. She was a proud and independent woman whose life centered around her home and the St. John the Fourth Baptist Church. She worked as a domestic, cleaning house and doing wash for people in the Garden District, and in late 1899 she was also working part-time as a laundress at a rooming house on North Liberty Street.[10] Alice apparently did not see Manuel Hall after 1898; he remarried in 1901.[11] She never remarried, though she went with several other men over the years and did, at times, have common-law relationships after

8. Campbell and Ertugin, interview with Ory, April 20, 1957, in Hogan Jazz Archive.
9. Bechet, *Treat It Gentle*, 84–85.
10. Author's interview with Jackson and Lawes, June 25 and July 2, 1971.
11. Marriage certificate of Manuel Hall, December 10, 1901, New Orleans Vital Statistics Records.

Buddy left home. She never changed her last name, in 1913 being listed in the city directory as Mrs. Edward Bolden, in 1923, perhaps erroneously, as Mrs. Silas Bolden.

Alice was not musically inclined. She did not sing in the church choir, there was never a piano in the house, nor was the Bolden home a drop-in rendezvous for musicians. The musicians who played with Buddy sometimes stopped by to check on a job or pick him up for a gig and Alice and Cora knew them, but these were not social relationships. Neither of the women attended the dances. Their acquaintance with Buddy's playing came from hearing him practice at home and play in the parades that passed near their corner. They clearly neither wanted to see nor hear any indication of questionable activity or wrongdoing on his part.[12] Family ties among the three were close—perhaps because of the family deaths in the early 1880s— and Alice and Cora may have been overprotective of Buddy, not wanting to see him go out on his own. Cora, though she was younger than he, seemed to feel the concern of an older sister. Even Louis Jones, who knew both of them well, referred to her as Buddy's older sister.[13]

Around 1902 Buddy became acquainted with Nora Bass, an attractive, lively girl who had much more class than some of his other admirers. Nora was a mulatto whose family had lived in New Orleans for a long time. She was born in January, 1880; in 1901 her family moved to 2405 First Street, a block from the Bolden home. Nora had two brothers, Arthur and Andrew, and three sisters, Dora, Nettie, and Bendetta. Dora married Edward Rose, Jr., in 1899, and though the marriage evidently did not last long, an interesting aside is that Rose's sister, Ida Rose, played piano with the Bloom Philharmonic Orchestra which included A. J. Piron, Dee Dee Brooks, Octave and Vic Gaspard, Alphonse Picou, George Moret, Jim Humphrey, Alcibiades Jeanjacque, and Louis Tio. Thus Buddy may have met Nora through her sister. The Bass family was very religious and Buddy's first dates with Nora consisted of taking her

12. Author's interview with Jackson and Lawes, June 25 and July 2, 1971; Allen and Russell, interview with Jones, January 19, 1959, in Hogan Jazz Archive.

13. Allen and Russell, interview with Jones, January 19, 1959, in Hogan Jazz Archive.

and Dora to church at the First Street Baptist Church or to the First Methodist Episcopal Church where Nora's brother Arthur was the Sexton. One can imagine that Arthur took a dim view of some of Buddy's activities, since he is known to have at one time signed a letter of complaint concerning a "questionable house" whose inhabitants were very disturbing to the neighbors.[14]

Although they did not have an official wedding ceremony, in 1902 Buddy and Nora set up housekeeping at 2719 Philip Street. Elizabeth Morton, an aunt of the previously mentioned Beatrice Alcorn, remembered that Nora had lived near her on Philip between Magnolia and Clara streets, and the 1903 city directory has Bolden living on both Philip and First Streets.[15] Nora was not a part of the sporting crowd and although she probably made adjustments to Buddy's ways and may even have accompanied him to some of his band jobs, she did not comfortably fit into that type of life. His musical world was undoubtedly rougher than the world she was accustomed to. She may have reconciled herself to the fact that Buddy was going to continue to drink a lot and spend time in an environment that was alien to her, but most likely she did not allow his world to encroach very heavily upon her own. And Buddy apparently spent as many nights at his old home as he did with his wife. Nora said that she knew Willie Cornish and Brock Mumford because they would come to see Buddy on band business, but, as in the Bolden family home, there was little socializing with the musicians or their families. Nora remained close to her own mother and sister Dora but did not get along well with Buddy's family, referring to them as "funny."[16] This is probably why she and Buddy lived on Philip Street rather than with Alice and Cora.

14. The details on the Bass family background come from the 1870 and 1880 census records for the City of New Orleans; *Soards' New Orleans City Directory*, 1875 to 1910; Hogan and Crawford, interviews with Russell, August 31 and September 4, 1962, in Hogan Jazz Archive. Arthur Bass was a complainant in a report made by George Long to the New Orleans First Precinct on September 20, 1907, in Louisiana Division, New Orleans Public Library.

15. Author's interview with Elizabeth Morton, June 23, 1971. In 1973 Mrs. Morton was still alert at age ninety-four.

16. Hogan and Crawford, interviews with Russell, August 31 and September 4, 1962, in Hogan Jazz Archive.

Around 1903 a daughter, Bernedine, was born to Buddy and Nora. Little can be documented about the relationship between father and daughter, but there is some indication of concern from a letter Bernedine wrote in 1927 to East Louisiana State Hospital, inquiring about "My father Charlie Bolden."[17]

From 1900 on Hattie, Buddy's first common-law wife, had begun using her maiden name of Oliver again and was living at 2018 South Liberty with Charles, Jr. Buddy was no longer contributing to their support and Hattie must have had a hard time making ends meet. Charles, Jr., who was eight years old in 1905, was an undisciplined youth who was frequently left to his own devices.

After Buddy had become serious enough about Nora to move away from his family, Cora took up with a man fourteen years her senior. On September 10, 1902, when she was twenty-two, she married Alex Reed. The marriage, however, seems to have been very short-lived, as police arrest records from 1903 indicate that Reed was already single again. He is not mentioned by anyone who knew the family, though Cora continued to go by the name Cora Reed.[18] Cora and Alice were close to very few people. Lena Kennedy and Gertrude Peyton, both first cousins of Alice and members of the same church, indicated that they had nothing to do with the two Boldens.[19] Sometime late in 1903 or early 1904, Alice and Cora moved from the long-time residence at 2309 First, almost directly across the street to 2302. By mid-1904 Buddy was living there too.[20]

17. Charles Bolden file, Southeast Louisiana State Hospital, Jackson, Louisiana.
18. Marriage certificate of Cora Bolden to Alexander Reed, September 11, 1902, New Orleans Vital Statistics Records. In May, 1903, Alexander Reed was arrested for driving a hack without a license, according to New Orleans Police Department Arrest Records, First Precinct, May 21, 1903, in Louisiana Division, New Orleans Public Library.
19. Author's interviews with Jackson and Lawes, June 25 and July 2, 1971.
20. *Soards' New Orleans City Directory*, 1902 to 1905.

8

How and What
He Played

DORA BASS said Buddy "broke his heart when he played."[1] That his sound was unique and affected people deeply despite any reservations they might have had about his technical abilities comes through in any number of interviews. And because there are no recordings to hear, we have only words to use in reconstructing that sound and the aura it created. Nobody played exactly like Bolden. Some who came before and after played better and there were men like Edward Clem and Fred Keppard who could have given reasonable imitations. But Clem never recorded either, and by the time Keppard put his music to wax he was past his prime and had been away from New Orleans long enough to have progressed from the basic jazz that Buddy played.

George Baquet recalled the effect Bolden's music had on him the first time he heard it at Odd Fellows Hall:

> Nobody took their hats off. It was plenty rough. You paid fifteen cents and walked in. The band, six of them was sitting on a low stand. They had their hats on and were resting, pretty sleepy. All of a sudden, Buddy stomps, knocks on the floor with his trumpet to give the beat and they all sit up straight. They played "Make Me a Pallet." Everybody rose and yelled out "Oh, Mr. Bolden, play it for us, Buddy, play it!" I'd never heard anything like that before. I'd played "legitimate" stuff. But this, it was something that pulled me in. They got me up on the stand and I played with them. After that I didn't play legitimate so much.[2]

1. Hogan and Crawford, interviews with Russell, August 31 and September 4, 1962, in William Ransom Hogan Jazz Archive, Tulane University, New Orleans.
2. Baquet, "Baquet on Bolden."

Creole violinist Paul Dominguez indicated that nobody's playing was quite so "legitimate" after Bolden, saying in *Mister Jelly Roll*: "Bolden cause all that. He cause those younger Creole men like Bechet and Keppard to have a different style all together from the old heads like Tio and Perez. I don't know how they do it. But, goddam, they'll do it. [They] can't tell you what's there on paper, but just play the hell out of it."[3]

What was it that sounded so different to Baquet and brought about the changes Dominguez mentions? It was not so much an improvised quality, since the terms "jazzing" or "ragging" as applied to Bolden's music did not mean the same as the improvisation that was later to be identified with jazz. It was more a matter of adding extra touches to the music. Indeed, Kid Ory, Bud Scott, Mutt Carey, and others attributed Bolden's fame to his ability to fake; if he forgot a passage he would introduce embellishments that his listeners often enjoyed more than the music originally written.[4] Bob Lyons thought the difference was that early bands like Bolden's, though not yet playing real jazz, "weren't restricted by classical music laws, so they improvised and this came out as their feeling unrefined."[5] Some of this feeling is captured by Bill Matthews, an old-time trombone player, as he describes Bolden's sound:

> When it came to playing sweet music; waltzes, there was nobody in the country could touch him. He played something on the order of Wayne King. He was one of the sweetest trumpet players on waltzes and things like that and on those old slow blues, that boy could make the women jump out the window. On those old, slow, low down blues, he had a moan in his cornet that went all through you, just like you were in church or something. Everybody was crazy about Bolden when he'd blow a waltz, schottische or old low down blues. He was the sweetest trumpet player in the world. He'd tell his boys to get low, they'd get low and he'd take it. . . . Louis Armstrong, King Oliver, none of them had a tone like Bolden. Bunk Johnson got his style

3. Lomax, *Mister Jelly Roll*, 86.
4. Campbell and Ertugin, interview with Ory, April 20, 1957, in Hogan Jazz Archive.
5. Goffin, *La Nouvelle Orleans, Capitale du Jazz*, 50–51.

following Buddy with his sweetness, but could never play rough and loud like Bolden.[6]

Matthews went on to say that Buddy always had his horn with him, "in a pool room, everywhere. Bolden would pull out his cornet in a barroom, him and his derby, when he'd get drunk." And Tom Albert said, "He played like he didn't care."[7]

Armand Hug, New Orleans piano player, also hinted at some of the feelings behind the new music: "The Quadrille was a proper dance, usually limited to a certain social strata, but the Uptown bands changed it to their own style. Jazz enabled the musician to let off steam. They played in the butler's pantry because they weren't allowed in the parlor. Some became brassy and egotistical as a compensation. They were impulsive, played blues and gut bucket. Depended on what people wanted to hear."[8]

The unwritten flourishes and the underlying feelings, combined with a different beat—which William "Bebe" Ridgely called a two beat slower than the later "double beat which is fast 4/4 time"—made Bolden's music compelling and controversial. Tom Albert said Bolden sometimes confused the dancers by blowing high, spirited notes and chords, then suddenly fading out with a mournful tone. Kid Ory said he didn't play high, but loud, "and people loved it. Bolden wasn't really a musician. He didn't study, I mean, he was gifted, playing with effect, but no tone." Albert Glenny, on the other hand, believed that Bolden "had a right good tone, too, and a lively style. With all those notes he'd throw in and out of nowhere, you never heard anything like it." Sidney

6. Collins and Russell, interview with Bill Matthews, March 10, 1959, in Hogan Jazz Archive. Matthews' birthday is usually given either as 1896 or 1899. However, his marriage certificate of September 21, 1909, in New Orleans Vital Statistics Records, indicates that he was born around 1889, and that extra ten years would make him old enough to have had firsthand knowledge of Bolden.

7. Collins and Russell, interview with Albert, September 25, 1959.

8. Televised interview with Armand Hug in 1963, Station WYES-TV, New Orleans. There is no written or taped record of the interview but its substance was verified in a telephone call from the author to Hug on August 26, 1976. Hug was not born until 1910 but has done considerable research into New Orleans jazz history.

Bechet thought that others played "a lot deeper into the music" but that Bolden attracted people by showmanship.[9]

Some differences of opinion concerning Bolden's music can be expected simply because of the different values and approaches taken by Creole musicians and Uptowners. One characteristic nearly all commentaries agree on, however, is that Bolden's sound was loud. A good percentage of the stories that emphasize his power are just passed-on tales, but the tales are myriad. Among those who elaborated were Albert Glenny, Vic Gaspard, Alphonse Picou, Bob Lyons, Thomas "Mutt" Carey, William "Bebe" Ridgely, Frank Amacker, Tom Albert, Wooden Joe Nicholas, Peter Bocage, Roy Palmer, and Bill Matthews. The statements were also sometimes extreme. Frankie Dusen told people that "Bolden blew the loudest horn in the world"; Jelly Roll Morton agreed that he was "the most powerful trumpet player in history." Morton continued: "I remember we'd be hanging around some corner, wouldn't know there was going to be a dance out at Lincoln Park. Then we'd hear old Buddy's trumpet coming on and we'd all start. . . . The whole town would know Bolden was at the park, ten or twelve miles from the center of Town. He was the blowingest man since Gabriel."[10]

Some ridiculed Jelly Roll for saying you could hear Buddy over such a long distance; others have told of hearing him in New Orleans proper when he was playing at the Pecan Grove across the river in Gretna. Several people have offered explanations for the phenomenon. For one thing the distance from the center of town to Lincoln Park seemed further than it actually was, for although the streetcar trip was six miles or more, the straight-line distance was closer to two miles. Also Buddy, at least some of the time, was no doubt playing for loudness. Many early music jobs were outside, either in parades or at outdoor concerts or dances where the music had to reach the back rows without a mi-

9. Collins and Russell, interview with William "Bebe" Ridgely, June 2, 1959, in Hogan Jazz Archive; author's interview with Albert, July 10, 1962; Campbell and Ertugin, interview with Ory, April 20, 1957, in Hogan Jazz Archive; Albert Glenny as quoted in Sancton, "Libretto," 1, 8, 13; Bechet, *Treat It Gentle*, 83–84.

10. Frankie Dusen quote from original p. 228, Lomax, *Mister Jelly Roll*, 57–60.

crophone. And the best way for a band to advertise was to play loud enough to be heard as far away as possible.

Manuel Manetta pointed out, too, that "in those days with no traffic noises, it was surprising how far you could hear, especially over water." Manetta lived across the river and swears that from the levee there he could hear Bolden playing at Globe Hall. "On a quiet night, you could hardly miss hearing a loud band."[11] Danny Barker has offered another explanation, saying that New Orleans sits below sea level on a spongy plain and acts as an echo chamber. The music thus reverberates rather than being absorbed; the sound carries long distances in the humid air and water-locked ground.[12] Even today when one walks toward the corner of St. Peter and Bourbon streets where a couple of bands are usually playing, in spite of traffic noises, jukeboxes, and other city interferences, if Sam Alcorn, Wallace Davenport, or Teddy Riley blow a few hot riffs in the doorway, you hear it from blocks away.

Many who spoke of Bolden did so by comparing his abilities as a cornetist with either his contemporaries or those who played later. Mostly older musicians, those interviewed sometimes used terminology based on a later frame of reference, and they ranged from those who thought no one ever played better than Bolden to those who thought many did. Guitarist Carl Davis, who, as a teenager, once passed through New Orleans, declared, "The greatest thing I ever heard was Buddy Bolden's horn." And Wooden Joe Nicholas, born in 1883, said he learned to play the cornet by listening to Bolden, following him wherever he played. Nicholas liked Bolden better than any cornet player in the world. Alphonse Picou, whose musical career spanned from 1894 until his death in 1961, granted that Bolden was a strong player, but qualified his praise, saying, "He was best at ragtime. Perez, Oliver and Keelin were better musicians. The ability to read and write music and accuracy and finesse that went with it, was highly valued by the old musicians." Frank Amacker, born in 1890 and still listening to and oc-

11. Allen, Campbell, Ertugin, and Russell, interview with Manetta, March 21, 1957, in Hogan Jazz Archive.
12. Hentoff and Shapiro (eds.), *Hear Me Talking to Ya*, 38–39.

casionally playing the music in 1975, placed Bolden further down the scale in comparison to his contemporaries. "Keppard was a master, so was Perez, but the most masterful master of all was James McNeil, who was college trained. George Moret, Andrew Kimball and Alcibiades Jeanjacque were fine 'Street' men, all readers. In contrast Bolden played this old lowdown music." Tom Albert thought Bunk Johnson was a better musician than Bolden, observing that "Bunk played from the 'Red Book of Rags,' Scott Joplin's numbers. . . . Bolden and the Uptown didn't bother with that, they couldn't play it." Albert also said, however, that he thought Bolden's band was "about the best. . . . a ragtime band, with the blues and everything." Manetta compared Bolden with two who came later, Keppard, who "played in a more dixieland style," and Wooden Joe Nicholas, who was a "jazzier" player.[13]

Peter Bocage's 1959 interview touched on Buddy's reading ability and the type of music he played, as well as comparing him with Keppard and Perez.

Q. Who do you think was the first band to play jazz or ragtime?

A. Well, I attribute it to Bolden. Bolden was a fellow, he didn't know a note as big as this house, whatever they played, they caught [learned by hearing], or made up. They made their own music and they played it their own way. So that's the way jazz started. Just his improvisation. And the surroundings were a fast type—exciting! But the old-time musicians, they didn't play nothing but music.

Q. When did you hear Bolden?

A. I heard him when I was a kid. I was just fixing to start, you know, a young man. He played over here [in Algiers] and I heard him play. He wasn't old.

Q. You remember about what year?

A. That was around I might say 1906. Now he was a fine-looking

13. Ralph W. Miller, "Carl Davis," *Jazz Report*, Vol. V (n.d.), No. 4, p. 3. Charles DeVore and Russell, interview with Wooden Joe Nicholas, November 12, 1956; Collins, Al Rose, and Russell, interview with Alphonse Picou, April 4, 1958; Allen and Crawford, interview with Frank Amacker, July 1, 1960; Collins and Russell, interview with Albert, September 25, 1959; and Allen, Campbell, Ertugin, and Russell, interview with Manetta, March 21, 1957, all in Hogan Jazz Archive.

fellow and a healthy-looking fellow, but the life, ya understand. That fast life just broke him up.

Q. How did he sound?

A. Oh, yeah. He was powerful. Plenty of power. He had a good style in the blues and all that stuff.

Q. Did anybody or does anybody play like Bolden?

A. Keppard, they were most on the same style. The improvisations is always gonna be a little different, no two men alike.

Bocage continued: "He had a good tone, didn't know what he was doing, didn't read. He played everything in b-flat. He played a lot of blues, slow drag, not too many fast numbers. Those fellows played b-flat, e-flat or f-sharp, but get three or four flats or three or four sharps and they was out of it. Blues was their standby, slow blues. They played mostly medium tempo. Perez had a better tone, sweeter than Buddy, he was taught."[14]

The controversy over whether Bolden was a reading musician seems to turn on whether or not the musician judging was a good reader himself. Bocage says Bolden didn't read, and Papa John Joseph, too, said "he wasn't much of a musician [reader], but he was a good player." Joseph recalled that the time Professor Holmes hired Bolden to play in Lutcher, Holmes "couldn't understand how a man could play that much music and couldn't read." Joseph added: "Bolden outplayed Robichaux's band in a way, cause they used to play them blues. But Buddy Bolden, nobody could read in his band and he used to kill Robichaux anywhere he went for colored. What made his band different from country bands, was more jazz to it." Louis Jones thought the big difference between Bolden's band and earlier ones was that Bolden's band could fake. According to Roy Palmer, a trombone player born in Carrollton in 1892, "Buddy would never bother with written music, he faked all the time."[15]

14. Allen and Russell, interview with Bocage, January 29, 1959, in Hogan Jazz Archive.

15. Allen and Russell, interview with Joseph, November 26, 1958; Allen and Russell, interview with Jones, January 19, 1959; Roy Palmer quoted from Hogan and Crawford, interviews with Russell, August 31 and September 4, 1962, all in Hogan Jazz Archive.

But Willie Parker, who, being identified with the Uptown musicians did not have the Downtowners' refined ideas about musicianship, replied when questioned about Bolden's ability to read, "Yeah, he could read. All of 'em could read." And many of those who said Bolden didn't read did not say he couldn't. The comments indicating that he didn't bother, that he could "fake," and those like Tom Albert's, saying, "he could hit the notes, but I never saw him read a piece of music," show that he must have kept most of the music in his head. But the fact that he played with brass bands and that then, as now, most brass bands played with written music, would imply that if the musicians interviewed had remembered seeing Bolden on the street they would almost certainly have seen him reading music.[16]

The question of whether Bolden stood up or sat down when he played is another that draws conflicting comments. Wooden Joe Nicholas thought he always stood up, never even taking his horn down. Roy Palmer, in describing how the leader stomped three times so the band could begin playing on the fourth beat, then stomped at the beginning of the last chorus to signal a stop, ended by saying that Bolden "would do all that while sitting down." Traditionally New Orleans bands sit except for solos and Bolden probably stood up at least on the numbers in which he featured himself.[17]

The Bolden band played any music they could get their hands on and could adapt to their own style. Some of the tunes were just popular sheet music numbers of the time, making their appearance and then fading out, much as "top forty" hits do today. The musicians' interpretation of a song was more important than the written version, and Bolden applied his unique style to whatever he played, just as now Louis Cottrell, Jr., Kid Sheik, or Kid Thomas can give almost any tune a New Orleans treatment. As to Bolden's repertoire, Palmer said, "He only played a few numbers, that he was used to. All of them had their own tunes and

16. Author's interview with Willie Parker, April 19, 1962; Collins and Russell, interview with Albert, September 25, 1959, in Hogan Jazz Archive.

17. Palmer quoted from Hogan and Crawford, interviews with Russell, August 31 and September 4, 1965, and DeVore and Russell, interview with Nicholas, November 12, 1956, both in Hogan Jazz Archive.

breaks, played their own music. Never played too many different numbers.'' But Nicholas again disagreed, saying, ''He played all kinds of numbers, including many blues. He played everything, every piece that came out.'' Some of the songs Bolden played are lost, but even a list of titles people have mentioned him playing would be burdensomely long.[18]

The type of music the band used depended on the occasion and clientele. Louis Jones said that for dances they played waltzes and mazurkas, no ragtime, ''except in the quadrilles or late at night.'' He also mentioned that although Bolden played mostly blues, in some halls around midnight the group might play a schottische and follow that with a variety, ''a long thing made up of waltzes and all kinds of time.'' They played all the popular dance tunes, plus polkas and Joplin's rags. And on that fabled cylinder, according to Willie Cornish, they had recorded a couple of marches.[19]

Tom Albert said the bands caught ''ratty'' tunes from one another; he remembers playing songs similar to those Bolden was doing, including ''If You Don't Shake It, You Don't Get No Cake.'' Another number that Bolden and most everyone in New Orleans played was the tune later known as ''Tiger Rag.'' Frank Amacker recalled Bolden's playing ''The House Got Ready,'' a tough, fast number the dancers liked. Jones mentioned ''Make Me A Pallet on the Floor'' as a song Bolden's band did in ragtime, and Susie Farr remembered the words to Buddy's version:

> Make me a pallet on the floor,
> Make me a pallet on the floor,
> Make it soft, make it low,
> So your sweet man will never know.

Mrs. Farr also recalled the words to ''Careless Love,'' a song Wooden Joe Nicholas believed Buddy wrote:

> Ain't it hard to love another woman's man.
> Ain't it hard to love another woman's man.

18. *Ibid.*
19. Allen and Russell, interview with Jones, January 19, 1959, in Hogan Jazz Archive.

> You can't get him when you want him,
> You have to catch him when you can.

Some of the spirituals and hymns Bolden played, according to Nolan Williams, included "Ride On, King," "I'm Going When Jesus Calls Me," and "Go Down, Moses." "Nearer My God to Thee" and "What a Friend We Have in Jesus," were commonly used by bands accompanying the horse-drawn hearses to the cemetery, whereas on the return trip they used more spirited hymns, as "Just a Little While to Stay Here" and "Lord, Lord, Lord," plus "good-time" music like "Didn't He Ramble" and "Panama."[20]

A number of tunes were considered specifically Bolden's—ones that he or the band wrote or adapted to their uses. He is said to have written words to "The Old Cow Died and Old Brock Cried," a song about Mumford in which the entire band sang the chorus.[21] One of his theme songs was "Don't Go 'Way, Nobody,"[22] and he played "Bucket Got a Hole in It" when he spotted friends or some of the sporting crowd and wanted to liven things up. He used certain quadrilles and waltzes to encourage dancing. The last number of the evening was also a special theme song, but it differed according to the audience. One person might say the closing number was always "Get Out of Here and Go on Home"; another would comment, "You never had to look at no clock, when it was time to go they played 'Home Sweet Home.'" "Get Out of Here" seems to have been the dismissal number for rougher places like Funky Butt or Odd Fellows halls, whereas "Home Sweet Home" signaled the close of more polite gigs.

The number that sticks out in everyone's mind as being Bolden's number is "Funky Butt" or "Buddy Bolden's Blues." This was the

20. Author's interview with Albert, July 10, 1962; author's interview with Amacker, June 15, 1962; Allen and Russell, interview with Jones, January 19, 1959, in Hogan Jazz Archive; author's interview with Susie Farr, August 8, 1971; DeVore and Russell, interview with Nicholas, November 12, 1956, in Hogan Jazz Archive; Nolan Williams quoted in Hogan and Crawford, interviews with Russell, August 31 and September 4, 1965, in Hogan Jazz Archive.

21. Ramsey and Smith (eds.), *Jazzmen*, 17.

22. "Don't Go Away, Nobody" was written by Percy Cahill and was included in a list of new music received by the New Orleans *Item* from Grunewald's Music Store, published October 7, 1906, p. 8. The exact date the song was written and published is not known.

crowd pleaser, the one that broke things up, and Bolden must have used it as a novelty number. Different people remember different words to the song, this being another instance when Bolden tailored his material to fit the situation. (It could be compared to Papa Celestin varying the lyrics to "Marie Laveau" or Louis Armstrong taking liberties with "Rocking Chair" or "Hello Dolly.") There were versions of "Funky Butt" made up on the spot and never written down—which may be good news to bluenoses since although some verses were comical and light, others were crude and downright obscene. Some versions were put-downs, often done under the breath so the people they were aimed at couldn't make out the words; only the band and a few friends and hangers-on around the bandstand would catch their significance.

E. Belfield Spriggins, in his 1933 *Louisiana Weekly* articles on jazz, gave Willie Cornish's story of the origin of "Funky Butt" and its immediate success.[23] The crowd loved the song. Whether or not Bolden intended to make it his theme song, it soon became so by popular acclaim. And because Bolden was also identified with Union Sons Hall, before long the sporting crowd that frequented the hall renamed it "Funky Butt Hall" in honor of the Bolden band. Few people later remembered the hall's correct name.

The tune of the song was catchy and conducive to parodies and extemporaneous words. It was sung in the towns up and down the Mississippi and had probably been carried to New Orleans by upriver boatmen. Whatever its origins, the tune was ideal for Bolden and his singing sidemen. The words they set to the basic chorus, according to Lorenzo Staulz, were: "I thought I heard Buddy Bolden say,/ Funky butt, funky butt, take it away." Another lyric was:

> I thought I heer'd Abe Lincoln shout,
> Rebels close down them plantations and let all them niggers out.
> I'm positively sure I heer'd Mr. Lincoln shout.

23. Spriggins, "Excavating Local Jazz," April 22, 1933, p. 5. Spriggins, undoubtedly a source of great importance, is still living in New Orleans, but in 1965 Hurricane Betsy struck his house and totally destroyed all the notes and records of his very early jazz research. His wife reports that he has been in such a serious state of depression since then that he will not or cannot speak to anyone including herself.

> I thought I heer'd Mr. Lincoln say,
> Rebels close them plantations and let all them niggers out.
> You gonna lose this war, git on your knees and pray,
> That's the words I heer'd Mr. Lincoln say.[24]

On a *General* label record issued in 1940 Jelly Roll Morton sang the following version of "Buddy Bolden's Blues":

> I thought I heard Buddy Bolden say,
> You're nasty, you're dirty, take it away.
> You're terrible, you're awful, take it away.
> I thought I heard him say.
> I thought I heard Buddy Bolden shout,
> Open up that window and let that bad air out.
> Open up that window and let that foul air out.
> I thought I heard Buddy Bolden say.
> Thought I heard Judge Fogarty say,
> Thirty days in the market, take him away.
> Give him a good broom to sweep with, take him away.
> I thought I heard him say.
> Thought I heard Frankie Dusen shout,
> Gal, give me the money, I'm gonna beat it out.
> I mean give that money like I explain you,
> I'm going to beat it out.
> 'Cause I heard Frankie Dusen say.[25]

The judge mentioned was J. J. Fogarty who presided in the First Recorders Court of New Orleans. Some of Bolden's boys had done business with him for minor infractions. Cornelius Tillman, for example, was picked up in 1904 for being drunk at Lincoln Park; in 1905 Henry Zeno, listed as a teamster, was picked up for "failure to straddle the car tracks" with his wagon at Camp and Common streets; in 1904 Frank Dusen was nabbed for loitering at Newton and Teche. The frequent penalty for such offenses was a fine or a period of cleaning up in one of the markets.[26]

24. Danny Barker, "Memory of King Bolden," *Evergreen Review*, March 1965, 67–74.
25. Morton, "In New Orleans, The Bolden Legend."
26. New Orleans Police Department Arrest Records for September 6, 1904, April 6, 1905, and September 13, 1904, in Louisiana Division, New Orleans Public Library.

The popularity of Willie Cornish's original ditty was widespread. Roy Carew, born in 1883, said he first heard a little blues across the river in Gretna, where bits of blues tunes, mostly ribald, were sung by the white office boy who was about thirteen years old. One of the fragments he heard was: "Thought I heard Miss Suzie shout,/ Open up the windows and let the breeze blow out." Carew said the boy had a lot of variations to the song, probably picking them up from his older brothers.[27]

Jelly Roll Morton made a recording of "Buddy Bolden's Blues," which Norwood Williams found "too slow." Sidney Bechet recorded a faster version called "Buddy Bolden's Stomp"—a really lively stomp being his idea of Bolden's up-tempo and driving style. Bechet, at one time a member of the Eagle Band ("Originally Buddy Bolden's Band" he said), thought that Bolden "was the best in New Orleans." He recalled: "When we started off playing Buddy's theme song, 'I Thought I Heard Buddy Bolden Say,' the police put you in jail if they heard you singing that song. I was just starting out on clarinet, six or seven years old, Bolden had a tailgate contest with the Imperial Band. Bolden started his theme song, people started singing, policemen began whipping heads. The Eagle Band was good for the blues, they played every Saturday night. They played Bolden's theme song, but they did not sing any words to it."[28]

27. George Kay and John Steiner, interview with Roy Carew, June 21, 1961, in Hogan Jazz Archive.

28. Norwood Williams quoted in Hogan and Crawford, interviews with Russell, August 31 and September 4, 1965, in Hogan Jazz Archive; Sidney Bechet, "Buddy Bolden Stomp," *The Grand Master of the Soprano Sax and Clarinet*, Columbia Record, CL 836, side 1, no. 4.

9

Demise as a Musician

AS 1906 DAWNED Buddy Bolden was the king of New Orleans black music. It was a perilous position, however, constantly threatened by those who were picking up on his ideas and doing other things with them. Bolden took on more and more jobs to keep ahead of his competitors and he tried to get deeper into the music, realizing that the style his band had developed in 1900 was no longer new. This was a music that would keep changing; its audience would be fickle.

As he became aware of his limitations Buddy began clashing with his music. Frustrated, he began to drink even more than usual, perhaps trying to wash from his mind the musical ideas that besieged him and with which he could not cope. In fits of depression he blamed his friends, as well as strangers and sometimes even his cornet, for his imagined shortcomings. He could no longer keep the various elements of his world in their proper places. Taking too much upon himself, he saw the lines between his responsibilities to the music, his band, his family, and other interests become fuzzy and overlap, to the detriment, mostly, of himself.

He began having severe headaches in early March, 1906. His wife Nora mentioned these bad spells and said that he seemed to be afraid of his cornet. Her sister Dora recalled that Buddy's playing began to cause him anguish—seemed to tear him up—and his headaches gave him so much pain he would play wrong notes. She used to go to Adam's Drug

Store on Howard Street to get medicine for him when he was suffering.[1] Buddy continued to play, but on Saturday, March 23, he was ill enough to be confined to bed. At this time he was staying with his mother and sister at 2302 First Street, though evidently Nora was staying with him. His mother-in-law, Ida Bass, and Dora visited him, and this may have been when Dora remembered getting medicine. He remained in bed over the weekend, not improving, and on Monday while Mrs. Bass was there, he suddenly became violent and under the delusion that his mother was giving him a deadly drug, he jumped out of bed and hit his mother-in-law on the head with a water pitcher, giving her a minor scalp wound. The women were able to calm him down somewhat with the aid of a doctor, but because they were afraid he might lash out again he was taken into custody at the Twelfth Precinct Police Station later in the evening, until his fit of insanity passed. The reports of this incident in the *Daily Picayune* and the New Orleans *Item,* ironically, constitute the only newspaper coverage given Charles Bolden during his lifetime. The *Daily Picayune* called his mother-in-law "Mrs. Ida Beach," but both papers did mention that he was a musician.[2] The March 27, 1906, arrest record states:

NAME: Bolden, Charles
RESIDENCE: 2302 First
COLOR: C
AGE: 35
NATIONALITY: U.S.
OCCUPATION: Musician
MARRIED OR SINGLE: S
READ OR WRITE: yes
CHARGE AND LOCATION OF ARREST: Insane, Residence
NAME OF COMPLAINANT: Alice Bolden, 2302 First[3]

1. Hogan and Crawford, interviews with Russell, August 31 and September 4, 1962, in William Ransom Hogan Jazz Archive, Tulane University.
2. New Orleans *Daily Picayune*, March 27, 1906, p. 2; New Orleans *Item*, March 28, 1906, p. 3.
3. New Orleans Police Department Arrest Records, Twelfth Precinct, March 27, 1906, in Louisiana Division, New Orleans Public Library.

In Search of Buddy Bolden

Buddy was probably released in a day or two, but his spells of depression increased and became apparent in disputes with some of his closest musical cohorts. Even the men who had come up the hard road with him over the previous ten years had trouble understanding the changes that were overtaking their friend and leader. Loyal as they were to Buddy, they undoubtedly were puzzled and saddened by his behavior. In some cases their patience eventually just gave out. Willie Cornish, Brock Mumford, Jimmy Johnson, and Cornelius Tillman all left the band in 1906, either fired by the inconsonant Bolden or leaving, in anger, of their own accord. They were replaced by Frankie Dusen on trombone, Lorenzo Staulz on guitar, Bob Lyons and others on bass, and a host of drummers and clarinet players. This is the period when so many musicians claimed to have played with Buddy Bolden.

Those who spoke of Bolden in a demeaning way, mentioning his drinking, unreliability, erratic personality, most often mention Dusen and Staulz at the same time, indicating that they saw Bolden around mid-1906 or later, when he was going downhill and had already suffered fits of insanity. They berated him, not having known him before and probably not realizing that he was sick. His behavior was not erratic before 1906.

Dusen was soon exerting his influence and brought Staulz and Lyons into the band. The three did not have good reputations with other musicians because they sometimes failed to pay off on their jobs. According to Clarence Vincent, Staulz was not a particularly strong guitar player and was hired primarily for his ability to improvise dirty lyrics.[4] Dusen and Staulz were close friends. Staulz ran the Red Cross Pressing Club at 1427 Leontine and Dusen lived at 1425.[5] By mid-1906 Buddy was no longer dependable for jobs and Dusen had taken over a lot of the booking and leadership chores. More and more often Edward Clem took Buddy's place on the cornet.

Several musicians saw Bolden during this time and their comments

4. Allen and Crawford, interview with Vincent, November 17, 1959, in Hogan Jazz Archive.
5. *Soards' New Orleans City Directory*, 1905–1908.

document the deterioration of "the most famous band in the city." Alcide "Slow Drag" Pavageau remembered a band contest at Globe Hall
scheduled between Bolden and a band that had Manuel Perez on cornet
and Big Eye Louis Nelson on clarinet. Bolden didn't show up, implying
that he was scared of a cutting contest with Perez. But Pavageau goes on
to say that two of Bolden's sidemen were Dusen and Staulz, thus locat-
ing the incident during the time when Bolden sometimes failed to keep
his engagements.[6] Manuel Manetta recalled that Bolden had fired Cornish and hired Frankie Dusen. Manetta played a few jobs with Bolden
around that time and said he was very eccentric and Dusen was actually
running the band, with Clem frequently replacing Bolden on cornet.
Dusen apparently bragged that he had Buddy Bolden in his band.[7] Kid
Ory recounted his version of one of Bolden's last jobs:

> Last time I saw Bolden, I saw him at Masonic Hall. He had a little trouble
> there. I stayed there until the dance was over on a Monday night. He was
> short. He had spent all the deposit he received on the engagement. When
> they paid him the rest, he didn't have enough money to finish paying the
> boys. So he started issuing it out. He said, "Here's your car ride, boys." He
> looked in his hand. He had sixty cents left. He said, "This is for Chookie.
> Ain't anyone going to get this but Chookie," and he walked away.[8]

Chookie's identity remains a mystery, and Ory said that the next he
heard Buddy was in Jackson.

Tom Albert, too, saw one of Bolden's last jobs, saying: "I saw him at
the Odd Fellows Hall. By this time Bob Lyons was playing bass and
some others who I didn't know. It was the first time I was up close to the
band and Buddy could still play. I stood there with my mouth open so
long, it got full of dirt. Shortly after that Bolden went crazy."[9]

Louis Jones's wife remembered that during this time Buddy on occasion didn't even recognize his old friends. He would get into scraps with

6. Author's interview with Alcide "Slow Drag" Pavageau, May 29, 1962.
7. Allen, Campbell, Ertugin, and Russell, interview with Manetta, March 21, 1957, in Hogan
Jazz Archive.
8. Campbell and Ertugin, interview with Ory, April 20, 1957, in Hogan Jazz Archive.
9. Collins and Russell, interview with Albert, September 25, 1959, in Hogan Jazz Archive.

Nora and his sister Cora; his mother would run over to get Louis to go over and settle Buddy down. Louis was about the only one who could handle him then. Susanna Pickett said her husband Bob mentioned that Buddy thought everyone was his enemy and was out to get him. Alphonse Picou said that in the end "all his good friends left him."[10]

Another account tells of the band members having trouble with Buddy over the money they were supposed to be paid for some of the jobs. Buddy did not satisfy their objections and Dusen called Clem for the next job they had booked, one scheduled for Odd Fellows Hall. As the band was about to stomp off the opening number, Buddy walked up to the bandstand to see what was going on. "We don't need you anymore," Dusen told him.[11] Eyewitnesses say Buddy didn't utter a word, just turned around and shuffled out of the hall. None of his fans screamed "King Bolden, King Bolden!" No one encouraged him to stay and play. The crown was lost on the sawdust floors of the Uptown saloons and in the muddy gutters of South Rampart Street, which somehow seemed to parallel the muddy recesses of a mind no longer controlled by reason.

Buddy's last music job was at a Labor Day parade in 1906. In this important yearly parade each union had its own brass band. Nearly every musician in the city would have marched, and some were probably imported from the country towns and plantations. The *Times-Democrat* reported the temperature on that day as a humid 91 degrees. The parade route was long, starting at Elks Place and reaching from Canal to Carondelet to Gravier, from Gravier to Camp to Poydras to St. Charles, from St. Charles to Washington to South Rampart to Philip (Bolden's neighborhood). Then came a thirty minute rest, which usually meant a drink or two at a convenient corner saloon or hall. From Philip the marchers went to Howard, then to Baronne, to Gravier, down North Rampart to Esplanade and then through the French Quarter, on Royal Street to Toulouse, from Toulouse to Chartres, and back up to Canal, returning

10. Author's interview with Mrs. Jones, April 9, 30, and May 7, 1971; author's interview with Mrs. Pickett, August 5, 1971; Collins, Rose, and Russell, interview with Picou, April 4, 1958, in Hogan Jazz Archive.
11. Ramsey and Smith (eds.), *Jazzmen*, 17-18.

finally to Elks Place where the parade was reviewed by the city council.[12]

The New Orleans *Item*'s long report on the colored parade described each union's representation, the attire of the rank-and-file marchers, names of union officials who rode in carriages, the floats, and names of parade organizers.[13] No mention, however, was made of Buddy Bolden, who at some point dropped out of the parade, either from exhaustion, or, perhaps more likely, from some conduct that caused concerned musicians or friends to take him home.

The rest of the week was a bad time for Bolden and his family; by Saturday his dementia was serious enough to cause his mother to call for the police. He was placed under arrest at four A.M. on Sunday, September 9, 1906, and again booked for insanity. Mrs. Bolden for some reason gave the residence and place of arrest as 2104 Jackson, which turns out to be a vacant lot directly across the street from Louis Jones. It may be that neither Mrs. Bolden nor Louis could handle Buddy and that they preferred not to give their correct addresses. The arrest record incorrectly states Bolden's age as twenty-seven, indicates that he is married—though Nora had certainly left him before this—and lists him as a musician, still able to read and write.[14]

After being released Buddy continued to drink and dissipate, forgetting the band, jobs, music, and friends. His conduct caused the neighbors to complain, and partly because of this, partly for lack of rent money, the Bolden family moved from 2302 First Street to a much shabbier residence at 2527 First.[15] Buddy never recovered. He stayed close to the house, going to a nearby bar to get drink to bring home or to nurse on a corner curb or stoop. He no longer cared about what he wore or how he looked. His mental state ranged from periods in which he directed his fears and violent actions at people—his musicians and Bob Pickett in

12. New Orleans *Times-Democrat*, Tuesday, September 4, 1906.
13. New Orleans *Item*, September 3, 1906.
14. New Orleans Police Department Arrest Records, Twelfth Precinct, September 9, 1906, in New Orleans Vital Statistics Records.
15. *Soards' New Orleans City Directory*.

particular—and such objects as his cornet, to periods of blank tranquility.

Clarence "Little Dad" Vincent, who, when he was fourteen years old lived on Second Street just around the corner from the Bolden home, saw Buddy during this period. Once when Little Dad was passing the Bolden home at 2527 First, Buddy called to him, "You're John's brother, isn't you?" Then he told Little Dad to go get him fifteen cents worth of beer. The boy went down to a saloon on Howard Street where someone would answer his knock and get the bucket. He carried the beer back to Buddy. Another day Buddy told Little Dad to come into the house. One of the neighbors saw the boy accept the invitation and ran to tell Little Dad's brother that he was with Buddy Bolden. His brother came down, knocked on the door, and told Buddy that he had come for his little brother, that they had to go somewhere. The two men talked for a while and Little Dad didn't notice anything peculiar about Buddy's actions. After they left, however, his brother told him to stay away from Bolden; "He's nuts, you know." [16]

Louis Jones did not talk much about Bolden's insanity and was not even too sure when he was committed or when he died. It may be that Buddy had dismembered this friendship, too, or Louis may simply have been reluctant to talk about his old friend's bad days.

Buddy's condition must have kept the household in turmoil throughout the winter, no doubt putting a great deal of pressure on Mrs. Bolden and Cora. They probably did not consider that Buddy's loss of sanity could have causes other than his drinking too much. By spring he was a derelict, a drunk. He was impoverished and incoherent, a stranger to his mother and sister and a burden they could no longer endure. On March 13, 1907, almost exactly one year after his first attack, Mrs. Bolden again called the Twelfth Precinct and for the third time Charles Bolden was booked for insanity. He was no longer listed as literate, his age was given as thirty-six, nine years older than in September, 1906, and his

16. Allen and Crawford, interview with Vincent, November 17, 1959, in Hogan Jazz Archive.

occupation was changed to "laborer." He was remanded to the house of detention until officials could decide what should be done with him.[17]

To stick someone in Bolden's condition into a common jail cell, with little or no medical attention, would be considered a crime in itself today. But in 1907 psychiatric beliefs were much less sophisticated. The best denunciation of those conditions appears in a 1903 letter from Coroner M. V. Richards, M.D., clearly a humanitarian whose ideas were years ahead of his time:

> It again devolves upon me to respectfully submit to your honor that there are at present confined the following persons who have been declared insane. . . . The present state of affairs is to be regretted and I earnestly hoped for an amelioration of existing conditions. . . . I protest and will continue to oppose the operation of any measure whereby the city's insane are detained at any place or institution where no provision has been made for the care and attention that is absolutely necessary for this unfortunate class. The unsanitary and defective conditions, as well as the environs . . . are such that would tend to aggravate the condition of anyone afflicted mentally or physically, and I will be forced to recommend the release of the insane confined therein, if the situation remains unchanged.[18]

Richards' ideas were unpopular and went unheeded while he was in office, but by 1907 some progress had been made with the city administration. In 1907, when Martin Behrman was mayor of New Orleans, the following story appeared in the New Orleans *Item*:

> Mayor Behrman today addressed a letter to the superintendent of the State Insane Asylum at Jackson calling his attention to the fact that there are now thirty-seven insane persons confined at the House of Detention. . . . He asks that at least some of these unfortunate people be taken by the asylum at Jackson. . . . This letter was the result of a conference with President M. Heyman and Secretary F. S. Shields of the Prison Reform Society. They stated that the insane could not be properly cared for at the House of Deten-

17. New Orleans Police Department Arrest Records, Twelfth Precinct, March 13, 1907, in New Orleans Vital Statistics Records.
18. M. V. Richards, Coroner, to Mayor Paul Capdevielle, September 27, 1903, in Louisiana Division, New Orleans Public Library.

tion, and besides that they ought to have scientific treatment at a regular asylum for the insane.[19]

Mayor Behrman had considerable influence and the next day the same newspaper carried a follow-up report: "Coroner O'Hara has received a communication from the superintendent of the Insane Asylum at Jackson that they would take twenty-five patients from New Orleans. These unfortunates will be sent without delay. Commissioner Pujol has thirty-seven incarcerated at the House of Detention and he has stated that it is impossible to give them proper attention."[20]

On April 4, Buddy Bolden was still in the house of detention, but on that day, perhaps spurred by Mayor Behrman's action, Dr. J. O'Hara examined Buddy and twenty other inmates. Fifteen were declared insane by reason of alcoholism and two were suffering from syphilis as well. Three were prostitutes from around the Rampart and Perdido area. Seventeen, including Buddy, were committed to Jackson. The other four were returned to the care of their families.

It took nearly a month for the "Declaration of Insanity" to be reviewed by Judge T. W. C. Ellis and for him to judicially commit Charles "Buddy" Bolden to Jackson. The commitment document, the description part of which is exactly the same as the April 4 coroner's description report, is a depressingly blunt summation of a man who only a year earlier had moved to exhilaration almost the entire black population of New Orleans. It gives no hint that this man, with his silver cornet, held the dancers in the palm of his hand and inspired excited shouts of "King Bolden! King Bolden!"

The document, entitled "Description of the Insane Person Named in the Within Warrant" gives this picture of King Bolden:

1. NAME: Chas. Bolden
2. SEX: M   AGE: 26   COLOR: N [Negro]
3. COLOR HAIR: b[rown]   EYES: b[rown]
4. OCCUPATION: Lab.

19. New Orleans *Item*, April 3, 1907, p. 3.
20. *Ibid*, April 4, 1907.

5. SINGLE: yes
6. RESIDENCE: House of Detention and 2527 First
7. NATIVITY: La
8. CHARACTER OF DISEASE: Insanity
9. CAUSE OF INSANITY: Alcohol
10. IS THIS FIRST ATTACK? yes
11. HOW LONG BEEN INSANE? 1 mos.
12. IS PATIENT DANGEROUS TO HIMSELF OR OTHERS? to others
13. HAS SUICIDE EVER BEEN ATTEMPTED? no
14. IS THERE A DISPOSITION TO DESTROY CLOTHING, FURNITURE, ETC.? no
15. ARE THE PATIENT'S HABITS CLEAN OR DIRTY? filthy
16. WHAT WAS THE PATIENT'S NATURAL DISPOSITION? quiet
17. HAVE ANY MEMBERS OF THE FAMILY EVER BEEN INSANE? no
    WERE THE PARENTS BLOOD RELATIONS? no
18. HAS THE PATIENT EVER BEEN ADDICTED TO THE INTEMPERATE USE OF
    ALCOHOL, OPIUM OR TOBACCO? Alcohol
19. HAS THE PATIENT EVER HAD ANY INJURY OF HEAD, EPILEPSY OR
    HEREDITARY DISEASE, SUDDEN SUPPRESSION OF AN ERUPTION OR
    ACCUSTOMED DISCHARGE? no
20. WHAT IS THE CAUSE OF THIS ATTACK? Alcohol
21. HAS ANY MEDICAL TREATMENT BEEN INSTITUTED? yes
22. ANY RESTRAINT OR CONFINEMENT BEEN RESORTED TO: yes
    IF SO, WHAT KIND AND HOW LONG? House of Detention 1 mo.
23. GENERAL REMARKS:
    Received Thursday June 4th, 1907 and on Friday June 5th, 1907 I deliv-
    ered to Dr. Clarence Pearson, superintendant of the Insane Asylum at
    Jackson La. the within named Interdicted Insane Person[:] Chas. Bolden
    which will more fully appear by refering to the receipt of said superin-
    tendant herein filed and made part of this return Returned same day
                                                    G. A. Putfark
                                                    Deputy Sheriff[21]

Deputy Putfark, carrying this piece of paper, accompanied Buddy Bolden on the long ride from New Orleans to Jackson. As Bolden left the
city where he was born, struggled and won, struggled and lost, he apparently had no recollection of what had gone before.

---

21. Warrant for Commitment of Insane Person, judicial number 42791 and Description of
Person Named in Within Warrant, June 1, 1907 with G. A. Putfark's remarks of June 5, 1907.

Charles Bolden arrived at Jackson on the afternoon of Friday, June 5, 1907, to begin the last twenty-four years of his life in a tranquil, supervised atmosphere far removed from the excitement of the days when he was creating a new music and from the good time Charlies who had toasted him but were already forgetting him.[22] Strangely, the Bolden legend was just beginning. He was not yet thirty years old, but he would never talk to an interviewer or tell anyone what it was really like; he would leave no record of "Funky Butt" played as only he could play it. Some of those who were forgetting would remember him much later and say they had never forgotten.

22. Certification of Admittance to Insane Asylum of Louisiana of Charles Bolden, June 5, 1907.

10

Institutionalization
and Death

THE MANY SUPPOSITIONS about Bolden's insanity, made primarily by fellow musicians, friends, or jazz enthusiasts, range from superstition to sophisticated psychiatric terminology. The only official records are from the hospital at Jackson and from Coroner O'Hara's initial examination. Psychiatric care at the time, however, was still experimental enough to be subject to the whims of the particular institution's director. The personnel and facilities were not available to give much more than generalized treatment and diagnosis; there was little contact between doctor and patient or even between social worker and patient. Bolden was at Jackson ten years before he was given any identification other than "Col. male from Parish of Orleans; Reason for insanity: alcohol." He was committed at a time when a black male from New Orleans had little hope of ever returning home.

Some of the superstitions explaining Buddy's demise have a voodoo flavor about them and in New Orleans it is ticklish to ask questions about such topics. The few who will venture to say, "Voodoo is nowhere," are quick to add, "But I'm not knocking it you understand." Kid Ory said the story was going around that Buddy had lost his mind because of something someone put on his mouthpiece. Ed "Montudi" Garland said some women had removed the bow from the sweatband of Bolden's hat, a fatal move according to superstition. Others decided that Buddy's downfall was caused by having too many women, and indeed, it is easy to imagine frustrated women aiming love potions and hexes at him. The witches, queens, and doctors must have done a brisk business when he was in his prime.[1]

Another natural suspicion arising from Bolden's reputation as a ladies' man is voiced by Samuel Charters in *Jazz New Orleans 1885–1963* when he says, "Buddy began having spells of insanity, probably as a result of tertiary syphilis."[2] Dr. O'Hara's examination report, however, did not mention that Bolden had syphilis, whereas the disease was recorded in others the doctor checked at the same time. Also, the hospital in Jackson administered blood tests to the patients at regular intervals, and though many black males in residence at the time were syphilitic and the condition was thus not one that would have been overlooked, Bolden was not one who suffered from it.[3]

The official statement that Bolden's insanity was caused by alcoholism must be given some credence. Many people, including his wife Nora and Mrs. Louis Jones, have mentioned that Buddy drank a great deal. Some gave extreme descriptions of his drinking, such as Jelly Roll Morton's colorful statement, "He drank all the whisky he could find." Whether he could have drunk himself into a state of insanity by age twenty-nine is a medical judgment beyond the scope of this work. It seems possible, though, that alcoholism was a by-product of his insanity and neither a beginning nor an end—that Bolden's doubts and frustrations led him to drink excessively as a release. He was, after all, arrested for insanity, not drunkenness. His erratic behavior, which many attributed to alcohol, did not begin until after his March, 1906, outburst that occurred after he had been in bed for several days. It does not seem likely that a man with Bolden's proclivities would have been drinking heavily while confined to bed.[4]

The cause of Bolden's mental decline lies somewhere in the several

1. Campbell and Ertugin, interview with Ory, April 20, 1957, and Allen and Levin, interview with Garland, April 20, 1971, both in William Ransom Hogan Jazz Archive, Tulane University, New Orleans.

2. Charters, *Jazz New Orleans, 1885–1963*, p. 12.

3. Author's interview with Lionel Gremillion, Assistant Administrator, Southeast Louisiana State Hospital, Jackson, Louisiana, March 17, 1969.

4. Description and Record of Insane Person, Coroner's Office, New Orleans, April 14, 1907; Nora quoted from Hogan and Crawford, interviews with Russell, August 31 and September 4,

worlds he attempted to balance and give equal attention to. He was simultaneously trying to function as son, brother, husband, father, lover, band leader, musician, friend, idol, good guy, teacher, and pupil. Some of these roles fitted together naturally, some came through vocation and avocation; to fulfill them all equally well would not have been easy.

Buddy's family roles revolved around his close ties with his mother and sister. Fatherless by the time he was seven, reared by a working mother who brooked no interference from relatives or friends in the way she raised her children, Buddy must have at times found it difficult to follow the strict Baptist-influenced guidelines his mother set. And in matters of religion and propriety his sister Cora was very much like her mother. Mrs. Bolden apparently did not approve of her son's marriages, particularly his liaison with Hattie Oliver. Buddy's rejection of Hattie, and especially the consequence of losing track of his son, no doubt caused him some anguish. With both Hattie and Nora, Buddy was placed in the middle, attempting to minimize any friction between wife, and mother and sister. How long he would have remained with Nora is speculation. His mental state caused the final schism, though Nora's patience may have been giving out before that. After he left New Orleans his mother and sister made no attempt to maintain contact with his son, with Nora, or with his daughter Bernedine. From the little that can be documented about these relationships they seem to have declined because of mutual disinterest.

Buddy's roles as a musician also brought conflict. Music was his first love; he was thoroughly involved in it. His mother said he'd rather play music than eat,[5] and Nora, Louis Jones, and Papa John Joseph made similar comments. He was a leader, not a follower. For all the accolades he earned by his musical prowess, enough musicians have qualified their appraisals of him to establish that his lack of a complete musical education left him vulnerable. He went as far as he could, but nothing in his

---

1962, in Hogan Jazz Archive; author's interviews with Mrs. Jones, April 9, 30, and May 7, 1971; Lomax, *Mister Jelly Roll*, 60.

5. Author's interviews with Jackson and Lawes, June 25 and July 2, 1971.

training had prepared him to solve all the complexities of the musical world he was in. What he wanted most he was not capable of fully achieving. Neither was he prepared to cope with the overwhelming fame that came early in his adult life. He moved between a close-knit family and the hell-bent for high living atmosphere of New Orleans sporting life. He took an unrouted, sometimes hedonistic path, and unfortunately he did not have the benefit of learning from others how to handle this situation; no one of his circumstances had been there before.

The first view Bolden would have had of the Jackson hospital was the Administration Building with its giant columns. This imposing structure was built in 1848, was once restored, but still looks basically the same. Bolden would have been housed in one of the two dormitories for black male patients. The hospital records contain few official reports before 1925, when more consistent yearly examinations of patients were initiated. Some records were destroyed in 1940 by a fire, others were pilfered by a previous Bolden researcher. The official documents concerning Buddy Bolden are not very thorough and most information on his years at Jackson comes from Lionel Gremillion, the assistant administrator, who talked to many people who were on the staff or on the hospital grounds during Bolden's confinement.

Bolden was placed in a stereotyped category of manic depressive or paranoid schizophrenic. A person in this category would have demonstrated noticeably hostile behavior toward the norms of society—the paranoid venting his frustration overtly. These characteristics were, however, true of the majority of black male patients admitted in Bolden's time. A black man could be committed if a white person complained of being upset by or the target of such hostility.

During his early days at the hospital Bolden underwent a number of medical examinations but there was very little personal contact with psychiatric personnel. Eventually his raging subsided. The coherence of his speech varied and one ward worker remembers that a good deal of his talk had to do with earlier feminine conquests.[6] A typical paranoid

6. The ward worker was Sebe Bradham. Lionel Gremillion to author, June 8, 1971, updating and verifying a telephone conversation of June 5, 1971.

THE NEW ORLEANS ITEM.

MARCH 28, 1906.

STRIKES MOTHER
WITH WATER PITCHER

Thinking that he was being drugged by his mother, Charles Bolden, a negro, living at 2302 First street, jumped out of bed yesterday afternoon while in a state of dementia and struck her over the head with a water pitcher.

Bolden, who is a musician, has been sick for some time. His mother was by his bedside yesterday afternoon, giving him what succor she could, when suddenly his mind was carried away with the belief that she was administering some deadly drug to him. Grabbing the water pitcher, he broke it over his mother's head, inflicting a scalp wound, which was pronounced not serious.

THE DAILY PICAYUNE

TUESDAY, MARCH 27, 1906.

MAULED HIS MOTHER-IN-LAW.

Charles Bolden, a musician, of 2302 First Street, hammered his mother-in-law, Mrs. Ida Beach, in their house yesterday afternoon. It seems that Bolden has been confined to his bed since Saturday, and was violent. Yesterday he believed that his mother-in-law was drugging him, and getting out of bed, he hit the woman on the head with a pitcher and cut her scalp. The wound was not serious. Bolden was placed under a close watch, as the physicians stated that he was liable to harm some one in his condition.

The only newspaper coverage given to Bolden during his lifetime was following his first attack of insanity, when two New Orleans papers ran these items.

Forty-one patients from New Orleans traveling to the mental hospital at Jackson, Louisiana. Bolden made this trip in June, 1907.

The patients from New Orleans approaching the Jackson Administration Building.

Front view of the main hospital at Jackson.

An afternoon lawn concert at the hospital.

The mental hospital was segregated when Bolden was there and black patients were housed in this dormitory.

View of Section C in Holt Cemetery, the general vicinity of Bolden's burial spot.

characteristic is the inability to accept rejection. Buddy eventually burned out some of this frustration and the focus of his concerns became generalized rather than aimed at specific persons or objects. He was not considered dangerous and in time was free to move about the large grounds and do some work around the hospital.

Mrs. Bolden and Cora visited him occasionally when he was first admitted and found him to be in good physical health, though almost totally incommunicative. At one time, according to cousins Laura Lawes and Eugenia Jackson, they believed Buddy was well enough to return home, but the doctor told them that going back to New Orleans and his former life would be very bad for him. As the years wore on, his few coherent moments ceased almost entirely. By 1920 he no longer recognized his mother and sister and their visits ceased shortly thereafter. From the 1920s on, there are only handwritten notes on yellow-lined notebook paper from Alice Bolden and Cora. The letters, addressed to the doctor, asking about Buddy's welfare, indicate that he no longer had any remembrance of, or connection with, his family.

Late in the 1920s, Dr. E. M. Robards took over the administration of the hospital from Dr. Glenn Smith. Robards was a musician who played violin in the Peter Bocage style—soft, refined, and classical—but he also played jazz style piano. When Robards came to the hospital there was already a colored patients' band, but according to his daughter, Mrs. George Gayden, Robards and Smith introduced music therapy at Jackson. They had a truck set up on the grounds for minstrels and music. Some of the top bands in the South played there, as well as bands from Angola prison. The patients' band played during the noon-time meal, for Thursday afternoon and Saturday night balls, and for lawn parties, sometimes playing from the six-sided cupola that once stood in front of the Administration Building. Mrs. Gayden, who sometimes played saxophone with the band, recalled that a patient could be way out of things mentally, but would still be able to relate to music. "They could really shift gears," she said.[7]

7. Author's interview with Mrs. George L. Gayden, June 16, 1971.

The patients were segregated in those days and before he became administrator Dr. Robards was assigned to the colored section. He took a special interest in any of the patients who played music and was aware that Bolden had been a musician. Several people, in fact, remembered that Bolden played the horn while at the hospital. Sebe Bradham, a ward attendant at Jackson and later a Protestant chaplain there, described Buddy as around five-ten or eleven, slightly stocky, of medium color, with very prominent eyes. He said that when he felt like it, Bolden would go up on the bandstand and play, but he was not a member of the band. Bradham remembered that Bolden always started out quick (staccato) and would play a particular little phrase, walking around and frequently standing by the window when he played. And though Bradham personally knew little about music he said that when Bolden played, "you could tell he was better than the rest. He played over the rest and louder than most people."[8] Dr. Robards' widow verified Bradham's statements, saying that although she did not know Bolden, she remembered people talking about him playing music at times, on the stage and with the patients' band.[9]

Thus Bolden did occasionally play during the twenty-four years he was at Jackson and seemingly retained traces of his old touch and mannerisms. Few, however, were aware of his former reputation. He was just another black patient who talked to himself, babbled incoherently, and walked around ritualistically touching objects. Several rumors in the Bolden legend state that Buddy returned to New Orleans around 1917 or 1918, but according to members of the family he never left the hospital once he had been committed. Hospital spokesmen said that when patients, in his day, with his diagnosis, were sent to Jackson more than 99 percent of the time they were there to stay.[10] Bolden's mental condition

8. Lionel Gremillion to author, June 8 and 17, 1971. Bradham was described by Mrs. Gayden and Mrs. Glenn Smith, widow of the former administrator, as being very sincere and honest, a humanitarian who was one of the earliest employees of the hospital to take a personal interest in the patients. He had no particular interest in jazz, nor did he know much about the historical significance of Buddy Bolden. His recollections of Bolden can thus be considered authentic.

9. Mrs. Glenn Smith to author, June 15, 1971; author's interview with Mrs. E. M. Robards, June 26, 1971.

10. A hospital spokesman. Lionel Gremillion to author, June 17, 1971.

gradually deteriorated; he became subdued and cooperative but never improved.

Some chronology of these hospital years is available in letters and official records.[11] A routine psychiatric examination by Dr. S. B. Hays in 1925 stated:

> Accessible and answers fairly well. Paranoid delusions, also grandiose. Auditory hallucinations and visual. Talks to self. Much reaction. Picks things off wall. Tears his clothes. Insight and judgement lacking. Health good. Negative blood, looks deteriorated, but memory is good. Has a string of talk that is incoherent. Hears the voices of people that bothered him before he came here. History of one month in House of Detention on account of alcohol. DIAGNOSIS: Dementia praecox, paranoid type.

In March, 1926, his mother wrote: "Dr. will you please infrom [*sic*] me of my son Charley Bolden from his mother. Mrs. Alice Bolden, 2338 Philip St., N.O." The superintendent replied on March 10, 1926: "He is silly, does no work, and spends most of his time waving his hands about in the air and talking with imaginary voices."

On February 27, 1927, Mrs. Bolden wrote again, asking: "Dr., Will you please infrom [*sic*] me of my son health Charley Bolden please let me know if you received the package for Christmas from his mother, Mrs. Alice Bolden, 2338 Philip Street, New Orleans." The superintendent's brief reply assured her that Charley was in good physical health but was unchanged mentally.

A letter from Bolden's daughter, who had not seen him since 1906 when she was four years old said:

> August 20, 1927
> 135 Darrow Avenue
> Evanston, Illinois

Dear Sirs,

I am writing you asking for some information concerning my father Char-

---

11. The letters and psychiatric examinations are from the Charles Bolden file, Southeast Louisiana State Hospital, Jackson, Louisiana.

lie Bolden. Please inform exactly of his present condition. As I am very anxious to know just how he is getting along.

Yours truly,
Bernedine Bolden

The answer she received was a perfunctory, "I am sorry to say that he shows no improvement." Bernedine was old enough to be curious about her father and it is unfortunate that her contact could not have been one of the musicians or fans in New Orleans who could have told her of the high period in Bolden's life. Since her mother was never on good terms with Alice and Cora Bolden, it is unlikely that Bernedine would have thought of writing them. And in light of Nora's later comments, it is also unlikely that she told Bernedine very much about those exciting but hectic days around the turn of the century.

Another letter from Alice Bolden, on March 23, 1930, elicited the following reply:

March 28, 1930

Mrs. Alice Bolden
2338 Philip Street
New Orleans, La.

RE: Charles Bolden

Dear Madam:

Replying to your letter relative to your son, Charles Bolden, we are pleased to inform you that he continues to get along nicely. While on the ward he insists on going about touching each post, and is not satisfied until he has accomplished this at least once. He causes no trouble and cooperates well.

His general physical condition is satisfactory.

All of Alice Bolden's letters were the same, word for word, line for line, including the misspelling "infrom." Examination of handwriting samples indicate that the letters were written by Cora. The last letter from the family was, in fact, signed by Cora and in addition to the usual query about her brother's health included the brief notation, "We lost our mother a short time ago." Alice Bolden had died on August 11, 1931. The hospital's September 21 reply did not indicate that Buddy was at all cognizant of his mother's death, but it did inform Cora that Buddy was "now ill from heart trouble."

Buddy's physical health continued to deteriorate, he was put in Parker Hospital, the general medical hospital on the grounds, and on November 4, 1931, at age 54, his twenty-five years of life without living ceased. A simple scrap of paper, torn from a tablet, stated: "Chas. Bolden, died at 2 a.m., card 7276, service of Dr. Turner, attd., J. B. McNabb." The death certificate read: "Cause of Death; Cerebral Arterial Schlerosis."

Bolden's body left the morgue at Parker Hospital, was claimed by J. D. Gilbert, an undertaker from Baton Rouge, and was shipped to Geddes-Moss Undertaking and Embalming Co., 2120 Jackson Avenue, New Orleans, at the direction of his sister, Cora Bolden Reed. The route back was almost the same as the one that had carried him away from his beloved New Orleans years before. He would not have recognized the scene of his triumphs. His band was gone, Funky Butt Hall had become the Greater St. Matthew Baptist Church; Odd Fellows and Masonic Hall, Lincoln and Johnson parks were no longer in existence. The city was well into the great depression. Of the men who had played regularly with him only two were still living and one of those, Jimmy Johnson, had left the city. A man who had been a five-year-old boy in 1905, had lived around Perdido Street, and said that he used to sneak outside a dance hall to listen to Buddy Bolden play, was the king. Louis Armstrong's fame—the fame that Bolden's music had grown into—had moved beyond black New Orleans, was national in scope.

Only Buddy's sister Cora and first cousin, Ida Cambric Baker, were there to escort his remains back to the old neighborhood.[12] And even at his death there was controversy. About twenty documents in the files at Jackson relate to money required for the burial. It seems that five dollars was needed and either Cora could not come up with the money or because Buddy had been a ward of the State for twenty-four years, she felt the State should pay. If she fought the burial fee as a matter of principle,

---

12. Author's interviews with Jackson and Lawes, June 25 and July 2, 1971.

it was also true that her mother's sickness had drained the scant savings, and in 1931 a laundress would not have had many extra five dollar bills.

Bolden's body lay in state at the Geddes-Moss Funeral Home for only a day, and according to the witnesses, there were very few at the wake. Cora, of course, was there. Cordelia Alcorn, Alvin Alcorn's sister; Ida Baker, who had taken care of Alice Bolden in her final days; Lena Kennedy and Gertrude Petyon, both cousins, all paid their respects. Cordelia Alcorn remembered hearing that Buddy Bolden was being waked. She knew some of the Bolden cousins but had also heard some of the tales of Buddy's music and confessed to being a little curious. She recalled that he looked like an old, old man.[13] Few, if any, musicians came by; it is doubtful that many were aware of Buddy's death. There was no brass band to say farewell, nor even a former sideman to act as pallbearer or to "walk the final mile" with the "king." The job had to be done by Geddes-Moss employees.[14]

The pine-box coffin was taken to Holt Cemetery, a city-owned cemetery behind the Delgado Trade School, where many of the city's indigents were laid to rest. Bob Griffin, the caretaker and handyman, had dug out the customary six feet of hard, clayish earth and the remains of Buddy Bolden were lowered into plot C-623.[15]

The news on page one of the *Picayune* for that day was of an airplane crash in Camden, New Jersey, Huey Long, China asking for help against Japan, and Mussolini visiting the Vatican. The temperature was a cool 65°. There was a typhoid epidemic in New Orleans and Griffin was kept busy digging graves. On the Steamer Capitol, Charlie Creath's Orchestra was playing for evening cruise dances. Nowhere was there a mention of the passing of Buddy Bolden.[16]

Cora was unable to keep paying the upkeep on her brother's grave and

13. Author's interview with Cordelia Alcorn, June 23, 1971.

14. The Geddes-Moss Funeral Home went into receivership in 1940 and was taken over by Good Citizen's Funeral Home on Melpomene Street, according to Director S. A. Chapitol. All of the records that would have listed the Bolden mourners and other funeral particulars were destroyed at that time. The old Geddes-Moss establishment is now Gertrude Geddes Willis Funeral Home and their records only go back to 1940.

15. Author's interview with Bob Griffin, August 11, 1970.

16. New Orleans *Times-Picayune*, November 6, 1931, p. 1.

in accordance with Holt policy, after two years his remains were dug up, reburied deeper, and another burial made on top. The plot number C-623 was changed, with no record being kept of the original burial. Records were not accurately kept until the 1940s and there have probably been at least eight or nine burials since Bolden's in that spot.[17] Holt Cemetery today is overgrown with weeds. Even if one knew exactly where to look it would be difficult to locate Bolden's grave. It is possible to find Section C—about the size of a quarter of a city block and guarded by a wide-spreading majestic oak tree—and to know only that Bolden's grave lies somewhere in that space.

Bolden's departure from the New Orleans music scene did not at first make any noticeable ripple. Beatrice Alcorn said that John Robichaux began getting more and more jobs at Jackson Hall; Bolden just sort of faded away. "Then we realized he wasn't around any more."[18] It is almost certain that Bolden was no longer playing after September, 1906, though people have mentioned hearing him later. Harrison Barnes recalled that one afternoon in 1907 he was playing a Bolden number with a band in the District, when out of the houses and saloons came the guys and dolls, waving and laughing, expectantly shouting, "It's Bolden's Band! It's Bolden's Band!"[19] Few knew where Buddy was or what had happened to him, but the spell he had cast over black New Orleans lived on—for a time at least—without him.

17. Author's interview with Griffin, August 11, 1970.
18. Author's interview with Beatrice Alcorn, June 23, 1971.
19. Allen and Russell, interview with Barnes, January 29, 1959, in Hogan Jazz Archive.

APPENDIX I

The Music
and Musicians
After Bolden Left

MUSIC IN New Orleans flourished in the period after 1906. New jobs opened as cabarets and cafes began to employ six- and seven-piece bands for dancing. For many jobs small jazz bands were replacing string bands and larger society orchestras. The District was wide open and many of the country musicians who had previously come to New Orleans only for the larger parades began to migrate there in search of full-time musical employment. There were enough jobs that lesser musicians and a number of precocious youngsters were successful in "holding down chairs." The city was growing and prospering. For a young black music was the pot of gold and the men looked up to were the hot musicians who wore flashy clothes, ran with the best-looking women, and wore diamonds on their fingers, in their ties, and sometimes in their teeth. There was as much bad music as good. Some worked until they became competent musicians, others just became old men who could remember the old days when they played with the greats.

Many jumped on the band wagon that Buddy Bolden had once led through the music houses of the city. As a result things became competitive. One bad night or one incompetent player could mean a loss of employment for the entire band; a good reputation was important. The outstanding musicians rose to the top and several bands stood out above the rest. Many of the younger musicians had something Bolden had lacked—a firmer, more total grasp of music's technical aspects. They improved on the sounds that Buddy had helped pioneer. Strict musicianship, however, was not enough and it was in the early twentieth century that the personality cult of traditional music first appeared. Whether it was show-boating, charisma, or some combination of qualities, it helped sell the music. Bolden had it; so did Freddie Keppard, Joe "King" Oliver, and later Louis Armstrong.

There being no recordings of Bolden's music the younger musicians learned not from him, but from the old "heads"—Perez, George Moret, Professor Jim Humphrey, Andrew Kimball, George Hooker, the Tio brothers, Louis Cottrell, Sr., Joe Oliver, and Keppard. The bands were still of various sizes and make-up, but groups like the Eagle, Imperial, Peerless, and Superior bands were becoming stabilized and establishing bases for themselves at specific dance halls and cabarets. There were still definite lines drawn between black and Creole musicians (Perez, Robichaux, A. J. Piron, Sidney Bechet, and Peter Bocage represented the Creole bands whereas Keppard, Dusen, Clem, and Ory were probably closer to the Bolden tradition). But the most important contribution of the period from approximately 1906 to 1913 was its "melting pot" aspect. The best of Uptown and Downtown was blended by the older musicians; the younger men listened, and some were able to not only use what they interpreted as the best of what they heard, but they also added their own interpretation and innovations.

Perez, Robichaux, Clem, and Dusen had already established their styles while Bolden was still active. Ory, Oliver, Keppard, Johnny Dodds, and Bechet—who were to make their names known in the later teens, the twenties, and later—were still learning and experimenting. The latter five had stabilizing effects on the music, having a lasting influence on New Orleans jazz as it is known today. Perez, Keppard, and Oliver were to come to the fore as the city's hottest horn men. Perez had musicianship, Keppard had power, Oliver combined the two. None of the three had the upper hand, however, and this continued to be true with later trumpet players. Buddy Petit was highly thought of during the 1920s, but he, too, had serious challengers, including Chris Kelly, Punch Miller, and Sam Morgan. After Bolden left the throne was vacant. Various trumpeters, either through their own design or because of fans' acclaim, laid title to the empty chair. But no one individual would again reign as supremely as Buddy had. In his time there were no serious challengers. Later, only Keppard and Oliver actually achieved the title "king."

The careers of those mentioned prominently in this book are briefly sketched as a follow-through to the Bolden days. The information was obtained from the author's interviews with Beatrice Alcorn, Willie Humphrey, Jr., Mrs. Jefferson Mumford, Jr., and Don Albert; from Hogan Jazz Archive interviews with Barnes, Vincent, Matthews, Bella Cornish, and Picou; from the books *Treat It Gentle*, *Jazz: New Orleans, 1885–1963*, and *Hear Me Talking to Ya*; and from New Orleans Vital Statistics Records. The material on Freddie Keppard and Joseph "King" Oliver was written by Harlan Wood, contributing editor of *Second Line*.

Of the men in Bolden's band of 1905, only Willie Cornish and Jimmy Johnson outlived Buddy. Willie Warner stayed on with Dusen and the Eagle Band for awhile, then, around 1913, he went with Edward Clem to form the Pelican Orchestra. He also played in A. J. Piron's Orchestra, which was similar to Robichaux's in style. He was probably the most accomplished of the Bolden men and did some writing and arranging with Piron. He was also a printer by trade and according to Clarence Vincent worked all the time, either as a printer or a musician. The last trace of him in New Orleans is a 1914 city directory listing at 2707 South Liberty. Willie Humphrey, Jr., believed that Warner had moved to California, along with his two sons. Warner did not marry until 1911, so if he did make such a move it would have been around 1920 when he was doing some traveling with Piron's Orchestra. He apparently died in the early 1920s.

Frank Lewis played with Dusen for awhile, but concentrated less and less on music. In 1914 the city directory no longer listed him as a musician. In 1915 he moved across Lake Pontchartrain to the town of Mandeville and played a few music jobs there, seldom returning to New Orleans. He died in the early 1920s also.

Brock Mumford continued in music for only a short time after 1907. In that year he opened a barbershop on Cherokee and Ann streets near the Lincoln Park area and by 1910 was devoting full time to barbering. He would get his guitar out infrequently at family gatherings but never again played professionally. His son, Jefferson, Jr., joined him in the barbershop, and did not take up music. Brock died in 1927 and was buried in the Carrollton Cemetery. Jefferson, Jr., moved to New York City and while he was dying of cancer in the hospital his apartment was ransacked. Among the items lost or destroyed in the looting was his collection of pictures and memorabilia from his father's music days.

Cornelius Tillman left the music scene soon after Bolden went insane. There is no evidence of him playing drums after that. He went to work in a cotton plant as a screwman, lived the rest of his life at 2912 Philip Street, and died in 1928. He was buried in the Cotton Yardmen's Vault in Lafayette Cemetery #1 on January 16th of that year. His son, Cornelius, Jr., died in 1959 but did not play music and his two daughters refused to talk at any length about their father.

Jimmy Johnson continued to play in New Orleans with Manuel Perez and with Fate Marable on a riverboat. He joined Don Albert's band in November, 1929, and traveled with that group during the 1930s. He became sick on a job in Mobile, Alabama, in 1937 and returned to New Orleans where he died later that year.

Willie Cornish lived the longest of the intimate Bolden band members. He played a lot of parade jobs and was with John Casimer's Young Tuxedo Brass Band during the 1930s and early 40s. He did not marry until 1922 and lived the remainder of his life with his wife Bella on Perdido Street. Cornish suffered a stroke while playing a parade and fell at the corner of South Rampart and Julia streets. He was carried home and subsequently was struck several more times resulting in partial paralysis. After one of his strokes he made a strap to help him hold his trombone so he could play a few notes; it was extremely difficult for him to accept the fact that he could no longer play. He was forgotten by the old musicians except for a few like trombonist Albert Warner. His only visitors were people who dropped by to get information for jazz research and to "borrow" some of his music and pictures. Just before he died, with a discouragement and resignation that was atypical, he told his wife that he did not want any music at his funeral. "If I die in the morning, bury me in the evening." Willie was the last of the Bolden band and when he died on January 12, 1942, at the Veterans Hospital at Alexandria, Louisiana, the last tune of the Bolden band era was truly over.

John Robichaux remained active in music until his death in 1939. He left a collection of hundreds of musical scores, most of which are now housed in the Jazz Archive at Tulane University. Robichaux did not play jazz in the hot sense that Bolden did, but he contributed a structured form to the most embryonic stage of jazz development.

Manuel Perez made contributions to New Orleans jazz throughout the teens and twenties. He seemed to be everywhere, leading the Imperial and Onward bands. The many years of seeing compromises made and seeing less talented musicians win out time after time left him embittered. He retired from music around 1930 and returned to his trade of cigar making. The thirties were rough on Perez both physically and financially and by the mid-forties his once-brilliant mind had deteriorated badly. In the time before his death in 1946 he would sit on an old chair outside his shop, barely able to make intelligent conversation.

Frankie Dusen was another who was victimized by the depression years. Only the most outstanding musicians were able to survive by music alone during the 1930s, and Dusen, a nonreader, had neither the musical background nor a back-up profession to help him. Broke and in poor health, he died as the 1930s were coming to an end.

Lorenzo Staulz was active musically into the 1920s. He owned the Red Cross Pressing Club and did not rely entirely on music for his livlihood. He worked a lot of jobs with Bob Lyon's band until his death in 1924. Lyons remained in the Rampart-Perdido area when his playing days ended, reliving the old days while running a shoe shine and repair stand next to the old Odd Fellows Hall. He died in 1949.

Charley Galloway had his barbershop at 1326 Lafayette Street until 1907 when he moved it to 709 and later 725 Bolivar Street. He had long since given up playing the guitar professionally and was only 51 years old when he died in 1921.

Alphonse Picou was one of the early jazzmen who remained in the city and became financially independent. He worked as a tinsmith during the day. For years he played with Papa Celestin at the Paddock Lounge on Bourbon Street. Picou had invested his money in several Back of Town bars that became successful. He was one of the true living legends when he passed away on February 4, 1961. His musical career spanned almost seventy years. Nearly 25,000 people accompanied the brass band that took his body to the grave.

Bolden's old neighbor, Papa John Joseph, remained active as a musician until his last moment. In 1965 at age eighty-eight, in Preservation Hall, he finished a bass solo on "The Saints", turned to the piano player, Dolly Adams, and said, "That number about did me in." A second later he collapsed and died.

Manuel Manetta did not play professionally a great deal in his later years, but he taught a large number of aspiring musicians from his home on the West Bank. He was extensively interviewed about his days in jazz and this material, in the William Ransom Hogan Jazz Archive at Tulane, is a most valuable reference source. "Fess" died on October 10, 1969.

Ed "Montudi" Garland moved to California in the teens, not returning to New Orleans until the 1971 Jazzfest. At this writing he is still playing a lot of bass, though his eye sight is nearly gone. He now returns to New Orleans each year for the Jazzfest and frequently sits in on jam sessions until the early morning hours. As far as is known, he is the only person living who played with Bolden.

Kid Ory had an illustrious career in jazz, spanning the years with King Oliver and Louis Armstrong's Hot Five recordings and later settling in California with his own band. He returned to New Orleans to play in Jazzfest 1972 and died in his retirement home in Hawaii a year later at age 86.

Albert Glenny, at age eighty-one, played a five-hour job at a big wedding reception on Esplanade Avenue. In 1952, at age eighty-three, he recorded with a pickup band for Vogue (LDE 161). Glenny was a good bass player and his old friend, Alphonse Picou, described him as "a hell of a man. . . . At his age he could climb a ladder, sixty feet up and paint the shit out of a house." Glenny died June 11, 1958, at age eighty-eight.

Papa John Joseph, Bolden's old neighbor, died in 1965 at age eighty-eight.

—Photograph by Ione Anderson

Ed "Montudi" Garland lived the longest of those who played with the Bolden band. Garland moved to California before 1920 and was with Kid Ory's band for many years. He returned to New Orleans for the first time for Jazzfest 1971. Garland died on January 22, 1980, at age ninety-five.

Ida Cambric Baker, a first cousin of Buddy, nursed both Alice and Cora in their last illnesses. She bore a strong resemblance to Cora and was the relative who inherited the Bolden family heirlooms.

—Photograph from Eugenia Jackson and Laura Lawes

Mrs. Eugenia Jackson, shown here, and her sister, Mrs. Laura Lawes, are among the few living relatives of the Bolden family who have been located.

—Photograph by Don Marquis

The bedroom set of hand-rubbed cherry wood was Alice Bolden's prized possession and is now owned by Buddy's second cousins, Laura Lawes and Eugenia Jackson.

—Photographs by Fay Rogers

The goblet inscribed "Alice Bolden, New Orleans, 1891."

The only known photograph of Charles Bolden, Jr. (on left), was taken in 1919 during World War I. The sailor on the right is New Orleans clarinetist Albert Nicholas who, along with drummer Zutty Singleton, served with Bolden on the U.S.S. *Olympia.*

—Photograph from Danny Barker collection

Tom Albert lived into his nineties, spending most of his last years in his home on Burgundy Street in the French Quarter near Buster Holmes' Bar and Restaurant where a lot of the musicians hung out during the 1950s and later. Tom frequently sat on his porch stoop and talked about the old days of jazz with interested listeners. In the 1960s he was guest of honor at a New Orleans Jazz Club gala for the old musicians.

Peter Bocage was still playing trumpet in the Eureka Brass Band in the mid-1960s. He had played his first job with a New Orleans band in 1900. Bocage has also left a lengthy and valuable interview in the Hogan Jazz Archive. He died on December 3, 1967.

Two musicians who did not play with Bolden, but who saw him, are still living in New Orleans. Louis Keppard is eighty-eight, Henry "Booker T" Glass is ninety-four, and they were guests of honor along with the white bass player, Chink Martin, at a Roots of Jazz Concert in the summer of 1975. Keppard and Glass are no longer playing, but Martin, at age 88, is still active with some of the bands at Preservation Hall.

What happened to the two crown princes—Freddie Keppard and Joe Oliver—who, respectively, inherited King Bolden's title? Their stories parallel Bolden's. They rose to great heights, gained great acclaim for their contributions to New Orleans music, and met death in tragic obscurity.

Keppard began playing cornet around 1901, forming his own Olympia Orchestra in 1905 or 1906. During his New Orleans years, he worked many locations, including Pete Lala's 25, Groshell's Dance Hall at Customhouse and North Liberty, and George Foucault's (Fewclothes) Cabaret at 134 North Franklin. From time to time he played with the Eagle Brass Band. In the eyes of New Orleans musicians, Keppard became the acknowledged successor to Bolden. Thomas "Mutt" Carey, an important New Orleans cornetist in his own right, said, "Now, at one time, Freddie Keppard had New Orleans all sewed up. He was the King—yes, he wore the crown." It has also been said that Keppard's style was a logical extension of Bolden's.

Bill Johnson, a New Orleans bassist born in 1872, moved to California in 1909, and in 1913 put out a call to Keppard to bring a band westward. Keppard accepted the invitation; the first New Orleans band to leave the city began a five-year tour on the Orpheum Circuit. Playing theater dates in major cities, Keppard's Creole Orchestra was the first to bring New Orleans jazz to the rest of the nation.

It is reported that in 1916 Victor Records offered to record the Keppard group while they were in New York. Freddie, however, turned the offer down, afraid that his style would be copied. Like the Bolden myths, this story has persisted through the years. Members of the band have refuted it, and in 1959 a search of Victor's files revealed that a test pressing by a "Creole Jass Band" had been made in 1918. Sidney Bechet said that Keppard told him the refusal was based on Keppard's fear that records would commercialize jazz. In all probability, Victor's refusal to release the test pressing sprang from a fear that Keppard's music was "too hot and dirty" for its white audience. All record companies, in those days, followed very restrictive racial policies.

In 1918, Keppard took his band to Chicago where it was successful. A dispute between band members led to its break-up, and Freddie Keppard was never to be a leader again. He became a featured sideman and, eventually, just a sideman. In his remaining years, he played with important dance bands in Chicago and finally did record with some of them. Always a heavy drinker like Bolden, Keppard began to drink even more heavily. His playing was seriously deteriorating and in the end, as trombonist Preston Jackson said, "Poor Freddie Keppard drank himself to death." He died in Chicago on July 15, 1933.

When Keppard left New Orleans, A. J. Piron took over the Olympia Orchestra, and, ironically, he hired Joe Oliver to replace Keppard. Oliver had begun playing professionally as a substitute cornetist with the Onward Brass Band. At various times during his New Orleans days he worked with the Henry Allen, Sr., Brass Band, the Magnolia, Olympia, Melrose, and Eagle bands, and the Original Superior Orchestra. Like many musicians of the day, he had another occupation; he was a butler.

In 1918, Kid Ory led the house band at the "25" which was then managed by Clarence Williams. Ory hired Joe Oliver, and in a flair of advertising genius, he started billing Joe as "King" Oliver. Thus a new king was crowned—not by the dancers of the city as with Bolden, or by the musicians as was Keppard, but in an advertising stunt by the flamboyant Ory. Joe "King" Oliver nonetheless earned the crown, and his contributions to jazz can stand up under any critical scrutiny.

In 1918, the same Bill Johnson who had called Keppard out of the city asked Joe Oliver to come to Chicago. While playing with Johnson, Oliver also started doubling with Lawrence Duhe's band at the Dreamland Cafe. By 1920 he was leading his own band—billed as King Oliver's Creole Jazz Band—at the Dreamland. Kid Ory suggested that Oliver's band come to the West Coast, and during 1921 the band toured California. It was on his return to Chicago that Oliver's reputation really soared. Booked into the Lincoln Gardens, Joe "King" Oliver made a decision that was to change the future of jazz. He had decided that he wanted a second cornetist for his band, the call went down the Mississippi to New Orleans, the choice was Louis Armstrong.

King Oliver now had the band on which his lasting fame is based. It drew Chicago crowds in droves. Both traveling and local musicians came to pay tribute—especially young white musicians who in later years became jazz greats. The band recorded on the Gennett label in 1923, and this series of recordings shows the musical leadership of Oliver, his inventiveness, and his tremendous influence on future jazz. Oliver's group also toured the Orpheum Circuit.

In June, 1924, Louis Armstrong left Oliver to strike out on his own. Oliver's popularity continued, but he was changing his music to keep up with the times. He added a full reed section and adopted written arrangements, continuing to play in Chicago's Plantation Club until 1927. Then he went on the road, eventually ending up in New York. He did not have the success he expected, his band broke up, and from then until 1930, Joe Oliver had no permanent orchestra. He had to assemble a new band for playing dates and recording sessions. Records—sometimes good ones, sometimes bad—became his principal means of support. In 1931 Victor Records refused to renew his contract.

With a new band, Oliver went on the road again until he finally settled in Savannah, Georgia, in 1936. These were bitter and frustrating years for him. He was barely earning enough to stay alive, was often stranded in small towns, and was as forgotten as he had once been famous. His health was broken and he had lost his teeth. His clothes were ragged, he had been cheated out of money by bookers and managers, and he had no regular job other than selling vegetables on the street and sweeping out pool halls. He died of a cerebral hemorrhage on April 8, 1938. His unmarked grave is in New York City.

The Family
Up-to-Date
(1978)

THE MATERIAL on the Bolden family and their relatives comes from the following sources: author's interviews with Eugenia Jackson, Laura Lawes, Dave Dennis, and Mrs. Cecile Augustine; interviews with William Russell in the Hogan Jazz Archive; New Orleans Vital Statistics Records; Burial Ledgers; Criminal Courts Archives; and letters from Congressman F. Edward Hebert and Zutty Singleton. Some details of the search for Buddy's daughter, Bernedine, have been withheld because of the informants' reluctance to be identified with the Bolden story.

Alice Bolden was deeply affected, emotionally and financially, by her son's mental breakdown. After moving from their long-time residences at 2309 and 2302 First Street, she lived at 2527 First from 1907 until about 1926, then moved to 2338 Philip Street where she remained until her death. The house at 2338, which has since been razed, was another Victorian double cottage similar to the one at 2309 First. Mrs. Bolden began suffering from a heart ailment later in life and by 1930 was confined to her home. Her niece, Ida Cambric Baker, took care of her during the day. Mrs. Baker's two daughters, Laura and Eugenia, used to go to Mrs. Bolden's house for their meals and also helped care for "Aunt Alice." On August 11, 1931, Alice died in her home of cardio-renal disease. She was buried at Lafayette Cemetery Number 2 in the vault of Ladies of Providence.

Buddy's sister Cora, except for her short marriage in 1902, lived all of her life with her mother. She was a homebody, did most of the housekeeping, and occasionally helped her mother with some jobs. When Alice became terminally ill, Cora worked outside the home as a laundress. According to Nora Bass, Cora "went to pieces" after her mother and Buddy died. Both physically and emotionally shaken, Cora became ill, and again Ida Baker was called to a deathbed in the Bolden home. Cora died of a gastric ulcer and on December 19, 1931, she was buried near her mother in Lafayette Cemetery in the Unity Hope Tomb. Alice, Cora, and Buddy Bolden died within a period of four months.

Ida Baker bore a strong physical resemblance to Cora Bolden. She and her husband had known the Bolden family as well as anyone knew them. They inherited the Bolden family heirlooms—a bedroom suite, china closet, a goblet etched "Alice Bolden, New Orleans, 1891," and a portrait of Buddy, hitherto undiscovered outside of the family realm. Mrs. Baker passed away in 1960 at age seventy-nine and the Bolden possessions were handed down to her daughters, Eugenia Jackson and Laura Lawes. The daughters married and raised their families in a double home on Willow Street.

The bedroom suite, now a valuable, swirled cherry wood antique, dominates the bedroom of Laura Lawes's home. It consists of a bed, with a massive wooden headboard, an armoire, double-doored with full length mirrors on both doors, and a dresser with a circular mirror bordered in wood. All the pieces have exquisite hand carving. The glassed-in china closet contains Mrs. Lawes's family china and crystal and has family pictures on top. The goblet sits on a fireplace and the portrait of Buddy hangs on the living room wall with other family pictures. This bedroom suite and china closet had been given to Mrs. Bolden by her long-time employers, the Del Bondio family of 2511 Napoleon Street.

The sisters still attend the St. John Institutional Missionary Baptist Church on Jackson Avenue, the original church of the Bolden family. Eugenia sings in the church choir and Laura plays piano for two other small churches. They were second cousins of Buddy and Cora and are the only survivors with any blood connection to the Bolden line who were found who agreed to being interviewed. They filled in important information on the family, especially on Alice and Cora. Their gracious loan of Buddy's portrait to be copied for this work is, of course, of inestimable value.

Mrs. Jackson said that another cousin, Lena Kennedy, and her daughter, Gertrude Peyton, lived in New Orleans, but had little to do with their Bolden relatives. Buddy's aunt, Cora Bolden Dent Wimby, died at about age 80. The exact date of her death is uncertain since there is no obituary record on file and her death certificate is "off-limits." She is listed annually in the city directory through 1933, but not after that year. There was evidently no contact between her and the Bolden family after the very early days.

Harriet "Hattie" Oliver Bolden raised Charles, Jr., but she died when he was coming into his teens and he was raised by Hattie's sister, Felicie Milo, at 2139 Jackson. Charles Junior was not closely supervised and by the time he was sixteen he was already on the police blotters for minor offenses, mostly having to do with truancy. He had nothing to do with the Bolden family and when he enlisted in the U.S. Navy on July 17, 1917, he listed his aunt as next of kin.

While in the navy, he served on the U.S.S. *Olympia* with New Orleans drummer, Zutty Singleton, and clarinetist Albert Nicholas. Zutty, who was born in 1898, had known Charles, Jr., as a child and said that he was a tall, good-looking guy and that they were about the same age. Charles did not play any musical instrument, stated Zutty, nor did he talk much about his father or his family.

Charles, Jr., was discharged from the navy on November 23, 1919 and returned to New Orleans to live at 1013 Ninth Street. He married and moved to 3233 Franklin Street. His Aunt Felicie died in the early 1920s. His marriage produced a daughter, Harriet, and she was named as his beneficiary in 1925 when he sent to the Veterans Administration for an adjusted compensation. He moved his family to 1003 St. Philip in the French Quarter and worked as a laborer, but he, too, fell victim to heart disease and died on Christmas Day, 1930, at age thirty-three. He was buried at the National Cemetery in Chalmette, Louisiana, on December 27, in Section 159, Grave No. 12902. His death certificate noted that his parents were Charles Bolden, Sr., and Harriet A. Oliver, both natives of

Louisiana. The last trace of his family was in 1938, when his daughter, also called Hattie, was working as a laundress and living at 6317 McKenna, an area not too far from old Lincoln Park. She probably got married around this time, but what her married name became is unknown and no trace has been found of her. She is probably still living in New Orleans, but even if she were located it is highly unlikely she would be able to shed any light on the Bolden story.

Nora Bass Bolden left Buddy when he became incorrigible during 1906. Bill Russell traced her in June, 1942, after finding her whereabouts from her sister Dora who was then living in Los Angeles. Nora had moved to Chicago and then to Waterloo, Iowa. She seemed stunned to find that anyone still identified her with Bolden, and half-heartedly denied ever having been married to him. She said her present husband knew nothing of her life with Buddy and "those people" of whom she seemed so ashamed. She picked out Cornish and Mumford from the band picture, saying that they came to the house occasionally on business. She was very nervous lest her husband came home from work while Russell was there. Bill, noting her concern, cut the interview shorter than he had wished and promised that he would never bother her again nor divulge where she lived. Nora returned to New Orleans for her mother's funeral in July, 1951; she died in the late 1950s.

Buddy's and Nora's daughter, Bernedine, was said to be living around Chicago about 1940. Many New Orleans musicians had moved there during the twenties and for years Chicago had a regular New Orleans community. One of the musicians on a return visit to New Orleans had mentioned seeing Bernedine up there, but no one was able to locate her later.

Not everyone in New Orleans loved jazz. Some families tolerated it because it provided a living, but they did not care to be associated with it, especially its earlier connotations. To some jazz was sinful, and when the musician in the family died, the jazz was buried with him. In this work it was sometimes greatly frustrating to spend months of "detective" research trying to locate persons connected with the Bolden story, only to be met with denials of relationship or straight refusals to supply even basic dates and authentication. This was especially true in the case of Bernedine. After five years of attempting to determine whether she was still living or available for an interview, a family lead in New Orleans was found. This family, closely related to Bernedine, did acknowledge that she was living (as of December, 1975) near Chicago, but they would not supply her married name or any other information that might lead to a meeting with her.

Among the confusing stories about Buddy Bolden appears one claiming that there was more than one Charles Bolden who played trumpet. Sam Charters stated in *Jazz: New Orleans, 1885–1963*, that a Charles Bolden who played cornet in New Orleans later traveled to New York and played there in a minstrel show. Charters fails to document this statement and it contradicts anything actually found about Buddy. Charters also says that Bolden had as many as six jobs in one night and moved from place to place.

It is true that Papa Jack Laine once led bands that had six or seven jobs simultaneously, but Laine was acting as teacher, organizer, and business manager. He did not always participate as a musician or leader on those occasions. Through carelessness or anxiety Buddy may have accepted more engagements than he could possibly fill, particularly after 1906, and he may have had a morning, afternoon, and evening gig on the same day, but spreading himself so thin as to play six jobs in one evening is not a believable or authentic addition to the legend.

There were other persons in New Orleans who went by the name Buddy Bolden, none of whom were cornet players. One pushed a vegetable cart. Another, known as both Buddy Bolden and Buddy Boland, was frequently in hot water for vagrancy and for "not being able to give a good account of hisself." He was a great talker and sometimes redeemed himself by giving information to the police. His gossip-mongering may have had something to do with the story about a Buddy Bolden who put out a scandal and gossip sheet. Buddy Bartley, the aerialist, was also sometimes confused with Bolden. Charles Junior, around the streets as a teenager between 1910 and 1917 and again after his return from World War I, could possibly have been confused with his father by persons not very close to either.

The only other musician called Buddy Bolden who turned up was a man named Thomas Bolden, Jr. He was from St. Bernard Parish, was born around 1900, and came to New Orleans around 1917 or 1918. He played guitar and possibly some piano in the honky tonks, but was not very highly regarded musically. He left for Chicago in the early 1920s and died in the mid or late forties. He never went to New York and never played trumpet or cornet. He was an uncle of the Reverend Dave Dennis, who still resides in New Orleans and provided much of the information on him. There were numerous other Bolden families in New Orleans concurrent with Buddy's family, but checks through obituaries and interviews with surviving relatives reveal that none of them were related to the Boldens of this book.

Another misconception that should be cleared up appeared in Tom Sancton's article "Trouble In Mind" for the *Second Line*, January-February, 1954. One of the neighborhood old-timers Sancton interviewed remembered going to a funeral for a younger sister of Buddy's named Angelina. Angelina Bolden, who died in 1921 at age ten, was actually a daughter of Richard Bolden of 2222 Melpomene Street.

Mrs. Cecile Augustine, who lived at 2323 Second Street in 1971, was eighty-five years old when interviewed and had lived at that address "longer than she could remember." When asked about Buddy Bolden, she said, "Yes, indeed, his wife used to live right over there." She pointed to a vacant lot across the street. Upon further checking in the city directories, it was revealed that there was a Mrs. Virginia Bolden living at that location (2316) when Buddy would have been around. Possibly Virginia was one of Buddy's women. Whatever the case, the house was torn down many years ago and Virginia Bolden disappeared from any traceable source. Another enigma must be added to the legend.

On the male side it was an ill-fated family. West Bolden died at age thirty-two. His son Buddy went insane before he was thirty and died when he was fifty-four. Charles Junior was dead at age thirty-three. The patriarch, Gustavus, lived until 1866 when he was approximately sixty years old. Gustavus and Buddy's sister Lotta were buried in the Greenwood-Cypress Grove Cemeteries on City Park Avenue.

Of the young girls who were members of the Blue Ribbon Social Club at whose dances Buddy and his band disported themselves so gallantly, only Beatrice Alcorn, her sister Louise Terrillatte, and Mrs. Augustine are still living. They are now all in their upper eighties. The direct lines to the Bolden story become less accessible each year. Soon it will be completely a secondhand or thirdhand tale, as much of it is already.

APPENDIX III

Epilogue, 2005

IT IS HARD to believe that it has been twenty-seven years since *In Search of Buddy Bolden* first appeared in print via Louisiana State University Press. I am frequently asked whether anything has been found that would change the original text, and my answer is an emphatic no. Unless someone finds the legendary cylinder on which Bolden's music was recorded or Buddy's diary, the book stands as written. However, enough things have happened directly concerning Bolden since 1978 to merit this updated version. It also gives me an opportunity to expound on some questions or controversies which have arisen.

First of all, the question is asked, "Was Buddy Bolden really 'The First Man of Jazz,' as the title suggests?" My personal choice for the title was "In Search of the Bolden Legend." As the name "Bolden" was relatively unknown in 1978, an editorial decision was made to use "Jazz" in the title. Such a claim is not made within the book. I was once berated by a critic who thought that the title was misleading and also that the band picture was backwards. Obviously he got no farther than the cover because the picture was printed in reverse on the inside, with an explanatory caption. I told this critic, "I did not do the cover, I just wrote the book."

Although the tales about Buddy Bolden being a barber and editor of the *Cricket* have been pretty much disproven, a few stories pop up about who the clarinet players are in the Bolden band photograph. The doubters base what they have to say on what the instruments look like. The way I chose to identify them properly was through six musicians who knew Willie Warner and Frank Lewis personally, plus the word of Willie Cornish, who was in the photo. Warner is the one standing and Lewis the one sitting!

When the book was first published, I still had a couple of concerns. One was my belief that somewhere a close relative of Buddy was still living. Another was that no one knew exactly where he was buried and that he had no grave marker or tombstone. It was not until 1993 that some things began to come together. Following a three-part series in the New Orleans *Times-Picayune* on the early days of jazz, I received a call from Henry Brown. He informed me that he had a cousin in Chicago who was Buddy Bolden's granddaughter. Would I be interested in contacting her? I would.

Thus began a series of letters and phone calls to Mrs. Gertrude Bolden Tucker. Her father was Charles Bolden, Jr. She did not live under his roof very long and he died when she was eleven years old, but she was a direct link and had some information about the family. It was my desire to bring her back to New Orleans one day for some kind of special event.

In early 1996, Delgado Community College hired a new public relations director named Joe Brennan. Mr. Brennan called me in May and said, "I just read your book about Buddy Bolden. As I sit in my office which overlooks Holt Cemetery, I am reminded that he has no grave marker. Do you think we should do something about that?" I replied that such had been a longtime goal of mine but that I could get little support from the community.

What ensued was an initial meeting of some interested parties, including Joe Brennan, Jerry Brock, Bernie Cyrus, Jackie Harris, Tom Jacobsen, Dr. Frank Minyard, George Schmidt, Jack Stewart, members of the Delgado staff, and me. By the third meeting, things were falling into place. It was decided to erect a monument in Holt Cemetery, have a jazz funeral and invite Mrs. Tucker to New Orleans for that weekend, and to hold the event on September 6, 1996, which would be the 119th anniversary of Buddy Bolden's birth.

Everyone came through. Stewart Enterprises was contacted and promised to provide the monument. Orleans Parish coroner Dr. Frank Minyard said he would sponsor the Olympia Brass Band. Delgado would furnish the facility, food, and, importantly, the public relations. The college also took care of two round-trip airline tickets for Mrs. Tucker and her daughter, Mrs. Rita Camille Bell. Delta Airlines made available their VIP Room at the airport and gave permission for a brass band to meet the plane at the arrival gate. Mrs. Dian Coleman Winingder, owner of the Downtown/Superdome Holiday and who was responsible for the Buddy Bolden Breezeway murals in her hotel, offered rooms for the two women, plus any meals they cared to eat there. The New Orleans Jazz Club would send a 12-piece brass band to meet the plane and present T-shirts and posters to Gertrude and Rita. The Louisiana Music Factory set up a two-hour session for the Bolden descendants to sign copies of the books and other bits of memorabilia. Mrs. Nina Buck agreed to set up a birthday party at her Palm Court, complete with cake and second line.

THE ARRIVAL AND THE EVENT

The plane arrived on time on September 5. Gertrude and Rita were among the last to deplane. The Jazz Club's brass band, complete with a grand marshal, greeted them. Gertrude was welcomed by a cousin from Las Vegas, which was a pleasant surprise for her. It took about fifteen minutes to make it through the corridors to the VIP Room. Many passengers joined the parade. There were a lot of meetings, lots of talking in the VIP Room. Then to the Holiday to get checked in.

Beginning at 6:00 P.M. on September 6, the Olympia Brass Band marched for almost an hour all around Holt Cemetery accompanied by about two thousand second-liners and lots of media. The march ended at a stage set up near the grave marker. The monument was unveiled to thunderous applause. Stewart Enterprises had done a magnificent job. Mayor Marc Morial said some appropriate words and conferred honorary New Orleans citizenship on Gertrude and Rita. After more music, food, and drinks, it was off to the Palm Court. George and Nina Buck provided a large birthday cake, some more music, and another second-line march through the Court. Alvin Alcorn (who was eighty-four years old) was there. His mother had known Buddy Bolden and his family. Blue Lu Barker, Danny's widow, was present, as were many other jazz fans.

When the Palm Court closed at 11:00 P.M., Gertrude, Rita, and some others went to Funky Butt on North Rampart Street, where some great young trumpet players played a tribute to Buddy. Gertrude, at age seventy-five, stayed until 2:00 A.M. Her daughter and cousin stayed later.

On September 7, *Times-Picayune* writer and tour guide John McCusker and I took the Bolden relatives to see the house at 2309 First Street, the Odd Fellows and Masonic Hall, and some other pertinent landmarks. Later that day, Joe Brennan and I took Gertrude to the airport for breakfast and good-byes.

It had been one great weekend, and at last Buddy Bolden was given a proper farewell and a lasting monument for his contributions to jazz. An important aside is that the Bolden jazz funeral won awards from the New Orleans Press Club and a national Clio award for best public relations campaign of 1996.

A DIFFERENT TYPE OF MEMORIAL

I received an unusual call in late December of 1999. Ms. Terry Beisly, with the Ken Colyer Trust in West Sussex, England, wanted to have a memorial marker installed in Holt Cemetery. The piece would mark the spot where Terry had scattered the ashes of her husband, Lawrence "Loe" Beisly, in 1995. She, Mick Brocking, and Ron Drakeford, devoted fans of Buddy Bolden, would come to New Orleans for the installation and also wanted their ashes spread eventually near the jazz great's final resting place.

The cast-bronze plaque on the marker reads, "May These Ashes Rest in Harmony For Ever to Heed the Call of Buddy Bolden." In addition to Lawrence Beisly's plate, now in place on the marker, there is room for three more individual plates to be mounted as the ashes of each person are scattered.

The group was pleased with the results and were here again in April of 2004. I picked up Terry, Mick, and Ron from their Bourbon Street hotel along with some of their children and grandchildren. It was the first time the children had seen Lawrence's final resting place, and they were quite touched. It is moving to think that this group's love of jazz carries them so far even after death.

OTHER WORKS ABOUT BUDDY BOLDEN

A question I am sometimes asked is, "Is any further research being done on Buddy Bolden?" The first person to show an interest in a possible book was Fred Ramsey, Jr., who was one of the major contributors to the 1939 book *Jazzmen*. He interviewed Louis Jones in the 1950s but spent little time in New Orleans after that until about 1973. When I began my serious research, I asked Dick Allen, then curator of the William Ransom Hogan Jazz Archive at Tulane University, if anyone else was working on Bolden. He mentioned Fred but commented, "He has not been here for a number of years."

"Should I proceed?"

"Yes," he said.

Fred Ramsey moved to New Orleans for a couple of years around 1973, and we became friends. As my research was well along, we did not talk much about Bolden. He told me that his book would be different and there was room for both. He even autographed an original copy of *Jazzmen* on November 23, 1974: "To Don Marquis from Fred Ramsey, Jr. Best wishes, especially on Buddy Bolden."

We kept in touch, but unfortunately Fred died before he could publish his story. What happened to his notes I do not know, but I am sure they contained some important information.

Around 1977 I was visited in my office by Canadian author Michael Ondaatje. He said he was interested in writing a biography of Bolden and asked, "Do you know anything about him?" I told him my manuscript had been accepted by LSU Press and was in the printing stage.

"Well, I will forget that."

Ondaatje then wrote a very interesting novel based on Bolden, called *Coming Through Slaughter.* Another fine novel by David Fullmer, *Chasing the Devil's Tail,* came out a few years ago.

Ray Bisso of San Pedro, California, wrote a 57-page poem entitled "Buddy Bolden of New Orleans." Dan Hardie of Sydney, Australia, wrote a book about Bolden called *The Loudest Trumpet.* He is another old friend, and his book is mostly an attempt to chase down the original band members. Danny Barker wrote a book entitled *Buddy Bolden and the Early Days of Storyville,* which he admitted to me was mostly fiction. Interesting reading, however.

There have been numerous letters dating back to 1980 suggesting ideas for plays or movies, but either they never materialized or I never saw them.

In 1979, LSU Press granted paperback rights for *In Search of Buddy Bolden* to Da Capo Press in New York for a limited time. In 1993, LSU took the rights back from Da Capo and has kept the book in print since then. In 1989, a French translation was published by Editions Denoel in Paris.

While working on the Bolden book, I kept a journal of my research. At that time, one of my former professors at Goshen College in Indiana told me he was instituting a small publishing operation called Pinchpenny Press. He asked if I would have anything to contribute. At first I said no, but then I mentioned the journal. *Finding Buddy Bolden* had a first printing in 1978 and is now in its seventh printing. It has even been used by some schools as a model for how to do research.

Since 1980 there has been considerable international interest in Buddy. BBC London did a documentary, and I have given talks in Amsterdam, Brussels, Cologne, Copenhagen, Darmstadt, Hamburg, London, Melbourne, Paris, Sao Paulo, Stockholm, and Tokyo. Most folks in the audiences had read this book.

In 1986, England's great trumpet player Humphrey Lyttleton put together a band to make a long-play album entitled "The World of Buddy Bolden," in which they perform numbers the band was known to have played. They went to the extra effort of obtaining instruments from the 1905 era. It is a sterling attempt.

BUDDY BOLDEN PLACE

In May 2002, the New Orleans City Council passed an ordinance renaming the 4900 block of Toulouse Street, between City Park Avenue and Holt Cemetery, as Buddy Bolden Place. It was sponsored by Councilman Scott Shea. A brass band accompanied the event. It is interesting that the *Times-Picayune* gave it a thumbs-down rating. The razz is quoted:

> Charles "Buddy" Bolden deserves to be honored for his role in the history of jazz. But surely the New Orleans City Council could have done better than naming a single block after the legendary cornetist. Buddy Bolden Place, as it's now called, is the final block of Toulouse Street and has no residents living on it. The block lies between City Park Avenue and Holt Cemetery, where Mr. Bolden's body is buried in an unknown location. The fact that Mr. Bolden died in obscurity is sad enough without giving him an obscure memorial.

THE CYLINDER AND THE *CRICKET*

In 1999 I received a letter from Mrs. Bennie Jay Zahn, excerpted below. Sadly, it confirms that there is no extant recording of Bolden's music.

Dear Mr. Marquis:

Many years ago you contacted me seeking information for your book on Buddy Bolden. You said that you had information that my uncle Oscar Zahn had been instrumental in making a recording of Bolden.

Although I had, and still have, Oscar's Edison phonograph, I'd had a storage shed torn down and, unbeknown to me, Oscar's cylinder records were stored on the top shelf. Needless to say, they were destroyed in the demolition. This was in the early 60's before I realized the importance of even broken artifacts.

Mrs. Zahn also told me her grandfather was Alfred Gehrke, a bootmaker who owned property around Lincoln Park. According to her, the area now known as Gert-town, in Carrollton, was originally Gehrketown.

Yes, jazz fans, there was a *Cricket!* Jazz historian Larry Gushee, from the University of Illinois School of Music, turned up three issues—Volume I, numbers 1, 2, and 3—at both Duke and Tulane universities. The dates were March 21, April 4, and April 18, 1896. The editor and publisher was Lamar Middleton; he was assisted by Louise de Hubert Guyol. The headquarters were located in the respectable neighborhood of Common and Carondelet streets. The three copies found do not indicate that it was a scandal sheet, and its availability at D. H. Holmes and the St. Charles Hotel bear that out. It ran to about twelve pages.

Kevin Herridge, who moved to the West Bank of New Orleans from England in 1994, got caught up in New Orleans history and located a later copy of the *Cricket* at Xavier University, dated July 24, 1897. Although the masthead is the same, things had changed. It was published and edited by H. Benjamin Francois at 510 South Liberty and appeared every Saturday. The available issue indicates it covered a lot of ground, but was also a scandal sheet. In a column entitled "Back of Town" appeared the following:

That man Wm. Adams had better go back to his wife and let that woman Lottie G. alone, who lives on Poydras street not a stone throw from Franklin.

Frank Victor from Melpomene street, ought to stay at home when he gets drunk in place of going out to a Sunday School to carry on as he did.

A certain married lady living back of town, ought to give her husband a chance to get cold in the ground before she begins cohabiting with other men.

Nellie Hamilton who has been keeping an immoral house at the corner of Joliet and Levee streets for some time has been ordered to move. Nellie don't like it, but what can the poor girl do?

The woman who lives corner General Taylor and Coliseum isn't as careful as she might be with her tricks. THE CRICKET is dead onto you, lady. Be careful.

A little wench with corkscrew hair says she will raise sand if she is put in THE CRICKET. Well, we know a thing or two about you, Sis, and when we get your full name and a few other particulars, we propose devoting some space to you. You hear from us next week.

The *Cricket* had correspondents all over. They covered Algiers, Back of Town, Carrollton, Downtown, the Garden District, Houma, Jefferson, and even Plaquemines Parish.

How Buddy Bolden's name came up in association with the *Cricket* is unknown at this point. There was a man named Bolden who was arrested about that time and gave his occupation as "reporter." More research is needed.

THE BOLDEN FAMILY AND BAND MEMBERS

When I first began my search for Buddy Bolden, there was a reluctance among some individuals to admit any relationship because of illegitimacy and insanity. After the book was published, and fortunately, some people came forward. Some were authentic, but some not. Those with a true claim are included in the text or earlier in this Epilogue. Given Bolden's reputation as a ladies' man, it is likely he left some other descendants; however, my search did not turn them up. It might be a good research project for someone to follow through on that.

Of the musicians associated with Bolden or his era, new facts have come to light only about Frank Duson. Note that the name is spelled "Duson," not "Dusen." I was not aware of the correct spelling when *In Search of Buddy Bolden* was first published.

Barbara Harris Jones sent me letters and photos related to Duson. He was born in 1881 and married Ethel Wells in 1924. They had two daughters, one of whom, Thelma, was Barbara's mother. Evidently, the marriage did not work. A letter from Frank to his sister-in-law dated April 7, 1927, indicates he was out of touch with Ethel but concerned about the baby Thelma.

There are notes from Frank to Thelma in late 1930 and a letter to Ethel stating he wished he knew where to send a Christmas present. As Ethel died in 1930, it is possible she never received that letter. Ethel was born in 1907 and thus was twenty-six years younger than Frank. Pictures of her from the 1920s show a slim, young, good-looking girl. Frank Duson died on April 1, 1935, and was cremated. Ethel is buried in the Wells plot in Cottonport, Louisiana. There is no doubt a Duson family story is out there.

The last man to have actually played with the Bolden band, Ed "Montudi" Garland, died in California in 1980 at age ninety-five. Musicians who had heard Bolden play and who lived into their nineties—Louis Keppard, Tom Albert, Booker T. Glass, and Martin "Chink Martin" Abraham—are also long deceased.

Anyone who honestly heard the Bolden band in person would now be over one hundred years old, and I must admit I have stopped looking for such people.

SOME PSYCHIATRIC THEORIES

Beginning around 1999, psychiatrists and psychologists have written several works and conducted several symposia concerning the mental deterioration of Buddy Bolden. Some of them use terminology that neither I nor likely the average jazz fan understands. I do believe they were sincere efforts and therefore deserve a mention.

Dr. Sean A. Spence, Senior Clinical Lecturer in Psychiatry at the University of Sheffield in England, was a research fellow at the New York Hospital–Cornell Medical Center from 1999 to 2001. He gave a presentation in London and at an International Association of Jazz Educators' conference in New Orleans. Here are excerpts from a personal letter he sent me in August 1999:

I wondered what you might think about the following (which is highly speculative): that BB "improvised" from necessity, perhaps related to the onset of motor impairment and that the unusual manner in which he holds the cornet is (albeit very weak) evidence in favour of such a subtle impairment. . . . if BB's illness facilitated his improvisation, then that might have had profound implications for the way that jazz developed (maybe even initiating jazz as an improvising music rather than as a dance music per se). . . . It's speculation and it has the rather dangerous connotation that jazz might be thought by some to be a by-product of an illness, but for me it underlines the inter-connectedness of the personal with the public in an artistic endeavor. It also relates to the issue of whether some illnesses have advantages for the community, if not for the individual afflicted. If BB had not lived, would jazz have evolved as it did? Would it have emphasised improvisation as it did? I'd be interested in your view on this.

My view is that Buddy Bolden began playing his music years before he was afflicted with mental illness and that what he played came from a sound, creative mind. It was only after 1906 that we hear it mentioned that he performed "erratically."

Following Dr. Spence's original treatise, an article headlined "Did Schizophrenia Start the Jazz Age?" appeared in the London *Times* and was quoted in the *Times-Picayune*. The article inspired numerous letters to the editor, including one from a longtime successful musician: "When I told my parents that I wanted to be a Jazz musician, they said, 'You're crazy!'"

In early 2000, I received a letter from Ferdinand Jones, a Ph.D. in psychology at Brown University, bringing up to date a paper he and his wife, Myra, who holds an M.S.W., did on Bolden. The 14-page paper was presented at the International Association of Jazz Educators' 2000 meeting in New Orleans. In his letter Jones admits: "We were not able to be much more decisive about the issues than you and others have been. We always understood, of course, that this is the nature of attempting to reconstruct a subject without direct access to its most informative details."

Some excerpts from Dr. and Mrs. Jones's paper follow:

A myth associated with Jazz musicians maintains that they are more likely to be psychologically disturbed than a comparable number of individuals in other occupations (persists today). This idea, an extension of one that pairs creativity with craziness and defies actual facts, has been around for a long time in the popular images of the Jazz world. Buddy Bolden, whom legend names the first Jazz musician, spent the last 24 years of his life in a mental hospital. He has the dubious distinction of being the first personification of this myth. . . . We know little about Bolden's extended family, so there is no way to know if his family history might have played a role in the development of either his alcohol dependence or his psychosis. Obtaining the critical information about his childhood development and a comprehensive knowledge of the overall workings of his physical and cognitive systems would be the only way to pin down their involvement. We are left then with the inconclusive and imprecise impression that dual conditions—alcohol and a destructive mental process—were the likely causes of Bolden's psychological troubles. But, however these conditions interacted with his personal characteristics, his circumstances and his environment, THE SIMPLE FACTS THAT HE WAS BLACK AND THAT HE WAS A JAZZ MUSICIAN DO NOT CONSTITUTE A THEORY OF A VERY COMPLEX HUMAN TRAGEDY.

I should add that the Jones's paper contains much valuable psychiatric information with excellent documentation.

On December 14, 2002, Dr. Alan Newman, of the Department of Psychology and Neurology at Tulane University, gave a talk entitled, "Buddy Bolden: The Neuropsychiatric Decline and Fall of the Founder of Jazz." He was under the assumption that Buddy suffered from syphilis and talked about how that particular affliction may have affected him. I told him Buddy did not have that disease, and he responded, "Well, I sure enjoyed reading your book about him."

A final word: I think what *In Search of Buddy Bolden* has done for jazz history is to enable us to accept the man as a real person and not just a myth. Many dates, locations, and people are now documented, and some erroneous theories about those early days in New Orleans have been corrected. I hope this book will encourage other writers to realize that the research is never done.

Labor Day, 1906. This was the date of Buddy's last music job and a major breakdown.

— From New Orleans *Times-Democrat,* September 4, 1906

Nº 15 LOUISIANA STATE INSANE ASYLUM, JACKSON, LA.

A postcard mailed from Jackson on September 10, 1909.

2338 Philip Street, the last residence of Mrs. Alice Bolden and daughter Cora. This photo was taken around 1954 before the building was razed.

—Photograph by Tom Sancton, Sr.

Gertrude Bolden Tucker, Bolden's granddaughter, leading a twelve-piece jazz band on her arrival at the New Orleans airport on September 5, 1996, for Buddy's memorial ceremony. Behind her is her daughter, Rita Camille Bell, and to her right is Joe Brennan, the prime mover in the event.

—Photograph by Don Marquis

Panorama of the jazz funeral at Holt Cemetery. The Olympia Brass Band led nearly two thousand second-liners.

—Photograph by Dian Coleman Winingder

Grave marker, Holt Cemetery. Stewart Enterprises donated the stone and the engraving. It is just left of the entrance gate.

—Photograph by Don Marquis

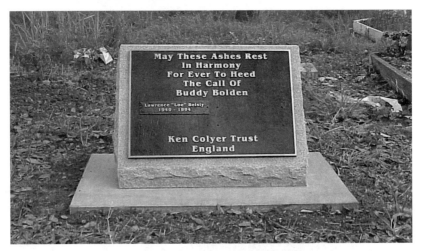

Memorial marker installed by the Ken Colyer Trust in England. Lawrence Beisly's ashes were scattered here in 1995, and three other Bolden enthusiasts plan to follow suit.

—Photograph by Fred Hatfield, courtesy Christine Robertson

Buddy Bolden Place, a one-block area with no homes. The reason for not extending it farther was that the residents affected would have had to change the address on their identification papers.

—Photograph by Don Marquis

Oscar V. Zahn (1876–1919). He recorded the
now-lost-forever Bolden cylinder.

—Photograph courtesy Mrs. Bennie Jay Zahn

The original Edison cylinder used to record Bolden's band.

—Photograph courtesy Mrs. Bennie Jay Zahn

Bibliography

PRIMARY SOURCES

OFFICIAL DOCUMENTS

CITY VITAL STATISTICS RECORDS

The City of New Orleans Vital Statistics Records were housed in City Hall for many years. Around 1973 these records were transferred to the State Office Building, which is across the street from City Hall and stands near the spot of old Union Sons (Funky Butt) Hall. Orleans Parish vital statistics records come under Louisiana Statute R. S. 40:158, Section C, which states, in part: "The registrar . . . shall not permit inspection of the records . . . unless he is satisfied that the applicant therefore has a direct and tangible interest in the matter recorded." Whereas in any other parish in Louisiana, the birth, death, and marriage statistics are a matter of public record, in Orleans Parish it is very difficult to obtain access to them.

The New Orleans Public Library was given microfilmed reels of death and marriage certificates up to the year 1914, primarily for genealogical research. They are not available for copying. There are legitimate reasons for the State's restrictions; they do, however, add to the difficulties of documenting a work of this nature with certified copies of vital statistic records.

In the summer of 1970, Assistant City Attorney Dave Cressy scrutinized my credentials and gave permission for several documents on the immediate Bolden family to be released for discriminate use in the book. These are now in the state office building but are not available for public inspection.

ARCHIVES OF THE CITY OF NEW ORLEANS
LOUISIANA DIVISION
NEW ORLEANS PUBLIC LIBRARY

166 Bibliography

BIRTH CERTIFICATES

Bolden, Lotta (Buddy's sister), June 24, 1875
Bolden, Charles, Jr. (Buddy's son), May 2, 1897, recorded August 16, 1897

DEATH CERTIFICATES

Bolden, Alice (Buddy's mother), August 30, 1931
Bolen [*sic*], Augustus (Buddy's grandfather), August 6, 1866
Bolden, Charles, Jr., August 30, 1931
Bolden, Frances (Buddy's grandmother), May 29, 1883
Bolden, Lotta, May 18, 1881

MARRIAGE CERTIFICATES

Marriage licenses verified family relationships, established exact dates, ages, and locations, and aided in the general accuracy of the book.

Alcorn, Oliver	March 18, 1905
Alexander, Adolphe, Sr.	September 25, 1897
Allen, Henry, Sr.	December 26, 1879
Amacker, Frank, Sr.	November 12, 1895
Avery, Joseph	April 23, 1902
Baquet, Achille	January 27, 1906
Baquet, George	November 18, 1905
Barbarin, Adolph	April 13, 1871
Barnes, Harrison	September 17, 1914
Bass, Andrew	November 3, 1909
Bass, Dora	June 26, 1899
Bass, Laura	March 14, 1907
Bechet, Homer	June 23, 1906
Bloom, Joseph	May 5, 1900
Bolden, Cora (aunt)	October 26, 1874
Bolden, Cora (aunt)	December 25, 1899
Bolden, Cora (sister)	September 11, 1902
Bolden, Westmore	August 8, 1873
Bontemps, Willie	December 3, 1914
Brundy, Walter	January 24, 1912
Carey, Thomas (Mutt)	June 13, 1913
Cato, August	September 21, 1904
Chandler, Edward (Dede)	May 21, 1891
Clark, Joseph, Sr.	July, 1874
Cornish, Marcus	December 19, 1894

Cornish, William	November 30, 1922
Cottrell, Louis, Sr.	March 19, 1903
Desvignes, Sidney	February 14, 1914
Dodds, Warren (Baby)	September 4, 1912
Dominguez; Paul	May 29, 1905
Dutrey, Honore	April 27, 1909
Dutrey, Sam, Sr.	June 12, 1912
Foster, George (Pops)	September 4, 1912
Frank, Gilbert (Babb)	August 17, 1891
Galloway, Charley	December 20, 1894
Galloway, Charley	February 17, 1901
Goldston, Christopher (Black Happy)	January 29, 1913
Hall, Manuel	July 8, 1880
Hall, Manuel	December 10, 1901
Hooker, George, Jr.	November 29, 1900
Humphrey, Will	September 5, 1900
Johnson, Jimmy	February 3, 1904
Kimball, Henry, Sr.	September 2, 1876
Landry, Tom	March 2, 1907
Lewis, Frank	February 17, 1904
Lyons, Bob	December 12, 1898
McCullum, George	April 27, 1905
McCurdy, Charles	December 23, 1895
McMurray, John	September 25, 1907
McNeil, James	July 23, 1900
Matthews, Bill	September 21, 1909
Mumford, Jefferson (Brock)	May 4, 1894
Nelson, Louis (Big Eye Louis)	March 5, 1910
Oliver, Felicie	February 9, 1907
Oliver, Joseph (King)	July 13, 1911
Olivier, Adam, Sr.	March 12, 1884
Olivier, Adam, Jr.	July 18, 1906
Ory, Edward (Kid)	October 26, 1911
Palao, Jimmy	October 3, 1913
Perez, Manuel	January 24, 1900
Perkins, Dave, Jr.	September 20, 1910
Petit, Joseph	November 19, 1898
Picou, Alphonse	October 28, 1901

Piron, A. J.	February 12, 1912
Remy, Dominique (T-Boy)	October 17, 1912
Ridgely, William (Bebe)	June 26, 1912
Riley, Amos	December 25, 1909
Rogers, Ernest (Duck)	January 6, 1912
Sayles, George	June 3, 1902
Staulz, Lorenzo	March 13, 1882
Tillman, Cornelius	January 9, 1890
Tillman, Lettie	September 6, 1909
Tio, Antoine	October 10, 1888
Tio, Lorenzo, Jr.	June 10, 1914
Valentin, Panquiette (Punky)	September 25, 1890
Warner, Willie	July 22, 1911
Williams, Claiborne	May 18, 1900
Wolff, Oscar	February 25, 1890
Zeno, Adam	May 30, 1907
Zeno, Henry	June 15, 1892

POLICE DEPARTMENT RECORDS

Specific dates are cited in the text.

New Orleans Police Superintendent's Office Reports of Homicide, cataloged under No. TP 205h, plus year.

Barroom Investigations and Permits, catalog numbers C676ti (1896–1901, 1902–1904, 1905–1911).

New Orleans Police Department Arrest Books, catalog numbers TP 35, plus date. These are on microfilm, each roll covering about one and a half months.

LETTERS

These letters, part of the city archives, are housed in the second basement of the New Orleans Public Library in document boxes. The first name is the addressee, followed by the sender and a short description of the contents.

Boyle, John P., Acting Inspector of Police, from Jim Driscoll, Commander, Fourth Precinct, July 10, 1907. Concerning Nancy Hank's Saloon.

Boyle, from William F. Azcona, Commander, First Precinct, August 28, 1907. Complaint on Nick Virget's Saloon, corner of Gravier and South Rampart.

Bishop, Frank, Commissioner of Buildings, from Widow St. Armand, July 20, 1902. Condition of building at 1320 Perdido Street.

Capdevielle, Paul, Mayor of New Orleans, from M. V. Richard, M. D., Coroner, July 27, 1903. Concerning placing insane persons in House of Detention.

Cooper, John B., Commander, Seventh Precinct, from D. S. Gaster, Superintendent of Police, October 16, 1899. Permission for dance festival at Electric Light Hall.

Fitzpatrick, John, Mayor of New Orleans, from Standard Marine Insurance Co., *circa* March, 1895. Concerning longshoremen's strike.

Fitzpatrick, from Ross Howe, Aaron Ferrow, A. K. Miller, and Andy Botto of L. Fornais and Co., Insurors, March 9, 1895. Concerning longshoremen's strike.

Gaster, D. S., Superintendent of Police, from Richard Walsh, Commander, Third Precinct, May 18, 1898. Refusal of application for entertainment with brass band at 99 St. Philip Street.

Gaster, from Walsh, November 6, 1898. Complaint about St. 'John Divine Church.

Gaster, from M. P. Creagh, Commander, Fourth Precinct, August 30, 1899. Complaint about church on Carondelet Walk.

Gaster, from G. Porteous, Commander, Second Precinct, December 14, 1899. Complaint about Spiritual Hall.

Gaster, from L. W. Rawlings, Commander, First Precinct, March 26, 1907. Concerning construction work and quoting law on bands playing music outside churches during services.

Long, George, Commander, Tenth Precinct, from Arthur Bass, September 20, 1907. Concerning complaint about questionable house at 728 South Salcedo.

McCabe, Joseph, Commander, Sixth Precinct, from Gaster, January 2, 1899. Permission for American String Band to play.

McCabe, from Gaster, July 4, 1899. Granting permit for entertainment at Mt. Zion Hall, corner of Philip and Liberty.

Reynolds, James W., Inspector of Police, from Joseph J. Cearns, Commander, Sixth Precinct, May 31, 1911. Investigation of complaint about lawn parties given by Babb Frank at 2917 South Rampart.

Whitaker, Edward S., Inspector of Police, from L. W. Rawlings, Commander, First Precinct, August 2, 1906. Complaint of barbershop at 427 South Rampart.

Whitaker, from Rawlings, September 1, 1906. Complaint of ship captain being rolled by prostitute.

Whitaker, from Louis Madere, Commander, Seventh Precinct, September 4, 1906. Complaint of brass band music at Electric Light Hall.

Whitaker, from Rawlings, October 23, 1906. Complaint about string band playing at Fishers Barroom.

Whitaker, from Rawlings, November 9, 1906. Investigation of complaint about Carrington Saloon at 818 South Rampart.

Whitaker, from James W. Reynolds and John Dauterive, detectives, September 8, 1907. Investigation of complaint about George Foucault selling catarrh powder containing cocaine at 135 North Basin St.

DIRECTORIES AND GUIDES

Atlas of the City of New Orleans, Louisiana. Based upon surveys furnished by John F. Braun, Surveyor and Architect, compiled by and under the supervision of E. Robinson and R. H. Pidgeon, Civil Engineers. Published by E. Robinson, 82–84 Nassau Street, New Orleans, 1883, catalog number Lou R 917.631 R67a.

New Orleans Guide, compiled by James S. Zacharie, 1902. Catalog number Lou R 917.631 Z16 1902.

New Orleans Police Department History, January 1, 1900. Catalog number Lou R v. 352.2 N53. A guide to police officers, containing numerous advertisements for cabarets.

Official Souvenir and Handbook, United Confederate Veterans Reunion, May 19–22, 1903.

Soards' New Orleans City Directory, published by Soards' Directory Co., 606 Commercial Place, New Orleans. These directories were extensively consulted from 1870 to 1930.

Wood's Directory of Colored Businesses in New Orleans, 1913 and 1914. Catalog number 917.631 W89.

MISCELLANEOUS

Administrations of Mayors of New Orleans. Compiled and edited by Works Project Administration, Project 665-64-3-112, catalog number AAU11 1803–1936, March, 1940.

Board of Assessors, Real Estate Tax Assessments. These are microfilms, catalog number CJ 431, plus municipal district, assessment district, and date.

Cemetery Records
　Holt Cemetery Burial Ledgers, 1895–1930
　Lafayette Cemetery No. 1 and 2 Burial Ledgers, 1910–August 30, 1943

Charity Hospital of New Orleans, Admission Book, Vol. 40, December 1883–November 1885, catalog number 65-36-60.

City Ordinances
No. 1260, New Council Series. Ordinance establishing Lincoln Park, May 30, 1902.
No. 3131 O.S. Permission to Be Obtained for Balls, May, 1859. Amended by No. 7944 Council Series, August 15, 1893.
No. 12, 485, C.S. Establishing boundaries of Storyville, July 6, 1897.
No. 13,032, C.S. Establishing certain guidelines for the behavior of "public prostitutes or notoriously lewd and abandoned women," January 26, 1897.
Coroner's Office
Description and Record of Insane Person. Charles Bolden, catalog number TH 427, 1900–1908, p. 408.
Mayoralty Permits for Music and Dancing
No. 398, January 24, 1910. For Young Men's High Arts Social Club at Odd Fellows and Masonic Hall, 1116 Perdido Street.
No. 594, January 28, 1913. For Groshell's Dance Hall, Customhouse and North Liberty streets.
No. 3490, March 12, 1913. For George Foucault [Fewclothes Cabaret], 134 North Franklin Street.
Petition for permission to create Johnson Park, submitted by George W. Johnson, approved April 14, 1902.
Street Number Changes, 1894. New Orleans City Engineers Office. Five rolls of microfilm, catalog number KJ6, alphabetical by streets.

FEDERAL ARCHIVES

United States Bureau of the Census Population Schedules of City of New Orleans, Wards 1 and 2, for the years 1860, 1870, 1880, cataloged under number 310U, plus year.

CONVEYANCE ORDER BOOKS

To trace property ownership in New Orleans, it is first necessary to go to the Division of Real Estate and Records Office at City Hall, 1300 Perdido Street. There one must locate the proper square number on a large map, then consult the corresponding folder containing current ownership of all the property in one square block. After obtaining the conveyance order book and folio numbers of the last act of sale, the searcher must then go to the Civil District Courts Building basement, 421 Loyola Avenue. Each previous act of sale goes back to an earlier conveyance order book; therefore, properties that had few changes of ownership or successions are much easier to trace than those that changed hands frequently. The following conveyance order books and folios provided valuable information on Johnson Park, Lincoln Park, Odd Fellows Hall, and Union Sons (or Funky Butt) Hall:

Johnson Park

(No book given) P. Bordenave to Jean Marie Larroux, October 23, 1873

Book 184, Folio 78,	January 6, 1902
Book 223, Folio 635,	February 5, 1909
Book 339, Folio 469,	September 28, 1921
Book 339, Folio 568,	October 19, 1921
Book 365, Folio 140,	March 24, 1923
Book 385, Folio 338,	December 3, 1924
Book 421, Folio 420,	February 12, 1927
Book 429, Folio 572,	January 4, 1928
Book 448, Folios 53 to 81,	January 9, 1929

Lincoln Park

Book 5, Folio 144 (Carrollton),	June 8, 1869
Book 103, Folio 670,	April 3, 1875
Book 116, Folio 967,	April 23, 1883
Book 275, Folio 49,	July 15, 1902
Book 304, Folio 387,	September 2, 1921
Book 369, Folio 333,	October 29, 1923
Book 384, Folio 501,	January 28, 1925
Book 421, Folio 111,	September 22, 1926

Odd Fellows Hall

Book 102, Folio 505,	August 31, 1872
Book 128, Folio 971,	July 10, 1889
Book 162, Folio 369,	April 8, 1896
Book 166, Folio 417,	March 22, 1897
Book 173, Folio 268,	March 21, 1899
Book 195, Folio 205,	February 3, 1904
Book 368, Folio 81,	September 2, 1924
Book 399, Folio 230,	October 20, 1925
Book 449, Folio 410,	July 12, 1929

Union Sons Hall

Book 91, Folio 103,	March 6, 1866
Book 155, Folio 384,	May 5, 1895
Book 202, Folio 21,	September 6, 1904
Book 203, Folio 450,	April 14, 1905
Book 209, Folio 510,	February 8, 1907
Book 253, Folio 244,	September 19, 1912

Book 253, Folio 263,   September 25, 1912
Book 291, Folio 275,   April 11, 1917
Book 569, Folio 189,   March 10, 1950

NOTARIAL ARCHIVES

The New Orleans Notarial Archives are just down the hall from the Conveyance Order Book Office. Each conveyance order is notarized and by taking the name of the notary public and the date it is often possible to find more detail about the property being researched. The name of the notary is given first:

Dibble, Henry C., March 1, 1866. Folder contains the original incorporation papers for the Union Sons Benevolent Association of Louisiana.

Eustis, J. G., March 24, 1902. Folder has a letter containing the lease agreement between Elder Edward A. Higgins, pastor of First Lincoln Baptist Church, and Reuben Elmore, representing the Union Sons organization. The agreement was for Higgins' congregation to have use of the hall for Sunday morning religious services for the sum of $5.00 per month.

Henriques, Edward, February 6, 1907. This file holds a copy of the minutes of a February 6, 1907, meeting of the Union Sons and includes a slate of officers elected at that meeting. It also shows that William S. Kinney was first elected president on November 9, 1904.

Ory, Benjamin, March 7, 1897. Contains the Articles of Incorporation for the Odd Fellows and Masonic Hall Association to be domiciled at 1116 Perdido Street.

Upton, Robert, September 11, 1897. Contains the lease agreement between Jacob Itzkovitch and the heirs of Joseph B. Hubbard for the building at the corner of South Rampart and Perdido streets. Itzkovitch ran his Eagle Loan Office from 401–403 Rampart and subleased the large hall upstairs to the Odd Fellows. The hall's entrance was at 1116 Perdido and the rental was $125.00 per month.

CIVIL DISTRICT COURT CLERK'S RECORDS

The court clerk's office is on the third floor of the court building at 421 Loyola Avenue. As late as fall, 1974, the archives there contained the following documents on Charles Bolden:

Warrant for Commitment of Insane Person, Chas. Bolden, June 1, 1907, Judicial Number 42791.

Description of Person Named in Within Warrant, June 1, 1907.

Remarks of G. A. Putfark, Deputy Sheriff, acknowledging that he had received custody of Charles Bolden on Thursday, June 4, 1907, and that he delivered him to Dr. Clarence Pierson at Jackson, Louisiana, on June 5, 1907.

Certification of Admittance to Insane Asylum of Louisiana, Charles Bolden, June 5, 1907.

I had xeroxed copies of the above documents in 1970, but when I returned in the summer of 1976 to check the possibility of obtaining clearer copies for inclusion in this book the Bolden documents were missing.

EAST LOUISIANA STATE HOSPITAL, JACKSON, LOUISIANA

REPORTS AND EXAMINATIONS

Biennial Report of the Board of Administrators of the Insane Asylum of the State of Louisiana to the Governor. Baton Rouge: *Advocate*, Official Journal of Louisiana, March 17, 1904; March 17, 1906; March 15, 1908; March 1, 1910; March 1, 1912; March 1, 1914; March 1, 1916; March 31, 1918; March 31, 1920; March 1, 1922; February 28, 1924; February 28, 1926; and March 1, 1928.

Psychiatric Examination by Dr. S. B. Hays, dated 1925.

LETTERS

There are still some letters in the Bolden file at Jackson. Buddy's sister Cora evidently wrote letters for their mother, and these are signed "Mrs. Alice Bolden." They were all written in pencil on yellow, lined paper; the expressions and even the misspellings are the same in each letter. The descriptions of Buddy's habits in the superintendent's replies are written in terminology that no doubt would have been meaningless to Alice and Cora. There is one letter from Buddy's daughter, Bernedine, datelined "Darrow Avenue, Evanston, Ill., August 20, 1927," in which she inquires about the health of "My father Charley Bolden." Some of the hospital records were destroyed in a 1940 fire, and in addition some of the Bolden files at Jackson have been rifled. It is therefore uncertain at this point just what remains.

NEWSPAPERS

Louisiana Weekly, April 22, 29, 1933.

New Orleans *Daily Picayune*, 1900–1907.

New Orleans *Item*, 1895–1907.

New Orleans *Louisianian*, May, 1879–July, 1882.

New Orleans *Times-Democrat*, 1885–1906.

New Orleans *Times-Picayune*, January 7, 1940.

LETTERS

Gremillion, Lionel, to the author, April 27, May 11, 1967; March 17, 1969; June 8, 17, 1971; November 18, 1974.

Hebert, Congressman F. Edward, to the author, May 17, 27; June 8, 1971.

St. Cyr, John, to the author, August 10, 1962.

Singleton, Zutty, to the author, June 20, 1971.

Smith, Mrs. Glenn, to the author, June 15, 1971.

Stewart-Baxter, Derrick, to the author, July 5, 1971.

INTERVIEWS

WILLIAM RANSOM HOGAN JAZZ ARCHIVE,
TULANE UNIVERSITY,
NEW ORLEANS, LOUISIANA

These interviews are available on tape and many of them have also been transcribed into digest form. They were conducted by one or more of the following persons: Richard Allen, Danny Barker, Robert Campbell, Ralph Collins, Paul Crawford, Harold Dejan, Charles DeVore, Nesuhi Ertugin, William Ransom Hogan, George Kay, Floyd Levin, Bill Madden, Manuel Manetta, Al Rose, William Russell, John Steiner, and Johnny Wiggs. They are listed according to person interviewed and date.

Adams, Frank, January 21, 1959.

Albert, Tom, September 25, 1959.

Alexander, Adolphe, Jr., March 8, 1961.

Allen, Henry, Jr., August 1, 1966.

Amacker, Frank, July 1, 1960.

Bailey, Andrew, September 16, 1959.

Barbarin, Isidore, January 7, 1959.

Barnes, Harrison, January 29, 1959.

Beaullieu, Paul, June 11, 1960.

Bocage, Peter, January 29, 1959.

Burbank, Albert, March 18, 1959.

Carew, Roy, June 21, 1961.

Cornish, Bella (Mrs. William), January 13, 1959.

Foster, Willie, January 2, 1959.

Garland, Ed, April 20, 1971.

Jones, Louis, January 19, 1959.

Joseph, John, November 26, 1958.
Laine, Jack, April 21, 1951.
Lopez, Raymond, August 30, 1958.
Love, Charlie, December 9, 1959.
McCullum, Bertha (Mrs. George), October 16, 1960.
Manetta, Manuel, March 21, 1957.
Matthews, Bill, March 10, 1959.
Nicholas, Joe, November 12, 1956.
Ory, Edward, April 20, 1957.
Picou, Alphonse, April 4, 1958.
Ridgely, William, June 2, 1959.
Russell, William, August 31, September 4, 1962.
St. Cyr, John, August 27, 1958.
Shields, Harry, May 28, 1961.
Vincent, Clarence, November 17, 1959.

INTERVIEWS BY THE AUTHOR

Albert, Don, August 6, 1971.
Albert, Tom, July 10, 1962.
Alcorn, Alvin, June 23, 1971.
Alcorn, Beatrice, June 23, 1971.
Alcorn, Cordelia, June 23, 1971.
Amacker, Frank, June 15, 1962.
Anderson, Anita, April 30, 1971.
Augustine, Cecile, July 16, 1971.
Barbarin, Louis, May 13, 1962.
Barbarin, Paul, September 7, 1963.
Bocage, Peter, August 3, 1962.
Burbank, Albert, August 3, 1962.
Caesar, Paul, July 16, 1971.
Chapital, S. A., July 31, 1970.
Cottrell, Louis, Jr., July 30, 1973.
Dawson, Eddie, September 12, 1970.
Dennis, Dave, July 11, 1971.
Dulitz, Morris, July 11, 1971.
Dutrey, Sam, Jr., August 4, 1962.
Farr, Susie, August 8, 1971.

Foster, Abbey (Chinee), June 6, 1962.
Frazier, Cié, July 7, 1962.
Garland, Ed, April 23, 1971.
Gayden, Mrs. George L., June 16, 1971.
Glass, Henry (Booker T), May 10, 1962.
Griffin, Bob, August 11, 1970.
Hausey, W. E., July 31, 1971.
Hug, Armand, August 26, 1976.
Humphrey, Earl, September 12, 1970.
Humphrey, Willie, October 13, 1970.
Jackson, Eugenia, June 25, July 2, 1971.
Johnson, Leonard, July 16, 1971.
Jones, John L., September 17, 1970.
Jones, Carrie (Mrs. Louis), April 9, April 30, May 7, 1971.
Joseph, Papa John, July 3, 1962.
Joseph, Mrs. Nelson, April 30, 1971.
Jules, John, July 16, 1971.
Keppard, Louis, August 10, 1962.
Lamkin, Alberta, August 5, 1971.
Lawes, Laura, June 25, July 2, 1971.
Love, Charlie, September 3, 1962.
Manetta, Manuel, June 20, 1962.
Matthews, Bill, June 18, 1962.
Miller, Ernest (Punch), April 17, 1962, September 14, 1970.
Morris, John, April 30, 1971.
Morton, Elizabeth, June 23, 1971.
Mumford, Mrs. Jefferson, November 2, 1971.
Parker, Willie, April 19, 1962.
Pavageau, Alcide (Slow Drag), May 29, 1962.
Pickett, Susannah, August 5, 1971.
Robards, Mrs. E. M., June 26, 1971.
Robertson, Henry, May 7, 1971.
Robertson, Peter Martin, May 13, 1971.
Russell, William, September 12, 1970.
Ruth, Larry, August 7, 1971.
Sayles, Emanuel, June 15, 1962.
Tervalon, Clement, September 7, 1971.
Wilson, Andrew, August 5, 1971.

SECONDARY SOURCES

BOOKS

This includes all of the books consulted by the author while doing the Bolden research. Most of them had little about Bolden himself and very few of them contained material actually used in this book. They are not necessarily recommended reading on Bolden. They were read as part of the plan to cover everything available on the subject and background of the city and the times.

Armstrong, Louis. *Satchmo, My Life in New Orleans*. Englewood Cliffs, N.J.: Prentice-Hall, 1954.

Arthur, Stanley Clisby. *Old New Orleans*. New Orleans: Harmanson Publishers, 1962.

Asbury, Herbert. *The French Quarter*. New York: Alfred A. Knopf, 1936.

Barker, Danny and Jack V. Buerkle. *Bourbon Street Black*. New York: Oxford Press, 1973.

Baxter, Derrick Stewart. *Ma Rainey and the Classic Blues Singers*. London: Studio Vista, 1970.

Bechet, Sidney. *Treat It Gentle*. New York: Hill & Wang, 1960.

Berendt, Joachim. *The New Jazz Book*. New York: Hill & Wang, 1962.

Blassingame, John W. *Black New Orleans, 1860–1880*. Chicago: University of Chicago Press, 1973.

Blesh, Rudi. *Shining Trumpets: A History of Jazz*. New York: Alfred A. Knopf, 1949.

Blesh, Rudi, and Harriet Janis. *They All Played Ragtime: The True Story of an American Music*. New York: Alfred A. Knopf, 1950.

Bradford, Perry. *Born With the Blues*. New York: Oak Publications, 1965.

Brown, Sterling, Arthur P. Davis, and Ulysses Lee, eds. *The Negro Caravan*. New York: Citadel Press, 1941.

Brunn, H. O. *The Story of the Original Dixieland Jazz Band*. Baton Rouge: Louisiana State University Press, 1960.

Cajun, Andre. *Basin Street: Its Rise and Fall*. New Orleans: Harmanson Publishers, 1957.

———. *Stories of New Orleans*. New Orleans: Harmanson Publishers, 1957.

Cash, W. J. *The Mind of the South*. New York: Vintage Books, 1941.

Charters, Samuel B. *Jazz: New Orleans, 1885–1963*. New York: Oak Publications, 1963.

Chase, John, Herman Deutsch, Charles Dufour, and Leonard Huber. *Citoyens,*

Progres et Politique de la Nouvelle Orleans, 1889-1964. New Orleans: E. S. Upton Printing Co., 1964.

————. *Frenchmen, Desire, Goodchildren: And Other Streets of New Orleans*. New Orleans: Robert L. Crager, 1960.

Chase, Richard, comp. *American Folk Tales and Songs*. New York: New American Library of World Literature, 1956.

Chilton, John, Leonard Feather, and Max Jones. *Salute to Satchmo*. London: IPC Specialist and Professional Press, 1970.

————. *Who's Who of Jazz: Storyville to Swing Street*. Philadelphia: Chilton Book Co., 1970.

Crump, Charlie, and Tom Stagg. *New Orleans, The Revival*. London: Bashall Caves, 1973.

Davis, Edwin Adams. *Louisiana: The Pelican State*. Baton Rouge: Louisiana State University Press, 1959.

de Toledano, Ralph, ed. *Frontiers of Jazz*. New York: Frederick Ungar Publishing Co., 1962.

Dexter, Dave, Jr. *The Jazz Story from the 90's to the 60's*. Englewood Cliffs, N.J.: Prentice-Hall, 1964.

Dodds, Baby. *The Baby Dodds Story*, as told to Larry Garra. Los Angeles: Contemporary Press, 1959.

Edmonson, Munro S., and John H. Rohrer, eds. *The Eighth Generation Grows Up*. New York: Harper & Row, 1960.

Ewen, David. *History of Popular Music*. New York: Barnes & Noble, 1961.

Farrell, Jack W., and William L. Grossman. *The Heart of Jazz*. New York: New York University Press, 1956.

Feather, Leonard. *The Book of Jazz*. New York: Horizon Press, 1957.

————. *The New Encyclopedia of Jazz*. New York: Bonanza Books, 1960.

Foster, Pops. *The Autobiography of Pops Foster: New Orleans Jazzman*, as told to Tom Stoddard. Berkeley, University of California Press, 1971.

Gara, Larry. See Dodds, Baby.

Goffin, Robert. *La Nouvelle Orleans, Capitale du Jazz*. New York: Editions de la Maison Francaise, 1946.

Grauer, Bill, Jr., and Orrin Keepnews. *Pictorial History of Jazz*. New York: Crown Publishers, 1962.

Green, Benny. *The Reluctant Art: The Growth of Jazz*. New York: Horizon Press, 1963.

Hadlock, Richard. *Jazzmasters of the 20's*. New York: MacMillan, 1965.

Harris, Rex. *Jazz*. London: Penguin Books, 1953.

Harris, Rex, and Brian Rust. *Recorded Jazz: A Critical Guide*. London: Penguin Books, 1958.

Haskins, James. *The Creoles of Color of New Orleans*. New York: Thomas Y. Crowell Co., 1975.

Hentoff, Nat, and Nat Shapiro, eds. *Hear Me Talking to Ya*. New York: Rinehart, 1955.

Hentoff, Nat, Nat Shapiro, and Albert J. McCarthy, eds. *Jazz*. New York: Grove Press, 1959.

Hodeir, Andre. *Jazz: Its Evolution and Essence*. New York: Grove Press, 1956.

Jones, Leroi. *Blues People*. New York: William Morrow, 1963.

Kane, Harnett T. *Queen New Orleans: City by the River*. New York: William Morrow, 1949.

Kmen, Henry A. *Music in New Orleans: The Formative Years, 1791-1841*. Baton Rouge: Louisiana State University Press, 1966.

Lomax, Alan. *Mister Jelly Roll*. New York: Grosset & Dunlap, 1950.

Longstreet, Stephen. *The Real Jazz Old and New*. Baton Rouge: Louisiana State University Press, 1956.

———. *Sportin' House: New Orleans and the Jazz Story*. Los Angeles: Sherbourne Press, 1965.

Lynn, Stuart M. *New Orleans*. New York: Bonanza Books, 1949.

Martinez, Raymond J. *The Story of the Riverfront of New Orleans*. Gretna, Louisiana: Pelican Press, 1948.

Miller, Paul Eduard, ed. *Esquire's Jazz Book—1944*. New York: Smith & Durrell, 1943, 1944.

———, ed. *Esquire 1945 Jazz Book*. New York: A. S. Barnes, 1945.

Myrus, Donald. *I Like Jazz*. New York: MacMillan, 1964.

New Orleans City Guide. Written and compiled by the Federal Writers' Project of the Works Progress Administration for the City of New Orleans. Boston: Houghton, Mifflin, 1938.

New Orleans City Park: Its First Fifty Years, 1891-1941. Compiled by workers of the Writers' Program of the Works Project Administration in the State of Louisiana. New Orleans: Gulf Printing Co., 1941.

Niehaus, Earl F. *The Irish in New Orleans*. Baton Rouge: Louisiana State University Press, 1965.

Oliver, Paul. *Bessie Smith*. New York: A. S. Barnes, 1959.

Panassie, Hugues. *The Real Jazz*. New York: A. S. Barnes, 1942, 1960.

Ramsey, Frederic, Jr., and Charles Edward Smith, eds. *Jazzmen*. New York: Harcourt, Brace, 1939.

Ramsey, Frederic, Jr., *et al*. *The Jazz Record Book*. New York: Smith and Durrell, 1942, 1946.

Rose, Al. *Storyville, New Orleans*. University: University of Alabama Press, 1974.

Rose, Al, and Edmond Souchon. *New Orleans Jazz: A Family Album*. Baton Rouge: Louisiana State University Press, 1967.

Rosenthal, George, Rudi Blesh, and Frederic Ramsey, Jr., eds. *Jazzways*. N.p.: New York, 1946.

Sargeant, Winthrop. *Jazz: A History*. Original title, *Jazz: Hot and Hybrid*. New York: McGraw-Hill, 1938, 1946, 1964.

Seymour, William H. *The Story of Algiers, 1718–1896*. Gretna, Louisiana: Pelican Press, 1971.

Sims, Walter Hines, ed. *Baptist Hymnal*. Nashville: Convention Press, 1956.

Spears, John R. *The American Slave Trade*. New York: Ballantine Books, 1960.

Stearns, Marshall W. *The Story of Jazz*. New York: Oxford University Press, 1956, 1958.

Stoddard, Tom. See Foster, Pops.

Vetter, Ernest G. *Fabulous Frenchtown: The Story of the Famous French Quarter of New Orleans*. Washington, D.C.: Coronet Press, 1955.

Williams, Martin, ed. *The Art of Jazz: Essays on the Nature and Development of Jazz*. New York: Oxford University Press, 1959.

———. *Jazzmasters of New Orleans*. New York: MacMillan, 1967.

———. *Jelly Roll Morton*. New York: A. S. Barnes, 1962.

———. *King Oliver*. New York: A. S. Barnes, 1960.

Wilson, John S. *The Collector's Jazz*. Philadelphia, New York: J. P. Lippincott, 1958.

PERIODICALS

"Albert Nicholas Talking." *Jazztimes*, IV (July, 1967), pages not numbered.

Baquet, George. "Baquet on Bolden." *Downbeat*, VII (December 15, 1940), page numbers not available.

Barker, Danny. "Memory of King Bolden." *Evergreen Review*, IX (March, 1965), 67–74.

Charters, Samuel B. "The Birth of Jazz." *Music of New Orleans*, booklet in Folkways Records, album no. FA2464, IV, 1959, p. 2.

de Toledano, Ralph. "Duke Ellington." *Fortune*, VIII (August, 1933), 47–48, 90, 92, 94–95.

Fairweather, D. "Hey, Buddy Bolden." *Jazz Journal*, XXII (November, 1969), 39.

Marquis, Donald M. "Cornelius Tillman, Drummer." *Second Line* (July, 1976), 41–43.

"I Thought I Heard Buddy Bolden Say." *Melody Maker* (March 9, 1963), 14.

Sancton, Tom. "Libretto." *Second Line*, II (April, 1951), 1, 8, 13.

———. "Trouble In Mind, Part 1." *Second Line*, II (September, 1951), 9, 14, 18.

———. "Trouble In Mind, Part 2." *Second Line*, V (January-February, 1954), 1–8.

Smith, Charles Edward. "The Bolden Cylinder." *Saturday Review*, March 16, 1957, pp. 34–35.

Souchon, Edmond. "The End of an Era: Papa Jack Laine Answers the Last Call." *Second Line*, XVII (July-August, 1966), 79–85.

Williams, Martin. "Cultural Digging." *Downbeat*, XXXVIII (January 21, 1971), 12.

PHONOGRAPH RECORDINGS

Bechet, Sidney. *Grand Master of the Soprano Sax and Clarinet*. "Buddy Bolden Stomp." Columbia CL 836, side 1, no. 4.

Johnson, Bunk and His Superior Jazz Band. *Bunk Johnson Talking Record*. Goodtime Jazz M12048, June, 1942, side 2, no. 4.

Keppard, Freddie. *17 Rare Selections of the Finest Jazz Cornetist of the 1920s*. Herwin RLP.

Love, Charlie. *Music of New Orleans, Vol. IV*. "The Birth of Jazz" and "Buddy Bolden." Folkways, FA 2464, 1959, side 1, nos. 2 and 3.

Morton. Jelly Roll. *Piano Solos*. "Buddy Bolden's Blues." Original Commodore Jazz Classics. Mainstream S/6020, side A, no. 3.

———. *The Saga of Mr. Jelly Lord*. "In New Orleans, The Bolden Legend." Circle Records, Vol. XI, Pt. 1 and conclusion.

The earliest documentation of the Bolden family is the death certificate of Buddy's grandfather, Gustavus, dated August 4, 1866. The name is given as "Augustus Bolen," but the notation, "at the residence of Mr. W. Walker on Calliope Street near the RR Station," coincides with further findings.

Be It Remembered, That on this day, to-wit: the Thirtieth of May in the year of our Lord One Thousand Eight Hundred and Eighty Three, and the One Hundred and Seventh of the Independence of the United States of America, before me, JOSEPH JONES, M. D., President Board of Health and Ex-Officio Recorder of Births, Deaths and Marriages, in and for the Parish of Orleans, personally appeared:

Joseph Singleton , a native of La residing at 218 Erie Street who hereby declares, that Frances Bowling Col a native of Virginia , aged 54 years departed this life, yesterday (29 May 1883) at No 3634 Howard Streets, in this city Cause of Death Small pox Certificate of Dr. A. G. Gill.

Thus done at New Orleans, in the presence of the aforesaid J. Singleton as also in that of Messrs. B. B. Howard & P. H. Lavarge both of this City, witnesses, by me requested so to be, who have hereunto set their hands, together with me, after reading thereof, the day, month and year first above written.

President Board of Health and Ex-Officio Recorder

Death certificate of Buddy's grandmother, Frances Bolden, who died May 29, 1883.

𝔜 𝖉𝖔 𝖍𝖊𝖗𝖊𝖇𝖞 𝕮𝖊𝖗𝖙𝖎𝖋𝖞, that on the.............................

Aug 14 th 1873 *after having received the mutual consent of the Contracting Parties in presence of the undersigned Witnesses, I have celebrated the* **MARRIAGE** *of the within named Parties,*

West Bolden age 23 years

native of *Louisiana* Son of

Gustavus Bolden

and *Frances Bolden*

Alice Harrison age 18 years

native of *Louisiana* Daughter

of *Henry Harrison*

and *Leah Harrison*

Contracting
Parties, { West ✗ Bolden
                    mark

alice ✗ Harrison
            mark

Witnesses. { Mary her ✗ Harrison
                      mark

Greatine her ✗ Harrison
                   mark

Rev. G. Carter
            Minister

Marriage license of Buddy's parents, West Bolden and Alice Harrison, dated August 14, 1873. Although the marriage license records the name as Harrison, the name was really Harris.

Be it Remembered, That on this day, to wit the *Nineteenth* of *May* in the year of our Lord One Thousand Eight Hundred and *Eighty one*, and One Hundred and *Fifth* of the Independence of the United States of Ameri— before me, JOSEPH JONES, M. D., President Board of Health and Ex-Officio Recorder of Births, Deaths and Marri— in and for the Parish of Orleans, personally appeared:

West Bolden, a native of *Texas* residing *St Andrew near Locust St* who hereby declares, th— *Lotta Bolden* *Col:* a native of *this city*, aged *5 years* departed this life, yesterday, *18 May 1881*, at his aforesaid residence, in this — Cause of Death *Encephalitis* Certificate of Dr *George Stimpf*

This done at New Orleans, in the presence of the aforesaid *W. Bolden* as also in that of Messrs. *S. Peralta* & *J. H. Lanaux* both of this Ci— witnesses, by me requested so to be, who have hereunto set their hands, together with me, af— sealing hereof, the day, month and year first above written:

W x Bolden

J. H. Lanaux

W Peralta

Joseph Jones MD
President Board of Health and Ex-Officio Recorder

Death certificate of Buddy's older sister, Lotta, who died May 18, 1881, a few days before her sixth birthday.

Birth certificate of Charles Joseph Bolden, Jr., August 16, 1897, whose parents were "Charles Bolden and Hattie Bolden born Oliver."

1222 Josephine St

I do hereby Certify, That on the *17 day of Feb.*

*192_* , after having received the mutual consent of the Contracting Parties in presence of the undersigned Witnesses, I have Celebrated the MARRIAGE of the within named parties.

Frank Lewis

native of *La.* .... Son of

Gustan Lewis

and *Matthew Lewis*

Jennie Gould.

native of *La.* .... Daughter

of *Rev. Joseph Gould.*

and *Kate Gould.*

Contracting } *Frank Lewis*
Parties *Jennie Gould*
George Thackeston
Witnesses: *Chas. Bolden*
B. Vacquera Cornish
Officiating } *Rev. B. W. Toney.*
Party

Marriage certificate of Frank Lewis, Bolden's clarinet player, the only document found with Charles Bolden's actual signature.

No. 42791

STATE OF LOUISIANA,

CIVIL DISTRICT COURT FOR THE PARISH OF ORLEANS.

———

To *Hon H. B. Mc Murray* Civil Sheriff of the Parish of Orleans :

Having caused *Chas Bolden* an indigent (alleged to be a lunatic), to be brought before me in chambers, and having made proper inquiry into all the facts and circumstances of the case, and being of the opinion that the said *Chas Bolden* is insane, and ought to be confined in the Insane Asylum of the State at Jackson, Louisiana,

You are hereby commanded, by the authority of the State of Louisiana, to take the said *Chas Bolden* into your custody, and forthwith to convey the said indigent lunatic or insane person to the State Insane Asylum at Jackson, Louisiana, and safely deliver *him* to the Superintendent of said Asylum at the expense of the City of New Orleans. And this shall be your warrant, for the custody and conveyance of said indigent patient, as well as the warrant of the Superintendent, for the confinement and care of said indigent patient until recovered of insanity.

Witness my hand and the seal of the said Court, at New Orleans,

Louisiana, this *1st* day of *June* 1907

This commitment order signed by Judge T. W. C. Ellis and dated June 1, 1907, sent Charles Bolden to the insane asylum at Jackson, Louisiana.

DESCRIPTION OF THE INSANE PERSON

NAMED IN THE WITHIN WARRANT.

1. Name _Chas Bolden_
2. Sex _M_ . . . . . Age _26_ . . . . . Color _Ed_
3. Color—Hair _b_ . . . . . Beard . . . . . Eyes _b._
4. Occupation _Lab._
5. Single _yes_ . . . . . Married . . . . . Widowed
6. Residence _House of Detention 2127 First st_
7. Nativity _La_
8. Character of disease _Insanity_
9. Cause of insanity _Alcohol_
10. Is this first attack? _yes_
11. How long been insane? _1 Mos_
12. Is patient dangerous to himself or others? _to others_
13. Has suicide ever been attempted? _no_
14. Is there a disposition to destroy clothing, furniture, etc.? _no_
15. Are the patient's habits clean or dirty? _filthy_
16. What was the patient's natural disposition? _quiet_

Was there any peculiarity or eccentricity?. _?_

17. Have any members of the family ever been insane? _no_ Were the parents blood relations? _no_
18. Has the patient ever been addicted to the intemperate use of of alcohol, opium or tobacco, or indulged in any improper habits? _Alcohol_
19. Has the patient ever had an injury of head, epilepsy or hereditary disease, sudden suppression of an eruption or accustomed discharge? _no_
20. What is the cause of this attack? _Alcohol_
21. Has any medical treatment been instituted? _yes_
22. Any restraint or confinement been resorted to? _yes_

If so, what kind and how long? _House of Detention 1 Mo_

23. General remarks . . . _Received Thursday June 4th 1907 & on Friday June 5th 1907 I delivered to Dr. Clarence Pearson superintendant of the Insane Asylum at Jackson La. the within named Interdicted Insane person Chas Bolden which will more fully appear by referring to the receipt of said superintendant herein filed & made part of this return_

Returned same day

G. A. Putfark
V Deputy Sheriff

Description of the insane person, Charles Bolden, dated June 4 and 5, 1907, with remarks by G. A. Putfark, deputy sheriff, who delivered Bolden to Jackson.

INSANE ASYLUM OF LOUISIANA.

Jackson, *June* 5— 190_7_

This is to Certify that _____ *Chas Bolden* _____.

an insane _Col Male_ resident of the parish of _____ *Orleans* _____

was this day admitted as an inmate of the Insane Asylum of Louisiana.

Clarence Pierson M.D.
SUPERINTENDENT.

Per_____
CLERK.

Receipt for Bolden, signed at Jackson by Clarence Pierson, superintendent of the hospital, on June 5, 1907.

march 1926

Dr will you please inform me of my son health Charley Bolden from his mother Mrs alice Bolden 2338 Philip St N.O.

Letter from Buddy's mother to the Jackson hospital, one of a number of nearly identical letters in Bolden's hospital file. They were written by his sister Cora in pencil on lined yellow tablet paper.

Death certificate of Charles Bolden, Jr. (Buddy's son), who died December 25, 1930, at age thirty-three. His grandfather, West Bolden, died at age thirty-two, on December 3, 1883.

Be It Remembered, That on this day to wit: the **THIRTEENTH.** of August in the year of our Lord, One Thousand, Nine Hundred and **THIRTY ONE** and the One Hundred and **56** of the Independence of the United States of America, before me, **WM. H. ROBIN, M. D.**, Chairman of the Board of Health and Ex-Officio Recorder of Births, Deaths and Marriages, in and for the Parish of Orleans, and the City of New Orleans, personally appeared

A.ROUNDS. an undertaker notice of this city residing **AT No 2128 JACKSON AVE.** who hereby declares that **ALICE BOLDEN.** (**COL**) a native of **LA.** aged **54 YRS.** departed this life **ON THE ELEVENTH INST.** (11TH of August 1931) AT No **2338 PHILIP ST IN THIS CITY.** Cause of Death **CARDIO RENAL DISEASE.** Certificate of Dr **C.H.D.BOWERS.** **DECEASED WAS A WIDOW.**

Thus done at New Orleans, in the presence of the aforesaid **A.ROUNDS.** as also in that of **P. H. Lanauze and W. J. Prudhomme** both of this city, witnesses by me requested so to be, who have hereunto set their hands together with me, after reading hereof this day, month and year first above written

Chairman Board of Health and Ex-Officio Recorder.

I Certify That The Above Is A True Copy Of The Original Record Duly Recorded In The Office Of The Registrar Of Births, Marriages And Deaths For The Parish Of Orleans And City Of New Orleans.

Date: **AUG 26 1970**

Deputy Registrar

Death certificate of Mrs. Alice Bolden, who died August 11, 1931. The age fifty-four is obviously wrong, other documents indicating that she was about seventy-six. Before the end of that year, her son and daughter had died too.

Index